Generative Adversarial Networks (GANs)

GENERATIVE ADVERSARIAL NETWORKS (GANS)

Edited by

Adele Kuzmiakova

ARCLER PRESS

www.arclerpress.com

Generative Adversarial Networks (GANs)

Adele Kuzmiakova

Arcler Press
4164 Lakeshore Road
Burlington, ON L7L 1A4
Canada
www.arclerpress.com
Email: orders@arclereducation.com

ISBN: 978-1-77956-417-7 (Hardcover)

ABOUT THE EDITOR

Adele Kuzmiakova is a machine learning engineer working at the intersection of machine learning, computer vision, and natural language processing. Adele attended Cornell University in New York, United States for her undergraduate studies. She studied engineering with a focus on applied math. Some of the deep learning problems Adele worked on include predicting air quality from public webcams, developing a real-time human movement tracking, using 3D computer vision to create 3D avatars from selfies in order to bring online clothes shopping closer to reality, and creating visual stories and photobooks from photos on mobile devices. She is also passionate about exchanging ideas and inspiring other people and acted as a workshop organizer at Women in Data Science conference in Geneva, Switzerland in 2022 and 2023.

TABLE OF CONTENTS

LIST OF FIGURES

LIST OF TABLES

PREFACE

A generative adversarial network (GAN) is a class of machine learning frameworks. In short, GANs are a methodology for generative modeling using deep learning techniques. GAN is an emerging network in deep learning applications. GANs are ingenious techniques for training a generative model by framing the problem as a supervised learning problem. Still, GANs also have a scope of research for semi-supervised learning and reinforcement learning. GANs are a recent and rapidly changing field that is distributing the capability of generative models in their ability to generate genuine examples through a range of problem domains, most notably in image-to-image translation and video translation.

GANs have the feasibility to build improved models, as they can generate the sample data as per application requirements. There are various applications of GAN in science and technology, including computer vision, security, image editing, security, image generation, natural language processing, emotion detection, image translation, text-to-image synthesis, and video synthesis.

This book comprises of eight chapters; the first chapter highlights the history of GANs along with their working mechanism and structure. This chapter also describes the benefits and challenges of working with GANs. The second chapter discusses the architecture of GANs as well as the best practices in GAN architecture development.

The third chapter is about the different types of GANs which highlight their architecture, applications, and issues. The training process of GANs is discussed in the fourth chapter of this book, emphasizing the significance of preparing the environment for the training stage.

The fifth chapter describes the security issues in GANs with emphasis on the security attacks in GANs, such as cracking passphrases and forging facial detection. The sixth chapter deals with the process of editing images using GANs. Practical applications of GANs, including the utilization of GANs in the field of medicine and fashion, are discussed in seventh chapter. The final chapter navigates through the advanced concepts in GANs, addressing the future research directions in this field.

This book serves as a guide to the fascinating world of GANs, offering readers a solid foundation in understanding, designing, and applying GANs. Readers will find this book to be a valuable resource for learning about GANs, contributing to further advancements in the field of artificial intelligence.

CHAPTER 1

INTRODUCTION TO GENERATIVE ADVERSARIAL NETWORKS (GANS)

LEARNING OBJECTIVES

At the end of this chapter, readers will be able to:

1. Understand the working of GANs along with their history.
2. Comprehend key concepts in GANs such as adversarial training, loss functions, latent space, and mode collapse.
3. Understand the benefits and challenges of working with GANs.
4. Identify real-world examples of GAN applications.
5. Comprehend future directions in GAN Research.

INTRODUCTORY EXAMPLE

In recent years, Acme Innovations Inc., a leading manufacturer of consumer electronics, faced challenges in swiftly iterating and refining product designs to meet evolving consumer demands. Traditional design processes often resulted in lengthy development cycles and limited flexibility in exploring diverse design options. To address these challenges, Acme Innovations Inc. turned to Generative Adversarial Networks (GANs), a revolutionary approach to generative modeling that has gained significant traction across various industries. By harnessing the power of GANs, Acme aimed to accelerate product design iterations and unlock new avenues for innovation. Acme Innovations Inc has gained a competitive edge over the market by using GANs to solve practical problems.

UNIT INTRODUCTION

Generative Adversarial Networks (GANs) are deep learning models utilized to address various problems. GANs, first introduced in a 2014 publication by Ian Goodfellow and his team, have been applied in various domains including image-to-image conversion, generating realistic graphics, and producing lifelike images. Current research largely investigates prevalent flaws that make GANs susceptible to a wide range of failure situations. Their operation is based on a dualistic competitive approach that integrates generators and discriminators, aiming to optimize performance and enhance both components (Saxena & Cao, 2021). The generator network is responsible for producing synthetic data that closely mimics the training data, whereas the discriminator network's goal is to differentiate between real and generated data. Both networks are trained simultaneously in a two-player minimax game until the generator produces data that is identical to real data. GANs are highly versatile and may be applied across multiple fields such as natural language processing, computer vision, and audio processing. Computer vision has utilized GANs for several tasks including image generation, image resolution enhancement, image style translation, and creative style transfer. Natural language processing has various applications, including generating text, synthesizing images from text, and evaluating sentiment. GANs have also been employed in audio processing to generate music, synthesize speech, and transform audio into visuals. GANs have a significant advantage in that they are capable of generating novel data that closely mimics the data used for training, even when they do not explicitly model the data distribution. These attributes make them very suitable for data augmentation and synthesis jobs, which require more data to train ML models. GANs can also be utilized for unsupervised learning by utilizing unannotated training data (Alqahtani et al.,

2021). However, GANs do have their limitations. During the training process, one may encounter frequent problems such as instability, mode collapse, and a lack of variance in the generated data. Several strategies have been proposed to address these issues, such as utilizing diverse loss functions, implementing regularization techniques on the generator, and incorporating feedback from the discriminator into the generator. Overall, GANs are a powerful tool for creating data and have the potential to revolutionize various fields, including design, art, and entertainment. The concept of artificial intelligence (AI) and its capacity to revolutionize various fields, including art, design, and entertainment, is a topic that generates significant attention and enthusiasm. Figure 1.1 presents a visual comparison between genuine and artificially generated images of speaking headshots using face landmark tracks. On the left side (a) are the original pictures which serve as a point of reference. In contrast, the right side (b) displays the generated images that have been carefully crafted using GANs. The comparison provides a clear comprehension of the potential of GANs in creating realistic representations utilizing face landmarks, highlighting the advancements in image synthesis techniques. This chapter will present a thorough analysis of the history, operation, uses, and notable approaches of GANs (Arora et al., 2017) (Figure 1.1).

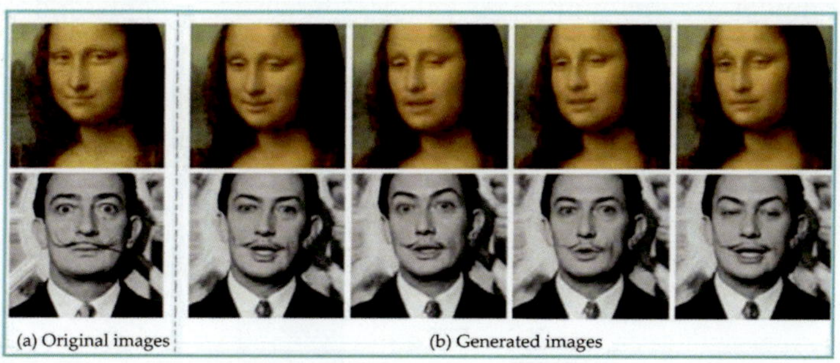

Figure 1.1. Examples of talking head image synthesis using face landmark tracks. (a) The left images are original. (b) The right ones are the generated images using GAN.

Source: Mehdi Ghayoum, Creative Commons License.

Did You Know?

The concept of Generative Adversarial Networks (GANs) was inspired by a game between two counterfeiters and a police officer, as described by Ian Goodfellow, the creator of GANs.

1.1. CONCEPT OF GENERATIVE MODELS

Learning objectives

- Comprehend the difference between discriminative and generative machine learning models

Before elucidating GANs, it is crucial to comprehend the distinction between the two categories of machine learning (ML) models. ML models can be classified into two categories: discriminative and generative. Discriminative refers to models utilized for classification, while generative refers to models that produce new data. According to Figure 1.2, the discriminative model functions as a classifier. The supplied data is ambiguous and does not account for the method of data generation (Lu et al., 2022). A discriminative model is a ML model that learns a function to assign input data to specific groups and may subsequently predict the class of new data instances. However, a generative model possesses the capacity to generate new data, as opposed to the discriminative model. Assume that a convolutional neural network (CNN) model is built to classify images of dogs and cats. The CNN model will be provided with images of cats and dogs, together with a class name that indicates their respective categories. The CNN model assigns numerical values, known as weights and biases, to each image. These values are used to calculate an output that categorizes the image either as a dog or a cat. What if the situation were flipped? Generative models employ a class label input to generate visual outputs.

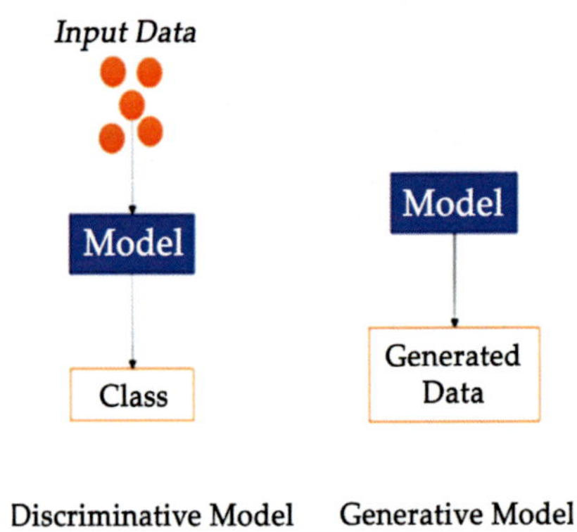

Figure 1.2. *Abstract definition of discriminative and generative models.*

Source: Sanaa Kaddoura, Creative Commons License.

These models generate output by processing input given to the computer. These methods are based on unsupervised machine-learning techniques. The generative model will undergo training using a dataset that has been specifically created for training. Afterward, it absorbs the patterns in the given data to generate new data using the acquired knowledge. Figure 1.2 illustrates that the discriminative model acts as a classifier, specifically for tasks such as classifying a picture as either a dog or a cat. Producing an image of a dog or cat includes employing a generative method to create a new picture (Gonog & Zhou, 2019).

The discriminative model calculates p(X|Y), which is the conditional probability. The set of features that the target produces for the object, such as a noticeable nose, long hair, whether it makes meow sounds or other attributes, is represented by the variable X. Whether it is a dog, or a cat is represented by the variable Y. The goal is to determine the probability that a class Y will exist given a set of qualities X. In the absence of labels, the generative model calculates the joint probability p(X, Y) or p(X). For example, it can produce realistic images of cats or dogs (Hardy et al., 2019). This model uses a random number, or a collection of numbers known as noise as its input data, such as [–3, 3.2, 5]. The model will generate a feature set X that closely resembles Y given the inputs. Every time, the noise is necessary to create a distinct image. As depicted in Figure 1.3, discriminative models establish a clear boundary to separate data points. Discriminative models create a decision boundary that effectively divides distinct classes. Yet, the generative model aims to understand the spatial distribution of data. The discriminative model attempts to distinguish between a cat and a dog image by creating a decision boundary. With precise delineation of the boundary, the model can distinguish a photograph of a cat from a photograph of a dog, even without prior knowledge of the data sets' arrangement. In contrast, a generative model aims to produce compelling images of dogs and cats that closely resemble the original photographs in the dataset (Wang et al., 2017) (Figure 1.3).

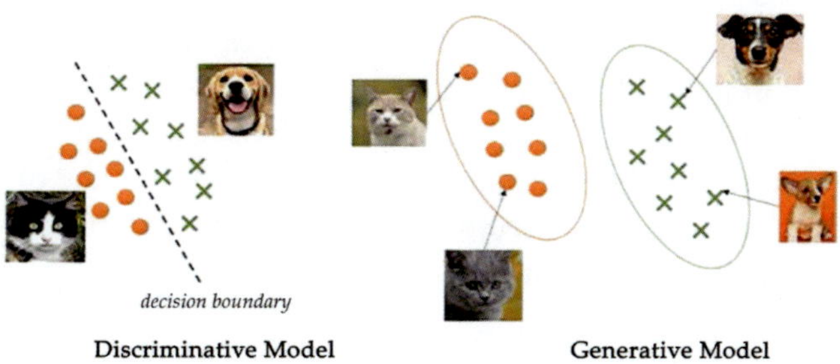

Figure 1.3. *Illustration of difference between discriminative and generative models*

Source: Sanaa Kaddour Creative Commons License.

1.2. HISTORY OF GANS

Learning objectives

- Understand the history of GANs along with some prior prominent generative models
- Comprehend notable advancements in GAN technology

Introduced in 2014 by Ian Goodfellow and his colleagues, GANs represent a noteworthy advancement in the realm of AI and deep learning. The seminal article named "Generative Adversarial Nets" was introduced at the Neural Information Processing Systems (NeurIPS) conference, demonstrating the innovative idea of simultaneously training two neural networks in a game-theoretic setting. This approach was groundbreaking, enabling algorithms to significantly enhance their capacity to produce exceptionally lifelike data, encompassing photographs, videos, and text. The idea of GANs originated from the desire to overcome constraints in current generative models and enhance the caliber of generated data. Before the advent of GANs, other generative models including Variational Autoencoders (VAEs) and Restricted Boltzmann Machines (RBMs) were widely used. However, these models had challenges such as generating low-quality images or requiring significant computational resources (Breckman, 2001). In the dynamic scenario of the GAN architecture, a discriminator network seeks to discern between authentic data and the data produced by the generator, while a generator network seeks to produce data that is identical to real data. The training procedure comprises a competitive mechanism whereby the generator continuously improves its ability to provide real data, and the discriminator constantly improves its ability to detect fake data. The minimax theorem in game theory serves as the basis for this antagonistic training technique (Offert, 2021). Its purpose is to reach a Nash equilibrium, which is reached when the discriminator can no longer distinguish between created and real data and the generator is able to produce perfect copies of the original data. Since they were first presented, GANs have undergone substantial development and growth. A multitude of variations and enhancements have emerged from the original GAN formulation to address different issues and limits. Significant progress has been made in various areas (MacMillan et al., 2004):

a. Conditional GANs (cGANs), allow the generation of data based on specified conditions, thereby giving more control over the characteristics of the generated data.

b. Deep Convolutional GANs (DCGANs), integrate convolutional neural networks into the GAN architecture, making it more effective for tasks involving image data (Li et al., 2021).

c. Wasserstein GANs (WGANs), introduce a new cost function to address the training instability and mode collapse issues, leading to more stable training of GANs.

d. CycleGANs, which facilitate the transformation of images from one domain to another without paired training data, enable applications such as style transfer and photorealistic image generation (Hacker et al., 2009).

The historical development of GANs also highlights the broadening of their application areas. Initially focused on generating realistic images, GANs have since been applied in diverse fields such as healthcare for the generation of synthetic patient data, in art for creating new forms of artwork, in fashion for designing new clothing items, and in video games for producing dynamic environments. Despite the progress and the expanding utility of GANs, their development has prompted discussions around ethical considerations, particularly concerning the potential for generating misleading or harmful content (Efron, 1997). The Al community continues to address these challenges, seeking ways to ensure the responsible use of GAN technology. In summary, the history of GANs is a testament to the rapid advancements within Al and machine learning, demonstrating the potential of deep learning models to not only understand but also generate complex data. The journey of GANs from their inception to their current state reflects a broader trend of innovation and exploration in the field, continually pushing the boundaries of what is possible with Al (Cohen et al., 2002).

1.3. WORKING OF GENERATIVE ADVERSARIAL NETWORKS

Learning objectives

- Understand the working of GANs.
- Comprehend the Generator and Discriminator networks.
- Comprehend the training process of a GAN.

GANs are a type of ML methods that involve two models trained simultaneously: the Generator, which generates artificial data, and the Discriminator, which learns to distinguish artificial data from real cases. The term "generative" signifies the primary objective of the model, which is to generate novel data. The generated data by a GAN is contingent upon the selection of the training set (Durgadevi, 2021). For instance, if the objective is to train a Generative Adversarial Network (GAN) to generate images resembling those created by Leonardo da Vinci, one would utilize a dataset consisting of da Vinci's artwork for training. The term "adversarial" refers to the competitive nature of the relationship between the two models in the GAN framework, namely the Generator and the Discriminator. The objective of the Generator is to generate samples that are indiscernible from the authentic data in the training set. In this current example, this entails creating artworks that closely resemble those of da Vinci (Navidan et al., 2021).

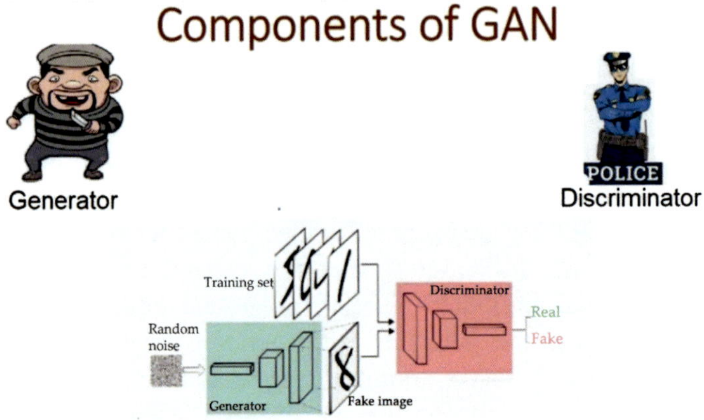

Figure 1.4. *Illustration of the components of GAN*

Source: Raghav Agrawal, Creative Commons License.

The mathematical principles that form the foundation of GANs are intricate; nonetheless, several real-world analogies help facilitate a better comprehension of GANs. In the previous discussion, the scenario of an individual who creates counterfeit artwork (referred to as the Generator) attempting to deceive an expert in the field of art (known as the Discriminator) was analyzed. The art expert's ability to discern the authenticity of false paintings is directly proportional to the level of skill demonstrated by the forger in creating convincing replicas (Pan et al., 2019). The same holds in the opposite scenario: when the art expert's ability to discern the authenticity of a specific picture improves, the forger must enhance their skills even further to evade detection. Another commonly employed metaphor to depict GANs, which Ian Goodfellow himself favors, is that of a counterfeiter (the Generator) and a detective (the Discriminator) attempting to apprehend the counterfeiter. The detective's ability to detect counterfeit bills must be commensurate with the level of authenticity they possess, and vice versa. Table 1.1 presents a succinct summary of the key aspects of the two GAN subnetworks (Iglesias et al., 2023).

Table 1.1. *Summary of Generator and Discriminator Subnetworks*

	Generator	**Discriminator**
Input	Random numbers vector	It gets input from two sources: • Real examples that come out from the training dataset. • Fake ones that come out from the Generator
Output	Fake examples that attempt to be as credible as possible	Predicted probability showing that the input example is truly real
Goal	Generate fake data, identical to members of the training dataset	Differentiate between the counterfeit instances generated by the Generator and the authentic ones derived from the training dataset.

Source: Jakub Langr, Creative Commons License.

Remember

The success of GANs relies on the delicate balance between the generator and discriminator networks. Training GANs requires careful tuning of hyperparameters and monitoring for stability.

1.4. KEY CONCEPTS IN GANS

Learning objectives

- Understand the key concepts in GANs including adversarial training, mode collapse, loss function and latent space.

GANs are underpinned by several key concepts that distinguish them from other models and methodologies in the ML landscape. This section delves into these core concepts, including the adversarial training process, loss functions, the role of latent space, and mode collapse, providing a comprehensive understanding essential for mastering GANs (Kazeminia et al., 2020).

1.4.1. Adversarial Training

The adversarial training procedure is the fundamental component of GANs. This procedure involves the concurrent training of two neural networks, namely the generator (G) and the discriminator (D), through a process that is more competitive than the other (Groenendijk et al., 2020). When compared to the discriminator, the primary responsibility of the discriminator is to discern between the output of the generator and actual data (Sajeeda & Hossain, 2022). The generator's principal purpose is to generate data that is almost identical to data that is collected from the real world. According to the equation that is presented below, this can be considered a game with no winners and no losers (Ni et al., 2018):

$$\min_G \max_D V(D, G) = \mathbb{E}_{x \sim p_{data}(x)}[\log D(x)] + \mathbb{E}_{z \sim p_z(z)}[\log(1 - D(G(z)))]$$

where p_{data} is the data distribution, p_g is the distribution of the generator's input noise, and V (D,G) is the value function that D and G optimize in opposition to each other (Mohamad Nezami et al., 2019).

1.4.2. Loss Functions

The choice of loss functions in GANs plays a critical role in the training process. Typically, binary cross-entropy is employed, reflecting the discriminator's task as a binary classification problem – real vs. generated. However, variants of GANs might utilize different loss functions, such as Wasserstein loss, to address specific challenges like training stability and mode collapse (Togo et al., 2019).

1.4.3. Latent Space and Sampling

Latent space refers to the high-dimensional space from which the generator samples input noise to produce output. Understanding and manipulating the latent space is pivotal for controlling the characteristics of the generated data. The richness and diversity of the generated data are often tied to the complexity and dimensionality of this latent space (Voynov & Babenko, 2020).

1.4.4. Mode Collapse

One of the significant challenges in training GANs is mode collapse, where the generator starts producing a limited variety of outputs. This occurs when the generator finds a particular subset of data that consistently fools the discriminator, leading it to neglect other portions of the data distribution. Addressing mode collapse requires careful tuning of the model architecture, training procedure, and regularization techniques (Kushwaha & Nandi, 2020).

Practice Problem

Describe the potential consequences of mode collapse in GANs and propose strategies to mitigate this issue.

Solution to Practice Problem

Mode collapse in GANs refers to a scenario where the generator fails to capture the full diversity of the training data, resulting in the generation of limited or repetitive samples. To mitigate mode collapse, techniques such as mini-batch discrimination, feature matching, and diversity regularization can be employed to encourage the generator to produce more diverse outputs.

1.5. BENEFITS OF GENERATIVE ADVERSARIAL NETWORKS

Learning objectives

- Understand the benefits of GANs in the field of artificial intelligence.

As a result of their unique technique of creating new data instances that closely mirror the distribution of a given dataset, GANs have attracted a significant amount of attention in the field of AI. This distinctive capability brings about several benefits across various domains, including but not limited to, enhanced realism in generated images, the ability to model high-dimensional data distributions, and significant contributions to semi-supervised learning, data augmentation, and domain adaptation. The following section elucidates these benefits in detail (Kusiak, 2020).

a. **High-Quality Data Generation:** The capacity of GANs to provide data of a high quality and a realistic representation is one of the most notable advantages of these systems. This is the case in the field of picture production, where GANs have proved successful in producing photorealistic images that are frequently indistinguishable from actual photographs. One of the primary factors that contributes to the quality of the data that is generated is the adversarial training process. During this process, the generator gradually acquires the ability to produce more authentic outputs to fool the discriminator (Karras et al., 2019).

b. **Understanding Complex Data Distributions:** GANs are adept at understanding and modeling complex, high-dimensional data distributions. This capability is of paramount importance in fields where the data is inherently complicated, such as genomics, financial modeling, and climate science. By capturing the underlying distribution of datasets, GANs facilitate more nuanced analyzes and predictions (Jeong et al., 2023).

c. **Data Augmentation:** In scenarios where data scarcity poses a significant challenge, GANs offer a powerful tool for data augmentation. By generating new data instances that accurately replicate the characteristics of the original dataset, GANs enable the expansion of datasets, thereby enhancing the performance of ML models trained on such augmented data. This is particularly beneficial in the domain of medical imaging, where acquiring large volumes of annotated data is often impractical (Biswas et al., 2023).

d. **Semi-supervised Learning:** GANs contribute significantly to semi-supervised learning, where they leverage a limited amount of labeled data alongside a larger pool of unlabeled data. Through the adversarial training process, GANs can learn useful feature representations that can improve the performance of classifiers trained on scant annotated datasets (Megahed & Mohammed, 2024).

e. **Domain Adaptation:** GANs are instrumental in domain adaptation tasks, where the goal is to train a model on a source domain and adapt it to perform well on a different target domain. By generating data that is representative of the target domain while retaining the characteristics of the source domain, GANs enable seamless domain adaptation, thus mitigating issues related to domain shift (Benjdira et al., 2019).

f. **Innovation in Creative Fields:** In creative domains such as art, music, and design, GANs have opened new avenues for innovation. By generating novel artistic content, GANs have given artists and designers new tools to explore creative ideas that would be difficult or impossible to realize by human means alone (Guo et al., 2019).

g. **Privacy Preservation:** GANs offer a method for generating synthetic data that can be used in place of real data, ensuring the preservation of privacy in sensitive applications. This is particularly relevant in fields such as healthcare, where sharing patient data is fraught with privacy concerns. By using GANs to create anonymized datasets, it becomes possible to conduct research and analysis without compromising individual privacy. Beyond these enumerated benefits, GANs continue to evolve, offering ever more sophisticated capabilities that promise to address some of the most challenging problems in AI and beyond (Montenegro et al., 2021).

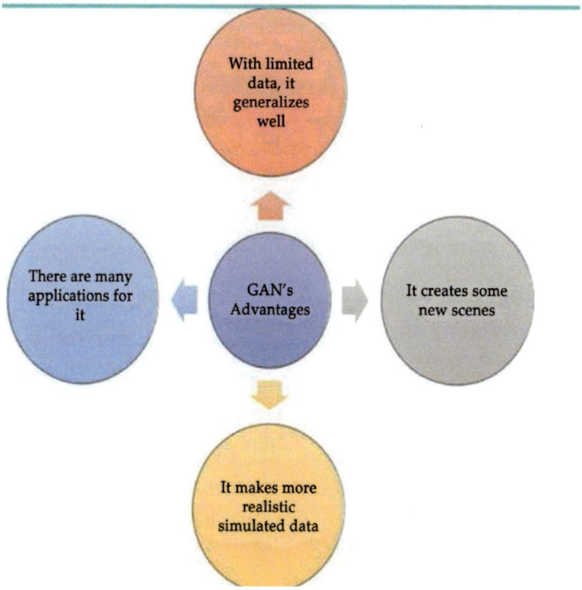

Figure 1.5. *Various advantages of GANs.*

Source: Mehdi Ghayoum, Creative Commons License.

1.6. ISSUES IN GANS

Learning objectives

- Understand the issue of instability during the training of GANs.
- Comprehend the challenges of mode collapse, computational cost and evaluation of generated data.

GANs have demonstrated their efficacy as a potent instrument for producing authentic and varied data, encompassing images, speech, and music. Nevertheless, GANs are accompanied by numerous concerns and obstacles (Lin et al., 2020).

1.6.1. Mode Collapse

Mode collapse is a phenomenon that can occur in GANs, where the generator fails to produce a diverse range of samples and instead focuses on only a few modes present in the real data distribution (Dai et al., 2024).

1.6.2. Training Instability

The training process of GANs can exhibit instability and difficulty in achieving convergence, particularly when there is an imbalance in strength between the discriminator and the generator.

1.6.3. Evaluation of Generated Data

The evaluation of the quality and variation in the generated data lacks a clear and definite method, and several measures may yield divergent outcomes.

1.6.4. Dataset Bias

GANs are highly responsive to the distribution of the training data. If the dataset is skewed or does not accurately match the actual data distribution, the generated data produced by GANs may exhibit bias or lack realism.

1.6.5. Computational Resources

Training GANs necessitates substantial computational resources like high-performance GPUs and extensive memory capacity, which can incur significant expenses and time consumption (Schonfeld et al., 2020).

1.6.6. Lack of Interpretability

GANs are commonly known as opaque models due to the challenge of comprehending the generator's process of generating samples and the specific attributes it derives from the input data.

1.6.7. Data Privacy and Security

GANs have the potential to be utilized for nefarious intentions, such as producing counterfeit information for fraudulent activities or impersonation, which gives rise to apprehensions over the privacy and security of data.

1.6.8. Transferability

GANs that are trained on a certain dataset may not have the ability to perform well on different datasets or domains. In order to make the model suitable for new data, it may be necessary to either fine-tune or retrain it (Salimans et al., 2016).

1.7. APPLICATIONS OF GANS

Learning objectives

- Understand the versatility and potential of GANs in diverse fields.

GANs have sparked significant interest across various domains given their unique ability to generate new, synthetic data that closely resembles authentic datasets. This section delves into several real-world applications of GANs, illustrating their versatility and transformative potential in diverse fields (Prajapati et al., 2021).

1.7.1. Image and Video Generation

One of the most prominent applications of GANs is in the field of computer vision, particularly for generating high-resolution, photorealistic images. GANs have been leveraged to create realistic human faces, animals, and natural scenes, which have applications in video games, film, and virtual reality. For instance, the use of GANs in video game development allows for the creation of diverse character appearances without manual design, enhancing the gaming experience with varied and realistic characters. In the entertainment industry, GANs can be used to generate lifelike animations and effects, reducing the time and cost associated with traditional computer graphics techniques.

1.7.2. Data Augmentation

ML models need large amounts of data to learn successfully. In situations where data is scarce or hard to come by, GANs can be used to create synthetic datasets that augment real data, enabling better model training and performance. This application is particularly valuable in the field of medicine, where GANs are used to generate synthetic medical images for training diagnostic models without violating patient privacy (Ma et al., 2018).

1.7.3. Style Transfer

GANs can modify the style of an image while retaining its content, enabling applications such as transforming photographs into paintings in the style of famous artists. This application is not only of interest to digital artists but also has potential implications in design and marketing, where visual content can be stylistically tailored to match brand esthetics or appeal to specific target audiences. Applications include transforming photos into artwork for personalized merchandise or creating stylized content for social media campaigns.

1.7.4. Text-to-Image Synthesis

GANs can also be used to generate realistic images from textual descriptions, a field known as text-to-image synthesis. This area holds promise for content creation where visual representations can be produced directly from textual ideas, streamlining processes in advertising, storyboarding for films, and more. An example includes automatically generating product images based on descriptive listings in e-commerce platforms (Berrahal & Azizi, 2022).

1.7.5. Drug Discovery

In the pharmaceutical industry, GANs are employed to generate molecular structures for potential new drugs, accelerating the process of drug discovery. By synthesizing molecular data, GANs can help identify promising compounds more efficiently than traditional methods, potentially reducing the time and cost associated with drug development. Synthetic datasets of molecular compounds generated by GANs can be used to train models that predict the efficacy and side effects of new drug candidates.

1.7.6. Anonymization of Data

GANs offer a novel approach to the anonymization of sensitive data, making it possible to share datasets for research without compromising individual privacy. By generating synthetic datasets that retain the statistical properties of the original data, GANs facilitate the advancement of research in fields where data privacy is a concern. This application is particularly relevant in healthcare research, where sharing medical data is essential for advancements in treatment and diagnosis but must be balanced with patient confidentiality. In each of these applications, GANs demonstrate a remarkable capacity to bridge the gap between creative ideation and technical realization, underscoring their role as a pivotal technology in data-driven innovation (Nikolaidis et al., 2021).

Did You Know?

GANs have sparked debates about the ethical implications of synthetic data generation, particularly in areas such as facial recognition, where generated images can be used to bypass privacy protections or perpetuate biases.

1.8. GANS VS. OTHER GENERATIVE MODELS

Learning objectives

- Comparison of other generative models such as VAEs, RBMs, Pixel RNN and Pixel CNN with GANs.
- Understand key strengths of GANs.

GANs have garnered significant attention in the field of ML for their ability to generate high-quality, realistic data. However, GANs are not the sole class of models capable of data generation. Other prominent generative models include Variational Autoencoders (VAEs), Restricted Boltzmann Machines (RBMs), and Autoregressive models like PixelRNN and PixelCNN. This section will delineate the operational principles, strengths, and limitations of GANs in comparison with these generative models (Han et al., 2018).

1.8.1. Variational Autoencoders (VAEs)

VAEs operate on the principle of encoding inputs into a latent space representation and subsequently reconstructing the input from this representation. Unlike GANs that utilize a discriminator to improve generation, VAEs optimize the reconstruction loss and a regularizer that ensures the latent space distribution closely approximates a prior distribution, typically a Gaussian. This results in VAEs being proficient at generating new data points similar to the original dataset but often lacking the sharpness and detail found in GAN-generated images due to the blurriness inherent in its reconstruction loss.

1.8.2. Restricted Boltzmann Machines (RBMs)

RBMs are energy-based models that learn a probability distribution over the input set. They consist of a layer of visible units and a layer of hidden units, with no intra-layer connections. While RBMs were once popular for their capability of feature learning and generation, their use has diminished over time, mainly due to the complexity of training and the rise of more effective models such as GANs and VAEs. Compared to GANs, RBMs struggle with generating high-fidelity samples in complex, high-dimensional spaces (Aslan et al., 2023).

1.8.3. Autoregressive Models (PixelRNN and PixelCNN)

These models generate data sequentially, predicting the next element in a sequence given the previous elements. They are explicitly designed to model the probability distribution of pixels in images, making them quite effective for tasks that require high levels of detail and consistency, such as generating textures. However, their sequential nature means they can be slower than GANs for generation tasks, and often, they do not produce as visually compelling results as GANs in tasks requiring the synthesis of complex, high-dimensional data (Metri & Mamatha, 2021).

1.8.4. Key Strengths of GANs

GANs distinguish themselves from these models through the adversarial training process, which is inherently competitive. Using this approach, the generator is encouraged to provide outputs that are progressively more realistic, even while the probability distribution of the input is not explicitly modeled. GANs have several major strengths, including:

a. **High-Quality Generation:** The adversarial process enables GANs to generate data that is often more realistic and detailed compared to other generative models.

b. **Flexibility:** GANs can be adapted to a wide range of data types and applications, from image and video synthesis to text-to-image generation.

c. **Improved Sample Diversity:** By effectively exploring the model's capacity, GANs can generate a diverse range of outputs, mitigating the mode collapse issue to some extent with advanced architectures and training techniques.

However, GANs also face challenges, such as training instability and mode collapse, where the generator starts to produce a limited variety of samples. Techniques such as Wasserstein loss, batch normalization, and architectural adjustments have been developed to address these issues, making GANs a robust and versatile choice among generative models.

While each generative model has its merits and use cases, GANs' ability to produce high-quality, diverse, and realistic outputs with considerable flexibility makes them a prominent tool in the generative modeling domain (Singh et al., 2024).

1.9. FUTURE DIRECTIONS IN GAN RESEARCH

Learning objectives

- Understand the potential future directions for GAN research highlighting areas for innovation and development.

GANs have transformed the landscape of AI by enabling the generation of highly realistic data across various domains. Despite their successes, numerous challenges and opportunities for advancement remain. This section delves into potential future directions for GAN research, highlighting areas ripe for innovation and development (Chang et al., 2017).

1.9.1. Improving Stability and Training Dynamics

An inherent obstacle in GAN research is the lack of stability that occurs during the training process. This problem develops because of the adversarial nature of the training mechanism, sometimes resulting in issues like mode collapse, when the generator begins to generate a limited range of outputs. Implementing advanced methods such as adjusting the loss functions, incorporating regularization terms, or utilizing alternate training methodologies may result in more reliable GANs. Research on new designs that naturally enhance stable training dynamics is also a crucial topic of investigation.

1.9.2. Enhancing Image Quality at Higher Resolutions

While GANs have proved outstanding success in creating high-fidelity images, achieving similar quality at significantly higher resolutions remains a challenge. Research could focus on developing more efficient architectures and training methods that can scale to larger images without compromising on generation quality or computational efficiency (Sun & Scanlon, 2019).

1.9.3. Expanding to Unexplored Domains

GANs have been primarily applied to visual data, but their potential extends to other domains such as audio, video, and even multi-modal data generation. Investigating GAN architectures tailored for these domains, which may require different considerations in terms of model complexity and data representation, represents a promising research path.

1.9.4. Improving Interpretability and Control

Achieving a higher degree of control over the generated outputs while maintaining or improving the quality of generated data is an important research area. This involves developing mechanisms to dissect and understand the latent space of GANs, allowing for precise manipulation of generation attributes. Techniques from the field of interpretable machine learning, when applied to GANs, could unlock new potentials in controlled generative processes (Abdullah et al., 2021).

1.9.5. Addressing Ethical and Societal Implications

As the capability of GANs to generate realistic data improves, so does the potential for misuse in creating deepfakes, misinformation, and other forms of digital manipulation. Research into methods for detecting GAN-generated content, as well as ethical guidelines for responsible use, is increasingly important. This includes technological solutions for the authentication of digital content and legal frameworks that consider the implications of generative AI technologies.

1.9.6. Enhancing Efficiency

Current GAN models, especially those generating high-quality outputs, are computationally intensive and require substantial resources. Optimizing GAN architectures for greater efficiency, enabling their use in resource-constrained environments, and reducing the carbon footprint of training large models are important future directions. Techniques such as pruning, quantization, and efficient network design principles can contribute towards more sustainable and accessible GAN technologies Anderson et al., 2018).

1.9.7. Integration with Other Machine Learning Paradigms

Integrating GANs with other ML approaches such as reinforcement learning, unsupervised learning, and semi-supervised learning opens new avenues for creating more robust generative models. For example, reinforcement learning can be used to automatically fine-tune the feedback loop in GANs for improved performance. Exploring these intersections could lead to breakthroughs in AI capabilities and applications.

The future of GAN research holds immense potential not only for advancing state-of-the-art generative modeling but also for exploring novel applications that impact society positively. By addressing the outlined challenges and exploring the suggested directions, GANs can continue to evolve and significantly contribute to the field of AI (Sarker, 2021).

SUMMARY

- This chapter presents an outline of GANs, covering their history, components, key concepts, benefits, challenges, real-world examples, and future directions.
- GANs belong to a category of ML algorithms. The system comprises two neural networks, namely the generator and the discriminator, which are trained in a competitive way. The generator produces artificial data samples by generating random noise. The discriminator differentiates genuine data from counterfeit data. Adversarial training involves the iterative improvement of both networks. The generator's objective is to produce realistic data, while the discriminator's objective is to accurately distinguish genuine and fake data.
- GANs were proposed to address the challenge of generating realistic data samples in unsupervised learning. Since their inception, GANs have undergone significant advancements, leading to improved performance and new applications. The key components of GANs are Generator, Discriminator, and Loss functions.
- The benefits and challenges of working with GANs are also discussed in this chapter. Some of the benefits include the ability to generate realistic data samples and data augmentation and synthesis for training other models.
- Real-world examples of GAN applications include image and video generation, style transfer, drug discovery, and data augmentation.

MULTIPLE CHOICE QUESTIONS

1. What are Generative Adversarial Networks (GANs)?

a) Supervised machine learning algorithms

b) Semi-supervised learning algorithms

c) Unsupervised machine learning algorithms

d) Reinforcement learning algorithms

2. How many neural networks are typically involved in a GAN architecture?

a) One

b) Two

c) Three

d) Four

3. Which component of a GAN generates synthetic data samples?

a) Generator

b) Discriminator

c) Loss function

d) Gradient

4. What is the primary objective of the discriminator in a GAN?

a) Generate realistic data samples

b) Classify real and fake data

c) Minimize the generator's loss

d) Maximize the generator's loss

5. Which of the following is NOT a key concept in GANs?

a) Mode collapse

b) Training stability

c) Gradient vanishing

d) Adversarial training

REVIEW QUESTIONS

1. Define Generative Adversarial Networks (GANs) and explain their primary objective in machine learning.
2. How do GANs work? Provide a step-by-step explanation of the training process.
3. Discuss the history of GANs, including their origins and notable advancements over the years.
4. What are the key components of GANs, and how do they contribute to the overall functioning of the model?
5. Explain the concept of adversarial training in GANs and its significance in the learning process.
6. What are some key challenges associated with working with GANs? How can these challenges be addressed?
7. Identify and discuss at least three benefits of using GANs in various applications.

Answers to Multiple Questions

1. (c) 2. (b) 3. (a) 4. (b) 5. (b)

REFERENCES

1. Abdullah, T. A., Zahid, M. S. M., & Ali, W. (2021). A review of interpretable ML in healthcare: Taxonomy, applications, challenges, and future directions. *Symmetry, 13*(12), 2439. https://doi.org/10.3390/sym13122439.
2. Alqahtani, H., Kavakli-Thorne, M., & Kumar, G. (2021). Applications of generative adversarial networks (GANs): An updated review. *Archives of Computational Methods in Engineering, 28*, 525–552. https://doi.org/10.1007/s11831-020-09466-y.
3. Anderson, T. J., Chowdhury, S., Aktas, O., Bockowski, M., & Hite, J. K. (2018). GaN Power Devices–Current Status and Future Directions. *The Electrochemical Society Interface, 27*(4), 43. https://doi.org/10.1149/2.F04184if.
4. Arora, S., Ge, R., Liang, Y., Ma, T., & Zhang, Y. (2017). Generalization and equilibrium in generative adversarial nets (GANs). In *International Conference on Machine Learning* (Vol. 2, pp. 224–232). PMLR. http://proceedings.mlr.press/v2/arora17a.html.
5. Aslan, N., Dogan, S., & Koca, G. O. (2023). Automated classification of brain diseases using the restricted Boltzmann machine and the generative adversarial network. *Engineering Applications of Artificial Intelligence, 126*, 106794. https://doi.org/10.1016/j.engappai.2021.106794.
6. Benjdira, B., Bazi, Y., Koubaa, A., & Ouni, K. (2019). Unsupervised domain adaptation using generative adversarial networks for semantic segmentation of aerial images. *Remote Sensing, 11*(11), 1369. https://doi.org/10.3390/rs11111369.
7. Berrahal, M., & Azizi, M. (2022). Optimal text-to-image synthesis model for generating portrait images using generative adversarial network techniques. *Indonesian Journal of Electrical Engineering and Computer Science, 25*(2), 972–979. https://doi.org/10.11591/ijeecs.v25.i2.pp972-979.
8. Biswas, A., Md Abdullah Al, N., Imran, A., Sejuty, A. T., Fairooz, F., Puppala, S., & Talukder, S. (2023). Generative adversarial networks for data augmentation. In *Data Driven Approaches on Medical Imaging* (Vol. 2, pp. 159–177). Springer Nature Switzerland. https://doi.org/10.1007/978-3-030-12385-7_10.
9. Breckman, W. (2001). Eduard Gans and the crisis of Hegelianism. *Journal of the History of Ideas, 62*(3), 543–564. https://doi.org/10.1353/jhi.2001.0026.

10. Chang, R. D., Zuo, J., Zhao, Z. Y., Zillante, G., Gan, X. L., & Soebarto, V. (2017). Evolving theories of sustainability and firms: History, future directions and implications for renewable energy research. *Renewable and Sustainable Energy Reviews, 72*, 48–56. https://doi.org/10.1016/j.rser.2017.01.007.

11. Cohen, L. J., Mcgeoch, P. G., Gans, S. W., Nikiforov, K., Cullen, K., & Galynker, I. I. (2002). Childhood sexual history of 20 male pedophiles vs. 24 male healthy control subjects. *The Journal of Nervous and Mental Disease, 190*(11), 757–766. https://doi.org/10.1097/01.NMD.0000046495.77498.3F.

12. Dai, Z., Zhao, L., Wang, K., & Zhou, Y. (2024). Mode standardization: A practical countermeasure against mode collapse of GAN-based signal synthesis. *Applied Soft Computing, 150*, 111089. https://doi.org/10.1016/j.asoc.2021.111089.

13. Durgadevi, M. (2021). Generative adversarial network (GAN): A general review on different variants of GAN and applications. In *2021 6th International Conference on Communication and Electronics Systems (ICCES)* (Vol. 2, pp. 1–8). IEEE. https://doi.org/10.1109/ICCES53269.2021.9489598.

14. Efron, N. J. (1997). Irenism and natural philosophy in Rudolfine Prague: The case of David Gans. *Science in Context, 10*(4), 627–649. https://doi.org/10.1017/S0269889700003680.

15. Gonog, L., & Zhou, Y. (2019). A review: Generative adversarial networks. In *2019 14th IEEE Conference on Industrial Electronics and Applications (ICIEA)* (Vol. 2, pp. 505–510). IEEE. https://doi.org/10.1109/ICIEA.2019.8834007.

16. Groenendijk, R., Karaoglu, S., Gevers, T., & Mensink, T. (2020). On the benefit of adversarial training for monocular depth estimation. *Computer Vision and Image Understanding, 190*, 102848. https://doi.org/10.1016/j.cviu.2019.102848.

17. Guo, T., Herber, D., & Allison, J. T. (2019). Circuit synthesis using generative adversarial networks (GANs). In *AIAA SciTech 2019 Forum* (Vol. 1, pp. 2350–2355). https://doi.org/10.2514/6.2019-2350.

18. Hacker, B. R., Wallis, S. R., McWilliams, M. O., & Gans, P. B. (2009). 40Ar/39Ar constraints on the tectonic history and architecture of the ultrahigh pressure Sulu orogen. *Journal of Metamorphic Geology, 27*(9), 827–844. https://doi.org/10.1111/j.1525-1314.2009.00829.x.

19. Han, L., Murphy, R. F., & Ramanan, D. (2018). Learning generative models of tissue organization with supervised GANs. In *2018 IEEE*

Winter Conference on Applications of Computer Vision (WACV) (Vol. 4, pp. 682–690). IEEE. https://doi.org/10.1109/WACV.2018.00102.

20. Hardy, C., Le Merrer, E., & Sericola, B. (2019). Md-gan: Multi-discriminator generative adversarial networks for distributed datasets. In *2019 IEEE International Parallel and Distributed Processing Symposium (IPDPS)* (Vol. 2, pp. 866–877). IEEE. https://doi.org/10.1109/IPDPS.2019.00090.
21. Iglesias, G., Talavera, E., & Díaz-Álvarez, A. (2023). A survey on GANs for computer vision: Recent research, analysis and taxonomy. *Computer Science Review, 48*, 100553. https://doi.org/10.1016/j.cosrev.2023.100553.
22. Jeong, S., Li, M., Berger, M., & Liu, S. (2023). Concept Lens: Visually analyzing the consistency of semantic manipulation in GANs. In *2023 IEEE Visualization and Visual Analytics (VIS)* (Vol. 2, pp. 221–225). IEEE. https://doi.org/10.1109/VISUAL.2023.00037.
23. Karras, T., Laine, S., & Aila, T. (2019). A style-based generator architecture for generative adversarial networks. In *Proceedings of the IEEE/CVF Conference on Computer Vision and Pattern Recognition* (Vol. 1, pp. 4401–4410). https://doi.org/10.1109/CVPR.2019.00452.
24. Kazeminia, S., Baur, C., Kuijper, A., van Ginneken, B., Navab, N., Albarqouni, S., & Mukhopadhyay, A. (2020). GANs for medical image analysis. *Artificial Intelligence in Medicine, 109*, 101938. https://doi.org/10.1016/j.artmed.2020.101938.
25. Kushwaha, V., & Nandi, G. C. (2020). Study of prevention of mode collapse in generative adversarial network (GAN). In *2020 IEEE 4th Conference on Information & Communication Technology (CICT)* (Vol. 2, pp. 1–6). IEEE. https://doi.org/10.1109/CICT50772.2020.9385473.
26. Kusiak, A. (2020). Convolutional and generative adversarial neural networks in manufacturing. *International Journal of Production Research, 58*(5), 1594–1604. https://doi.org/10.1080/00207543.2019.1679631.
27. Li, S., Wu, J., Xiao, X., Chao, F., Mao, X., & Ji, R. (2021). Revisiting discriminator in GAN compression: A generator-discriminator cooperative compression scheme. *Advances in Neural Information Processing Systems, 34*, 28560–28572. https://arxiv.org/abs/2110.14439
28. Lin, Z., Jain, A., Wang, C., Fanti, G., & Sekar, V. (2020). Using GANs for sharing networked time series data: Challenges, initial promise, and open questions. In *Proceedings of the ACM Internet Measurement Conference* (Vol. 3, pp. 464–483). https://doi.org/10.1145/3419394.3423643.
29. Lu, Y., Chen, D., Olaniyi, E., & Huang, Y. (2022). Generative adversarial networks (GANs) for image augmentation in agriculture: A systematic

review. *Computers and Electronics in Agriculture, 200*, 107208. https://doi.org/10.1016/j.compag.2022.107208.

30. Ma, Y., Liu, K., Guan, Z., Xu, X., Qian, X., & Bao, H. (2018). Background augmentation generative adversarial networks (BAGANs): Effective data generation based on GAN-augmented 3D synthesizing. *Symmetry, 10*(12), 734. https://doi.org/10.3390/sym10120734.
31. MacMillan, I., Gans, P. B., & Alvarado, G. (2004). Middle Miocene to present plate tectonic history of the southern Central American Volcanic Arc. *Tectonophysics, 392*(14), 325–348. https://doi.org/10.1016/j.tecto.2004.06.006.
32. Megahed, M., & Mohammed, A. (2024). Multi-GANs with shared generator: An approach for handling mode collapse issue. In *2024 6th International Conference on Computing and Informatics (ICCI)* (Vol. 2, pp. 483–489). IEEE. https://doi.org/10.1109/ICCI53214.2024.9763366.
33. Metri, O., & Mamatha, H. R. (2021). Image generation using generative adversarial networks. In O. Metri & H. R. Mamatha (Eds.), *Generative Adversarial Networks for Image-to-Image Translation* (Vol. 2, pp. 235–262). Academic Press. https://doi.org/10.1016/B978-0-12-820331-9.00009-6.
34. Mohamad Nezami, O., Dras, M., Wan, S., Paris, C., & Hamey, L. (2019). Towards generating stylized image captions via adversarial training. In *PRICAI 2019: Trends in Artificial Intelligence: 16th Pacific Rim International Conference on Artificial Intelligence, Cuvu, Yanuca Island, Fiji, August 26–30, 2019, Proceedings, Part I* (Vol. 1, pp. 270–284). Springer International Publishing. https://doi.org/10.1007/978-3-030-29908-8_21.
35. Montenegro, H., Silva, W., & Cardoso, J. S. (2021). Privacy-preserving generative adversarial network for case-based explainability in medical image analysis. *IEEE Access, 9*, 148037–148047. https://doi.org/10.1109/ACCESS.2021.3124138.
36. Navidan, H., Moshiri, P. F., Nabati, M., Shahbazian, R., Ghorashi, S. A., Shah-Mansouri, V., & Windridge, D. (2021). Generative adversarial networks (GANs) in networking: A comprehensive survey & evaluation. *Computer Networks, 194*, 108149. https://doi.org/10.1016/j.comnet.2021.108149.
37. Ni, Y., Song, D., Zhang, X., Wu, H., & Liao, L. (2018). CAGAN: Consistent adversarial training enhanced GANs. In *IJCAI* (Vol. 1, pp. 2588–2594). https://www.ijcai.org/Proceedings/2018/359 (accessed on 27 June 2024).
38. Nikolaidis, K., Kristiansen, S., Plagemann, T., Goebel, V., Liestøl, K.,

Kankanhalli, M., & Steinshamn, S. (2021). Learning realistic patterns from visually unrealistic stimuli: Generalization and data anonymization. *Journal of Artificial Intelligence Research, 72*, 1163–1214. https://doi.org/10.1613/jair.1.12494.

39. Offert, F. (2021). Latent deep space: Generative adversarial networks (GANs) in the sciences. *Media+ Environment, 3*(2), 98–100. https://doi.org/10.1525/elementa.2021.00085.
40. Pan, Z., Yu, W., Yi, X., Khan, A., Yuan, F., & Zheng, Y. (2019). Recent progress on generative adversarial networks (GANs): A survey. *IEEE Access, 7*, 36322–36333. https://doi.org/10.1109/ACCESS.2019.2906011.
41. Prajapati, K., Chudasama, V., Patel, H., Upla, K., Raja, K., Ramachandra, R., & Busch, C. (2021). Direct unsupervised super-resolution using generative adversarial network (DUS-GAN) for real-world data. *IEEE Transactions on Image Processing, 30*, 8251–8264. https://doi.org/10.1109/TIP.2021.3111670.
42. Sajeeda, A., & Hossain, B. M. (2022). Exploring generative adversarial networks and adversarial training. *International Journal of Cognitive Computing in Engineering, 3*, 78–89. https://doi.org/10.4018/IJCCE.2022070106.
43. Salimans, T., Goodfellow, I., Zaremba, W., Cheung, V., Radford, A., & Chen, X. (2016). Improved techniques for training GANs. *Advances in Neural Information Processing Systems, 29*, 321–325. https://papers.nips.cc/paper_files/paper/2016/file/8a3363abe792db2d8761d6403605aeb7-Paper.pdf
44. Sarker, I. H. (2021). Deep learning: A comprehensive overview on techniques, taxonomy, applications and research directions. *SN Computer Science, 2*(6), 420–425. https://doi.org/10.1007/s42979-021-00358-7.
45. Saxena, D., & Cao, J. (2021). Generative adversarial networks (GANs) challenges, solutions, and future directions. *ACM Computing Surveys (CSUR), 54*(3), 1–42. https://doi.org/10.1145/3459934.
46. Schonfeld, E., Schiele, B., & Khoreva, A. (2020). A U-net based discriminator for generative adversarial networks. In *Proceedings of the IEEE/CVF Conference on Computer Vision and Pattern Recognition* (Vol. 2, pp. 8207–8216). https://doi.org/10.1109/CVPR42600.2020.00828.
47. Singh, P., Dutta, S., & Pranav, P. (2024). Optimizing GANs for cryptography: The role and impact of activation functions in neural layers assessing the cryptographic strength. *Applied Sciences, 14*(6), 2379. https://doi.org/10.3390/app14062379.

48. Sun, A. Y., & Scanlon, B. R. (2019). How can Big Data and machine learning benefit environment and water management: A survey of methods, applications, and future directions. *Environmental Research Letters, 14*(7), 073001. https://doi.org/10.1088/1748-9326/ab1dc1.
49. Togo, R., Ogawa, T., & Haseyama, M. (2019). Synthetic gastritis image generation via loss function-based conditional PGGAN. *IEEE Access, 7*, 87448–87457. https://doi.org/10.1109/ACCESS.2019.2920271.
50. Voynov, A., & Babenko, A. (2020). Unsupervised discovery of interpretable directions in the GAN latent space. In *International Conference on Machine Learning* (Vol. 1, pp. 9786–9796). PMLR. http://proceedings.mlr.press/v119/voynov20a.html (accessed on 27 June 2024).
51. Wang, K., Gou, C., Duan, Y., Lin, Y., Zheng, X., & Wang, F. Y. (2017). Generative adversarial networks: Introduction and outlook. *IEEE/CAA Journal of Automatica Sinica, 4*(4), 588–598. https://doi.org/10.1109/JAS.2017.7510555.

CHAPTER 2

ARCHITECTURE OF GENERATIVE ADVERSARIAL NETWORKS

LEARNING OBJECTIVES

At the end of this chapter, readers will be able to:

1. Overview of GAN architecture.
2. Training procedure of GANs.
3. Concept of latent space in GANs.
4. Steps of developing GAN models.
5. Challenges in GAN architecture design.
6. Practices in GAN architecture development.

INTRODUCTORY EXAMPLE

A company in the fashion industry, "FashionX," generates realistic images of clothing items for its online catalog. By utilizing Generative Adversarial Networks (GANs), FashionX creates high-quality images of clothing items such as dresses, shirts, and pants. The generator model of the GAN produces diverse and realistic images of clothing based on input specifications, while the discriminator model ensures that the generated images closely resemble real clothing items. This enables FashionX to enhance its online shopping experience by providing visually appealing and accurate representations of its products, ultimately attracting more customers and driving sales.

UNIT INTRODUCTION

This chapter explores the intricacies of GAN architecture, including the roles and structures of these networks, the critical concept of latent space, and various architectural innovations that enhance GANs' capabilities (Karras et al., 2019). By examining the standard architectures as well as variations like DCGANs, cGANs, and CycleGANs, readers will obtain a comprehensive understanding of how GANs are built and how their design influences their ability to generate high-quality synthetic data (Gong et al., 2019).

2.1. GAN ARCHITECTURE

Learning objectives

- Understand the Generator and Discriminator model
- Comprehend the interaction between Generator and Discriminator

The phrases generator and discriminator will be used frequently. Although they are contrasting, they will be utilized in conjunction as they are the two fundamental elements of a GAN. These are neural networks designed to examine the fluctuations within the dataset. By employing two neural networks in a supervised manner, the GAN can solve the problem of unsupervised generation. This model is known as the generator, and it is responsible for producing novel and credible cases from the problem domain. The model known as the discriminator is responsible for determining whether instances are part of the problem area or whether they are simply the result of the generator's fake generation. For instance, when it comes to the process of making images of automobiles, the discriminator's job is to decide whether a particular image has the characteristics of a vehicle. The generator can generate data that is credible, while the discriminator is able to differentiate between genuine and fake data. Both abilities are acquired by the generator. To teach the discriminator to classify the input as real or counterfeit, genuine samples are used as teaching tools. The generated data that is produced by the generator is where the negative training examples are taken from. Through the process of assigning a score to the generator, the discriminator can place a penalty on the generator whenever it produces results that are not considered to be acceptable. The scores that are offered by the discriminator will be utilized by the generator to acquire knowledge regarding the enhancement of the quality of the data that is generated (Abdollahi et al., 2020) (Figure 2.1).

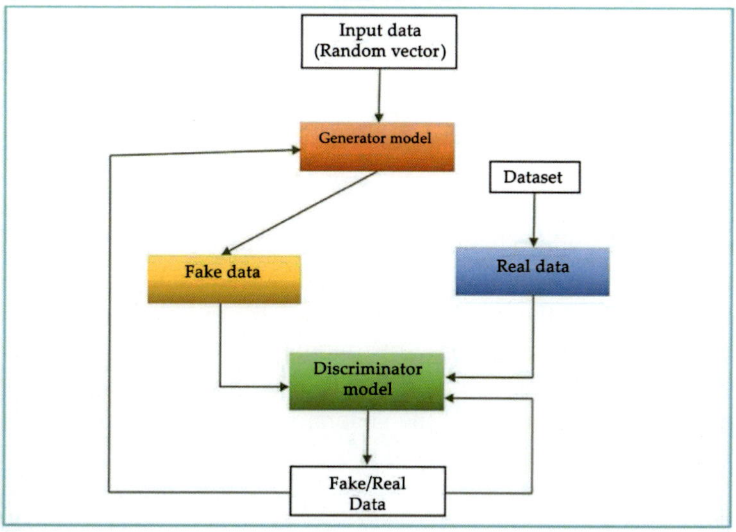

Figure 2.1. *Schematic of general GAN architecture.*

Source: Mehdi Ghayoum, Creative Commons License.

2.1.1. The Discriminator

In the GAN architecture, the discriminator is a key component because its major role is to determine the validity of the input data by categorizing it as either real or false. This is accomplished through the discriminator's classification system. The architecture can be different, although in most cases, it is made up of neural networks. The convolutional neural network (CNN) is the component that makes up most of the discriminative models that are utilized in GANs. Training the discriminator model with real-world data samples allows it to acquire knowledge about specific patterns that are present in the samples that are being used for training. The discriminator receives data that is a composite of two different sources while they are in the process of being trained. The first source is comprised of information that is genuine and has been obtained directly from the problem domain. Data that is obtained from the real world is referred to as real data. Real data can take numerous forms, including photographs, text, or a combination of the two. When it comes to the generation of lifelike photographs of human faces, for instance, the discriminator is given authentic images of human faces to work with.

On the other hand, when the goal at hand is to generate images from textual data, the discriminator will be provided with a combination of text and the image sample that would be linked with it as input. Because they are instances of actual data, this data source could be referred to as the positive samples. Additionally, the samples that are produced by the generator are included in the second data source. As a result of the fact that these data are fake, they might be referred to as negative samples. Following the provision of the discriminator with the input data, the discriminator will proceed to traverse through the layers and produce a bidirectional output. A genuine or created (counterfeit) data sample is indicated by the binary output, which indicates whether the input is authentic or not. While the discriminator is in operation, the generator weights are permitted to remain unchanged throughout the training phase. Now, the discriminator receives data from the generator for the purpose of training (Elazab et al., 2020). A binary cross-entropy loss function is utilized by the discriminator to assess the distance that exists between the output of the generator and the actual label of the data sample that is being collected.

Through the utilization of backpropagation, the accuracy of discriminator identification is effectively enhanced. As a result, it will be able to differentiate between genuine and fake samples with more efficiency. The quality of the samples that are created by the generator improves as the discriminator acquires more capabilities. This technique is repeated an infinite number of times until the generator produces samples that are indistinguishable from the ones that are real. A representation of the discriminator's architecture may be found in Figure 2.2. The layers that are subject to downsampling are represented by a sequence of consecutive rectangles that gradually decrease in size. On the left-hand side of the picture is a representation of the input data that is being fed into the discriminator. A representation of the binary classes that are produced by the discriminator can be found on the right side of the figure. These classes can either be fake or real (Li et al., 2021).

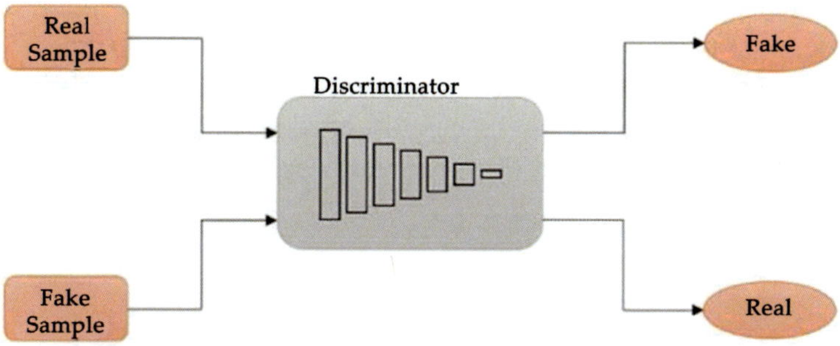

Figure 2.2. *Illustration of discriminator architecture.*

Source: Reem Nassar, Creative Commons License.

2.1.2. The Generator

The generator is the main component in GANs, responsible for generating data. The design may differ, but often it involves a neural network. The generator model of GANs typically has multiple up-sampling layers. The input data sample passes through a sequence of phases to attain the desired shape. For example, if the goal is to generate images of a human face with dimensions of 224 by 224 pixels and 3 color channels, the last layer in the generator will produce an image that meets these parameters. Usually, the input of the generator is dictated by the task being performed. In the context of image production, it will seem like random interference or disturbance. Text-to-image translation utilizes a combination of textual information and random data as input. In the context of picture-to-image translation, the source image will be used as the input. The generator receives input data continuously during the training process and produces the necessary output. The method will begin by generating random noise that is significantly far from the actual data (Durall et al., 2021). The goal is to trick the discriminator by evaluating the quality of the generated images using a designated loss function. The primary goal of the generator is to optimize the loss function by modifying the weights and biases, to produce high-quality data. The loss incurred by the generator at the onset of training is significant. While training the generator, the discriminator's loads remain unchanged. However, the generator modifies its loads based on the precision of the discriminator model. Similarly, the generator is trained using the backpropagation technique. During the training process, the generator iteratively modifies its loads based on the feedback received from the discriminator. After finishing the training procedure, the generator model can generate counterfeit samples that closely resemble genuine ones. The generator also aims to prevent overfitting the training data. Figure 2.3 depicts the arrangement of the generator. The gray box depicts the many stages of up-sampling in the generator model. The up-sampling layers are represented by a sequence of neighboring rectangles that gradually grow. The input to the generator, often a random noise, is illustrated on the left side of the diagram. The fake samples are exhibited on the right side of the illustration (Fetty et al., 2020).

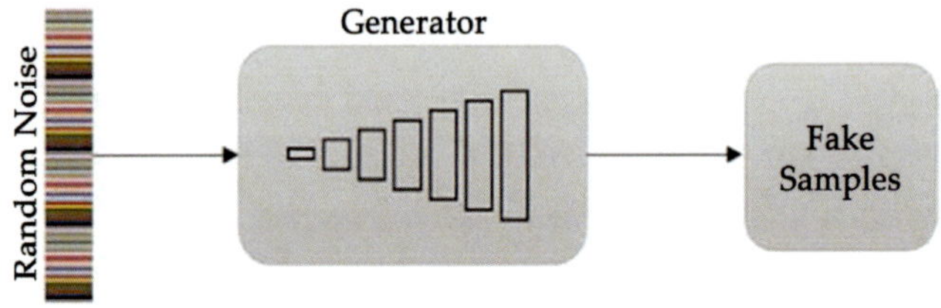

Figure 2.3. *Schematic of generator architecture.*

Source: Sanaa Kaddaoura, Creative Commons License.

Did You Know?

GANs have been used to create "deepfakes," which are synthetic media generated using AI algorithms to manipulate or replace existing content, such as videos or images. This technology has raised concerns about misinformation and privacy.

2.2. TRAINING THE GAN

Learning objectives

- Comprehend the procedure of training the components of GAN

It is necessary to train both the generator and discriminator networks, which are the GAN's constituent elements, to complete the process of training the GAN. To attain a state of equilibrium between the two networks, this technique calls for the training of both networks regularly. The training process in GANs alters the weights in both the generator and the discriminator in an iterative manner. After both models have reached a state of convergence, the method will be considered complete. The objective of the GAN training process is to arrive at a point when the discriminator is unable to differentiate between the data that has been created and the data that is authentic. In addition, the generator delivers data that is extremely similar to authentic data. The "Nash equilibrium" refers to the situation in which neither of the networks can increase their performance any further than they already have. To obtain data of exceptional quality, it is necessary to have a neural network model that is both reliable and robust (Padiyar & Ghosh, 1989). Consequently, it is of the utmost importance to meticulously optimize the hyperparameters, select the model architecture with great precision, and utilize an adequate number of additional layers. It is not always necessary to do a single endeavor in order to develop the generator model with an optimum design. One of the most notable characteristics of the training process for GANs is its protracted duration, which includes a great number of epochs and necessitates a considerable amount of time to accomplish completion. An increase in the number of epochs results in an improvement in the quality of the data; however, there is a possibility of overfitting. Additionally, a technique known as progressive training is utilized in several applications that make use of GANs. Initially, this method involves the generation of fresh data with a low resolution, which is then subsequently entered into a different GAN model to generate data with a higher resolution. In the field of image synthesis, it is typically utilized to allow the model to gradually acquire knowledge about the characteristics of the input and ultimately arrive at a more ideal solution. Training a GAN is illustrated in Figure 2.4, which shows the process explained (Parikh et al., 2018).

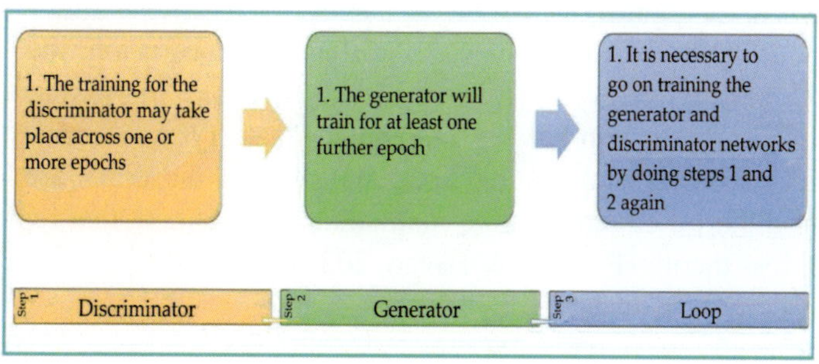

Figure 2.4. *Illustration of GAN training procedure.*

Source: Mehdi Ghayoum, Creative Commons License.

2.3. LOSS FUNCTIONS

Learning objectives

- Understand the concept of loss functions in GAN models

A min-max loss is a term that is typically used to refer to the loss function that is utilized for GANs. The purpose of the discriminator is to maximize the loss, but the objective of the generator is to increase the loss as much as possible to provide data of a high quality. When it comes to training their components, GANs make use of two different loss functions: the generator loss function and the discriminator loss function. To determine the quality of the data that is generated, the generator loss function is utilized. To put it another way, it measures the generator's capacity to make fake images that are very similar to real ones. The fundamental goal of the generator model is to lessen the magnitude of this loss function to produce images of a higher quality. To determine whether the model can deliver genuine data, the discriminator loss function is utilized. On the other hand, it provides a quantitative measure of the discriminator's capacity to discern between genuine and fake data samples. The discriminator model's goal is to optimize this loss function to improve its ability to discern between the two categories of data samples. This is the objective of the discriminator model. The goal of GANs can be accomplished by the utilization of a collection of different loss functions. The mean squared error, the binary cross-entropy loss, and the Wasserstein loss are the three functions that are applied the most frequently for various purposes. Binary cross-entropy loss is a method that is frequently used for estimating the difference between the output of the discriminator and the one that indicates whether the label is real or not. To compute the binary cross-entropy loss, the following equation is utilized. It is usual practice to use the mean squared error as a metric for quantifying the difference between the data samples that were generated and those that were collected. In the second equation, the expression for the mean squared error is displayed by the equation. In Wasserstein GANs (WGANs), the Wasserstein loss is utilized to quantify the inconsistency that exists between the data samples that are generated and those that are legitimate. Presented in the third equation is the mathematical statement that represents the Wasserstein loss theory (Fonseca & Bacao, 2023).

$$\mathrm{BCE} = \frac{1}{n}\sum_{i=1}^{n} y_i \log\left(p(y_i)\right) + \left(1 - y_i\right)\log\left(1 - p(y_i)\right)$$

The BCE loss refers to the binary cross-entropy loss. The label, denoted as y, can take on values of either 1 or 0. The predicted output, represented as p(y), is used in the calculation of the loss. Lastly, n represents the total number of samples.

$$\mathrm{MSE} = \frac{1}{\mathrm{n}}\Sigma\left(\mathrm{real} - \mathrm{fake}\right)^2$$

MSE stands for mean squared error. "Real" refers to the actual values of the data samples, "fake" refers to the created values of the data samples, and "n" represents the total number of samples.

$$Critic\_Loss = D(x) - D(G(z))$$

D(x) represents the mean evaluation score for genuine photos, D(G(z)) represents the mean evaluation score for created images, and G(z) represents the output produced by the generator. Alternative loss functions that can be employed in GANs include reconstruction loss and regularization loss. The first is employed in variational autoencoder-GAN (VAE-GAN) to quantify the resemblance between produced and authentic images. The latter, in this context, refers to a technique that helps minimize overfitting and enhances the model's ability to generalize by applying penalties to the weights of the network throughout the training process (Saxena & Cao, 2021).

2.4. LATENT SPACE IN GANS

Learning objectives

- Comprehend the properties of latent space
- Understand the importance of latent space in GANs

Generative Adversarial Networks (GANs) operate by learning the distribution of real data in order to generate new data points that are indistinguishable from real ones. A critical concept in the architecture of GANs is the latent space, a high-dimensional space that encodes various features and characteristics of the data. Understanding the role and properties of latent space is essential for grasping how GANs function and how they can be manipulated to generate diverse and complex synthetic data. The latent space, sometimes referred to as the hidden space or the Z space, is where the generator network finds the initial input to start the data generation process. It is essentially a compact representation of the vast, often high-dimensional, space of possible data points. Latent vectors, which are points in this space, are randomly sampled and fed into the generator, which then transforms them into output data that ideally resembles the real data distribution (Wu et al., 2016).

Remember

GANs have been used to generate realistic images of celebrities, animals, and even fictional characters, leading to the creation of various artistic and entertainment applications.

2.4.1. Properties of Latent Space

Latent space is characterized by several key properties:

a) **High-dimensionality:** Latent space is typically high-dimensional, allowing for the encoding of complex and varied data characteristics. This high dimensionality provides the generator with a rich and expressive input space.

b) **Continuity:** Points that are close to each other in the latent space correspond to data instances that are similar in feature space. This property enables smooth transitions and interpolations between generated data points.

c) **Learned Representation:** Unlike manually designed feature spaces, latent space is learned during the training process. This means it is optimized to best represent the underlying data distribution in a way that is useful for generation (Fonseca & Bacao, 2023).

2.4.2. Exploring and Manipulating Latent Space

The latent space of a GAN offers various avenues for exploring and manipulating the generated data.

2.4.2.1. Interpolation

By interpolating between two points in latent space and generating the corresponding data points, one can observe smooth transitions and explore the variations the generator can produce. This technique is useful for understanding how different features are encoded within space.

2.4.2.2. Vector Arithmetic

Certain arithmetic operations with latent vectors can lead to interpretable changes in the generated data, akin to semantic manipulations. For instance, adding the vector difference associated with a particular attribute (e.g., smiling vs. not smiling) to a latent vector can imbue the generated data with that attribute. These operations highlight the intriguing property of latent space where linear operations can result in nonlinear effects in data space, allowing for a powerful mechanism to control and understand the generation process (Huang et al., 2020).

2.4.3. Importance of Latent Space in GANs

The latent space is integral to the architecture and functionality of GANs, serving as the starting point for the generator's creative process. Its properties of high dimensionality, continuity, and learned representation enable the generation of diverse, high-quality data. By understanding and manipulating latent space, researchers and practitioners can unlock new potentials in data generation, from creating realistic synthetic images to exploring variations of existing ones. The concept of latent space is fundamental to the operation and versatility of GANs. Its exploration and manipulation not only provide insights into the generative capabilities of GANs but also open possibilities for novel applications and improvements in synthetic data generation. This later section dives deeply into the concept of latent space within GANs—its properties, significance, and how it can be manipulated to control data generation. It incorporates code snippets to demonstrate practical applications, leveraging continuous and high-dimensional characteristics of latent space for generating and modifying data (Peacock et al., 1995).

Practice Problem

Discuss the significance of the latent space in Generative Adversarial Networks. Describe how the dimensionality and distribution of the latent space can affect the quality and diversity of generated samples

Solution to Practice Problem

The latent space serves as the input for the generator and represents the space of all possible data samples that the generator can produce. The dimensionality and distribution of the latent space can impact the variety and quality of generated samples. Higher dimensionality and well-distributed latent space can lead to more diverse outputs.

2.5. DEVELOPING GAN MODELS

Learning objectives

- Understand the major steps for developing GAN models

There are several steps to creating a GAN model.

2.5.1. Analyze the Problem

It is essential to conduct an accurate analysis of the problem and determine all of its requirements, inputs, outputs, and characteristics.

2.5.2. Select GAN Architecture

An examination of some of the most prevalent GAN architectures has been carried out. It is of the utmost importance to ascertain which GAN architecture is appropriate for the data and the task at hand. Previous uses of GAN, comparable designs, characteristics of each GAN architecture, including advantages and disadvantages, and the objectives for utilizing GAN to solve the problem are all factors that can be considered while making this determination (Tanaka, 2019).

2.5.3. Train the Discriminator on Real Dataset

During this stage, the discriminator of the GAN is trained on the dataset by making use of historical data. Real data is included in this stage; there is no fake data. The discriminator is a tool that can differentiate between actual data and fake data that is either noisy or generated by a generator. It is recommended that the discriminator be trained solely on real data.

2.5.4. Train Generator

There will be some random noise introduced into the generator during this stage so that it can be trained. To train the initial generator, this kind of data is utilized (Fang et al., 2022).

2.5.5. Fake Data on the Discriminator

It is at this stage that the trained discriminator will be presented with the fake data that has been generated to decide whether it is genuine.

2.5.6. Train Generator

As part of this process, the feedback from the discriminator will be transmitted to the generator to enhance the data that is generated.

2.6. CHALLENGES IN GAN ARCHITECTURE DESIGN

Learning objectives

- Understand the challenges in the architecture design of GANs
- Comprehend the mitigation strategies to the challenges

Designing GANs presents a unique set of challenges that stem from its dual network architecture, the dynamic nature of its training process, and the complex balance required to achieve convergence between the generator and discriminator. The following discussion elaborates on these challenges, offering insights into their origins and presenting strategies aimed at mitigation (Pavan Kumar & Jayagopal, 2021).

- **Vanishing Gradients:** The discriminator, becoming too proficient in distinguishing real from fake data, can cause the gradients returned to the generator during backpropagation to vanish. This phenomenon impedes the generator's ability to learn and improve, essentially stalling the GAN's training process. The vanishing gradients problem often emerges when there is a significant disparity in learning capabilities between the generator and discriminator (Emon et al., 2022).
- **Non-Convergence:** GANs inherently involve a min-max game where the discriminator and generator networks compete to optimize opposing objectives. This adversarial setup can lead to non-convergence, where the networks oscillate between states without finding a stable equilibrium. This challenge is exacerbated by factors such as the choice of the cost function, network architecture, and training hyperparameters.
- **Balancing the Networks:** Achieving an optimal balance between the generator and discriminator networks is essential for the successful training of GANs. An excessively powerful discriminator can overwhelm the generator, leading to vanishing gradients, while a dominant generator can precipitate mode collapse by easily fooling the discriminator. Maintaining a delicate balance between these networks is critical but challenging, necessitating careful design and tuning of the network architectures and training parameters (Tey et al., 2022).
- To address these challenges, various strategies and best practices have been developed, including:
- **Modified Loss Functions:** Introducing modified or alternative loss functions has been a common approach to mitigate issues such as mode collapse and vanishing gradients. For instance, the Wasserstein loss function has shown promise in improving training stability and convergence.
- **Gradient Penalty and Regularization:** The implementation of gradient penalties or regularization techniques can assist in stabilizing the training process by preventing the discriminator from becoming too powerful and ensuring a smoother gradient flow to the generator (Aalaei et al., 2023).

- **Architecture Tweaks:** Adjusting the architecture of the GAN, such as through the introduction of skip connections, normalization layers, or carefully designed convolutional layers, can enhance learning dynamics and facilitate a more balanced and stable training process (Zhang et al., 2024).

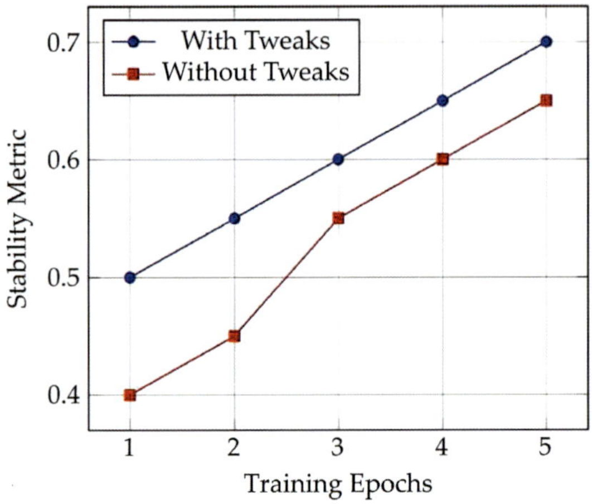

Figure 2.5. *Impact of architecture tweaks on GAN training stability.*

Source: Russ Elektran, Creative Commons License.

- **Careful Hyperparameter Tuning:** Meticulous, empirical tuning of training hyperparameters, including learning rates, batch sizes, and the ratio of generator to discriminator updates, plays a critical role in navigating and overcoming GAN training challenges (Zhan et al., 2022).

Understanding and addressing these challenges requires a deep knowledge of the underlying dynamics between the generator and discriminator alongside a continuous exploration of innovative solutions in architecture design, loss functions, and training strategies. By meticulously applying the methodologies discussed, progress can be made toward more stable, efficient, and effective GAN architectures (Shen & Zhou, 2021).

2.7. BEST PRACTICES IN GAN ARCHITECTURE DEVELOPMENT

Learning objectives

- Understand the best practices to enhance the performance of GANs.

Developing GANs encompasses numerous challenges, ranging from mode collapse to unstable training dynamics (Amirkolaee et al., 2022). To mitigate these issues and enhance the performance of GANs, certain best practices have been established by the ML community through empirical research and experimentation. This section provides a comprehensive overview of these practices, offering insights into achieving robust GAN architectures (Issenhuth et al., 2022).

2.7.1. Balanced Architectural Capacity

Ensuring a balance in the capacity between the generator and discriminator is crucial for effective GAN training. A too-powerful discriminator can easily distinguish between real and generated samples from the outset, preventing the generator from learning effectively. Conversely, an overly capable generator might not provide enough gradient information for the discriminator to learn (Recanatesi et al., 2021).

2.7.2. Use of Batch Normalization

The process of batch normalization is a method that is used to normalize the inputs to each layer inside a network in such a way that they have a mean of zero and a standard deviation of one within the network (Tran et al., 2020). By lowering the amount of internal covariate shift, its introduction into both the generator and discriminator networks has the potential to dramatically improve the stability of deep neural networks (GANs) (Sun et al., 2022).

```
# Example of incorporating batch normalization in a generator network.
from keras.models import Sequential
from keras.layers import Dense, BatchNormalization
model = Sequential()
model.add(Dense(units=256, input_dim=100))
model.add(BatchNormalization())
model.add(Activation('relu'))
model.add(Dense(units=512))
```

```
model.add(BatchNormalization())
model.add(Activation('relu'))
```

2.7.3. Gradual Learning Rate Decrease

Adjusting the learning rate over time can also contribute to stable training of GANs (Rubin et al., 2015). Implementing a schedule where the learning rate decreases gradually can help the networks fine-tune the adjustments in weights, leading to smoother convergence (Jahan et al., 2021).

2.7.4. Use of Label Smoothing

Label smoothing is another technique to prevent the discriminator from becoming too confident in its predictions. Rather than providing hard labels (0 or 1), slightly adjusted labels (e.g., 0.9 or 0.1) are used. This makes the discriminator's task slightly harder, allowing the generator more room to improve (Segal et al., 2021).

```
# Example of label smoothing in training GANs.
real_labels = np.ones((batch_size, 1)) *0.9
fake_labels = np.zeros((batch_size, 1)) * 0.1
```

2.7.5. Choosing the Right Activation Functions

The choice of activation functions significantly affects the performance of GANs. ReLU and its variants (e.g., LeakyReLU) are often preferred in generator networks for their ability to mitigate the vanishing gradient problem (Ismail et al., 2012). In contrast, sigmoid activations are commonly used in the output layer of the discriminator to classify real versus generated images (Ihle et al., 2019).

Did You Know?

The choice of activation functions, normalization techniques, and optimization algorithms can significantly impact the performance and stability of GANs during training. Experimenting with different architectural choices is crucial for achieving optimal results.

SUMMARY

- The chapter provides an in-depth exploration of the architecture of Generative Adversarial Networks.
- The generator typically comprises layers of neural networks, such as convolutional or fully connected layers, followed by activation functions. The discriminator also consists of neural network layers, tasked with classifying input as real or fake.
- The concept of latent space in GANs is also highlighted in this chapter. The latent space represents the space of all possible inputs to the generator. It is typically sampled from a probability distribution, such as Gaussian or uniform distribution, and serves as the input for generating data samples.
- The chapter also provides an insight to the challenges in GAN architecture design. Challenges include mode collapse, training instability, vanishing/exploding gradients, and achieving a balance between the generator and discriminator networks.
- Finally the chapter discusses the best practices in GANs architecture development. Best practices include careful selection of network architectures, optimization techniques, regularization methods, and evaluation metrics. Hyperparameter tuning, training strategies, and monitoring for convergence are essential for successful GANs development.

MULTIPLE CHOICE QUESTIONS

1. What are the two main components of a Generative Adversarial Network (GAN)?

a) Classifier and regressor

b) Generator and encoder

c) Generator and discriminator

d) Discriminator and encoder

2. What is the primary function of the generator model in a GAN?

a) Classify input data

b) Generate synthetic data samples

c) Discriminate between real and fake data

d) Encode input data into latent space

3. **Which neural network component of a GAN is responsible for distinguishing between real and fake data?**
   a) Generator
   b) Classifier
   c) Discriminator
   d) Encoder
4. **What is the latent space in a Generative Adversarial Network?**
   a) Space of all possible input data samples
   b) Space of real data samples
   c) Space of all possible output data samples
   d) Space of random noise input to the generator
5. **Which of the following is an architectural variation of GANs specifically designed for stability in training?**
   a) Deep Convolutional GANs (DCGANs)
   b) Conditional GANs (CGANs)
   c) Wasserstein GANs (WGANs)
   d) Autoencoder GANs (AEGANs)

REVIEW QUESTIONS

1. Describe the structure and function of the generator model in a Generative Adversarial Network (GAN). How does it generate synthetic data samples?
2. Explain the role of the discriminator model in a GAN. How does it distinguish between real and fake data samples?
3. What is the latent space in GANs, and why is it important? How is noise sampled from the latent space?
4. Discuss the architectural variations of GANs, such as Deep Convolutional GANs (DCGANs), Wasserstein GANs (WGANs), and Conditional GANs (CGANs). What are the specific characteristics and advantages of each variation?
5. What are some common challenges in GANs architecture design? How can these challenges be addressed or mitigated?

Answers to Multiple Questions

1. (c)   2. (b)   3. (c)   4. (d)   5. (c)

REFERENCES

1. Aalaei, M., Saadi, M., Rahbar, M., & Ekhlassi, A. (2023). Architectural layout generation using a graph-constrained conditional Generative Adversarial Network (GAN). *Automation in Construction, 155*, 105053. https://doi.org/10.1016/j.autcon.2022.105053.
2. Abdal, R., Zhu, P., Mitra, N. J., & Wonka, P. (2021). Styleflow: Attribute-conditioned exploration of StyleGAN-generated images using conditional continuous normalizing flows. *ACM Transactions on Graphics (ToG), 40*(3), 1–21. https://doi.org/10.1145/3459934.
3. Abdollahi, A., Pradhan, B., Gite, S., & Alamri, A. (2020). Building footprint extraction from high resolution aerial images using generative adversarial network (GAN) architecture. *IEEE Access, 8*, 209517–209527. https://doi.org/10.1109/ACCESS.2020.3034790.
4. Amirkolaee, H. A., Bokov, D. O., & Sharma, H. (2022). Development of a GAN architecture based on integrating global and local information for paired and unpaired medical image translation. *Expert Systems with Applications, 203*, 117421. https://doi.org/10.1016/j.eswa.2022.117421.
5. Durall, R., Frolov, S., Hees, J., Raue, F., Pfreundt, F. J., Dengel, A., & Keuper, J. (2021). Combining transformer generators with convolutional discriminators. In *KI 2021: Advances in Artificial Intelligence: 44th German Conference on AI, Virtual Event, September 27–October 1, 2021, Proceedings 44* (Vol. 2, pp. 67–79). Springer International Publishing. https://doi.org/10.1007/978-3-030-93466-3_6.
6. Elazab, A., Wang, C., Gardezi, S. J. S., Bai, H., Hu, Q., Wang, T., & Lei, B. (2020). GP-GAN: Brain tumor growth prediction using stacked 3D generative adversarial networks from longitudinal MR Images. *Neural Networks, 132*, 321–332. https://doi.org/10.1016/j.neunet.2020.08.020.
7. Emon, A. I., Mirza, A. B., Kaplun, J., Vala, S. S., & Luo, F. (2022). A review of high-speed GaN power modules: State of the art, challenges, and solutions. *IEEE Journal of Emerging and Selected Topics in Power Electronics, 11*(3), 2707–2729. https://doi.org/10.1109/JESTPE.2022.3151195.
8. Fang, T., Sun, R., & Schwing, A. (2022). Diggan: Discriminator gradient gap regularization for GAN training with limited data. *Advances in Neural Information Processing Systems, 35*, 31782–31795.
9. Fetty, L., Löfstedt, T., Heilemann, G., Furtado, H., Nesvacil, N., Nyholm, T., & Kuess, P. (2020). Investigating conditional GAN performance with different generator architectures, an ensemble model, and different MR scanners for MR-sCT conversion. *Physics in Medicine & Biology, 65*(10), 105004. https://doi.org/10.1088/1361-6560/ab8bb2.

10. Fonseca, J., & Bacao, F. (2023). Tabular and latent space synthetic data generation: A literature review. *Journal of Big Data, 10*(1), 115. https://doi.org/10.1186/s40537-023-00511-4.
11. Gong, X., Chang, S., Jiang, Y., & Wang, Z. (2019). Autogan: Neural architecture search for generative adversarial networks. In *Proceedings of the IEEE/CVF International Conference on Computer Vision* (Vol. 1, pp. 3224–3234). https://doi.org/10.1109/ICCV.2019.00329.
12. Huang, J., Le, Z., Ma, Y., Fan, F., Zhang, H., & Yang, L. (2020). MGMDcGAN: Medical image fusion using multi-generator multi-discriminator conditional generative adversarial network. *IEEE Access, 8*, 55145–55157. https://doi.org/10.1109/ACCESS.2020.2980782.
13. Ihle, S. J., Reichmuth, A. M., Girardin, S., Han, H., Stauffer, F., Bonnin, A., & Forró, C. (2019). Unsupervised data to content transformation with histogram-matching cycle-consistent generative adversarial networks. *Nature Machine Intelligence, 1*(10), 461–470. https://doi.org/10.1038/s42256-019-0101-4.
14. Ismail, H. M., Ng, H. K., Queck, C. W., & Gan, S. (2012). Artificial neural networks modelling of engine-out responses for a light-duty diesel engine fueled with biodiesel blends. *Applied Energy, 92*, 769–777. https://doi.org/10.1016/j.apenergy.2011.09.029.
15. Issenhuth, T., Tanielian, U., Picard, D., & Mary, J. (2022). Latent reweighting, an almost free improvement for GANs. In *Proceedings of the IEEE/CVF Winter Conference on Applications of Computer Vision* (Vol. 2, pp. 1668–1677). https://doi.org/10.1109/WACV51435.2022.00168.
16. Jahan, T., Guan, Y., & Van Kaick, O. (2021). Semantics guided latent space exploration for shape generation. *Computer Graphics Forum, 40*(2), 115–126. https://doi.org/10.1111/cgf.14307.
17. Karras, T., Laine, S., & Aila, T. (2019). A style-based generator architecture for generative adversarial networks. In *Proceedings of the IEEE/CVF Conference on Computer Vision and Pattern Recognition* (Vol. 2, pp. 4401–4410). https://doi.org/10.1109/CVPR.2019.00454.
18. Li, S., Wu, J., Xiao, X., Chao, F., Mao, X., & Ji, R. (2021). Revisiting discriminator in GAN compression: A generator-discriminator cooperative compression scheme. *Advances in Neural Information Processing Systems, 34*, 28560–28572.
19. Lu, F., Lee, H. P., & Lim, S. P. (2003). Modeling and analysis of micro piezoelectric power generators for micro-electromechanical-systems applications. *Smart Materials and Structures, 13*(1), 57–66. https://doi.org/10.1088/0964-1726/13/1/306.

20. Padiyar, K. R., & Ghosh, K. K. (1989). Direct stability evaluation of power systems with detailed generator models using structure-preserving energy functions. *International Journal of Electrical Power & Energy Systems, 11*(1), 47–56. https://doi.org/10.1016/0142-0615(89)90057-2.
21. Pang, B., & Wu, Y. N. (2021). Latent space energy-based model of symbol-vector coupling for text generation and classification. In *International Conference on Machine Learning* (Vol. 2, pp. 8359–8370). PMLR. https://proceedings.mlr.press/v139/pang21a.html (accessed on 27 June 2024).
22. Parikh, P., Wu, Y., Shen, L., Barr, R., Chowdhury, S., Gritters, J., & Asai, Y. (2018). GaN power commercialization with highest quality-highest reliability 650V HEMTs-requirements, successes and challenges. In *2018 IEEE International Electron Devices Meeting (IEDM)* (Vol. 1, pp. 19–27). IEEE. https://doi.org/10.1109/IEDM.2018.8614603.
23. Pavan Kumar, M. R., & Jayagopal, P. (2021). Generative adversarial networks: A survey on applications and challenges. *International Journal of Multimedia Information Retrieval, 10*(1), 1–24. https://doi.org/10.1007/s13735-020-00223-5.
24. Peacock, M., Turner, C. H., Liu, G., Manatunga, A. K., Timmerman, L., & Johnston, C. C. (1995). Better discrimination of hip fracture using bone density, geometry and architecture. *Osteoporosis International, 5*, 167–173. https://doi.org/10.1007/BF01623786.
25. Recanatesi, S., Farrell, M., Lajoie, G., Deneve, S., Rigotti, M., & Shea-Brown, E. (2021). Predictive learning as a network mechanism for extracting low-dimensional latent space representations. *Nature Communications, 12*(1), 1417. https://doi.org/10.1038/s41467-021-21301-0.
26. Rubin, E. S., Azevedo, I. M., Jaramillo, P., & Yeh, S. (2015). A review of learning rates for electricity supply technologies. *Energy Policy, 86*, 198–218. https://doi.org/10.1016/j.enpol.2015.07.009.
27. Saxena, D., & Cao, J. (2021). Generative adversarial networks (GANs) challenges, solutions, and future directions. *ACM Computing Surveys (CSUR), 54*(3), 1–42. https://doi.org/10.1145/3463254.
28. Segal, B., Rubin, D. M., Rubin, G., & Pantanowitz, A. (2021). Evaluating the clinical realism of synthetic chest x-rays generated using progressively growing GANs. *SN Computer Science, 2*(4), 321. https://doi.org/10.1007/s42979-021-00498-3.
29. Shen, Y., & Zhou, B. (2021). Closed-form factorization of latent semantics in GANs. In *Proceedings of the IEEE/CVF Conference on Computer Vision and Pattern Recognition* (Vol. 1, pp. 1532–1540). https://doi.org/10.1109/CVPR.2021.00162.

30. Sun, Q., Chen, Y., Tao, W., Jiang, H., Zhang, M., Chen, K., & Erdt, M. (2022). A GAN-based approach toward architectural line drawing colorization prototyping. *The Visual Computer, 38*(2), 1–18. https://doi.org/10.1007/s00371-022-02396-7.
31. Tanaka, A. (2019). Discriminator optimal transport. *Advances in Neural Information Processing Systems, 32*, 987–990.
32. Tey, F. J., Wu, T. Y., Wu, Y., & Chen, J. L. (2022). Generative Adversarial Network for Simulation of Load Balancing Optimization in Mobile Networks. *Journal of Internet Technology, 23*(2), 297–304. https://doi.org/10.3966/160792642022042302001.
33. Tran, N. T., Tran, V. H., Nguyen, N. B., Nguyen, T. K., & Cheung, N. M. (2020). Towards good practices for data augmentation in GAN training. *arXiv preprint arXiv:2006.05338, 2*(3), 3–7.
34. Wu, J., Zhang, C., Xue, T., Freeman, B., & Tenenbaum, J. (2016). Learning a probabilistic latent space of object shapes via 3D generative-adversarial modeling. *Advances in Neural Information Processing Systems, 29*, 987–990.
35. Xia, K., Yin, H., Qian, P., Jiang, Y., & Wang, S. (2019). Liver semantic segmentation algorithm based on improved deep adversarial networks in combination of weighted loss function on abdominal CT images. *IEEE Access, 7*, 96349–96358. https://doi.org/10.1109/ACCESS.2019.2923012.
36. Zhan, Z. H., Li, J. Y., & Zhang, J. (2022). Evolutionary deep learning: A survey. *Neurocomputing, 483*, 42–58. https://doi.org/10.1016/j.neucom.2021.12.001.
37. Zhang, W., Liu, H., Li, B., Xie, J., Huang, Y., Li, Y., & Ghanem, B. (2024). Dynamically masked discriminator for GANs. *Advances in Neural Information Processing Systems, 36*, 321–325.

CHAPTER 3

TYPES OF GENERATIVE ADVERSARIAL NETWORKS

LEARNING OBJECTIVES

At the end of this chapter, readers will be able to:

1. Comprehend the architecture of DCGANs.
2. Understand the implementation of cGANs.
3. Gain knowledge about the architecture, applications, and issues of CycleGANs.
4. Comprehend the implementation and issues of SGANs.
5. Understand the architecture, applications, and issues of LSGANs.
6. Gain knowledge about the architecture, applications, and issues of WGANs.

INTRODUCTORY EXAMPLE

In the realm of computer vision and image processing, "ImageTech Solutions" stands at the forefront, pioneering advancements in generative modeling with their innovative use of Generative Adversarial Networks (GANs). As a leading provider of image enhancement services, ImageTech Solutions leverages various types of GANs to transform ordinary photographs into stunning works of art, seamlessly removing imperfections, enhancing details, and even generating entirely new scenes based on user preferences. With their proprietary algorithms and cutting-edge research in GAN technology, ImageTech Solutions has revolutionized the way visual content is perceived and manipulated.

UNIT INTRODUCTION

Generative Adversarial Networks (GANs) have emerged as one of the most exciting and innovative developments in the field of deep learning, revolutionizing the way data is generated and manipulated. Since their introduction by Ian Goodfellow and his colleagues in 2014, GANs have evolved into a diverse family of models, each designed to address specific challenges or cater to applications. This chapter explores the fascinating world of GAN architecture, exploring the various types of GANs that have been developed over the years (Durgadevi, 2021).

From Deep Convolutional GANs (DCGANs) to Conditional GANs (cGANs), CycleGANs, Semi-Supervised GANs (SGANs), Least Squares GANs (LSGANs), and Wasserstein GANs (WGANs), each type of GAN offers unique advantages and capabilities. Through a comprehensive examination of these architectures, a deeper understanding of the architectures, issues, and applications of different types of GANs is developed.

By the end of this chapter, readers will gain insights into the rich landscape of GANs, empowering them to choose the most suitable architecture for their specific use case and inspiring further exploration and innovation in the field of generative modeling (Gui et al., 2021).

3.1. DEEP CONVOLUTIONAL GENERATIVE ADVERSARIAL NETWORKS (DCGANS)

Learning objectives

- Understand the architecture of DCGANs
- Comprehend the issues and applications of DCGANs

DCGANs are powerful generative models that leverage deep convolutional neural networks to learn and generate new data. They have successfully generated high-quality images and found applications across various domains. DCGANs excel in creating large, detailed images by capturing fine-grained features through their convolutional layers. However, they are not without challenges. Issues, such as mode collapse and training instability, can arise during training. Techniques, such as mini-batch discrimination, spectral normalization, and alternative loss functions, have been proposed to address these issues. In industries such as entertainment, fashion, and healthcare, DCGANs have the potential to be revolutionary. They offer a powerful means to generate high-quality images. Figure 3.1 showcases the architecture of a Deep Convolutional Generative Adversarial Network (DCGAN). The diagram is divided into two main sections: the generator and the discriminator. The generator is responsible for creating synthetic data, while the discriminator evaluates the authenticity of the generated samples against real data. The structure is designed to illustrate the intricate interplay between these two components, highlighting the iterative nature of their relationship as they compete to outperform each other. The representation serves as a visual guide to understanding the mechanics and intricacies of the DCGAN model (Gao et al., 2018).

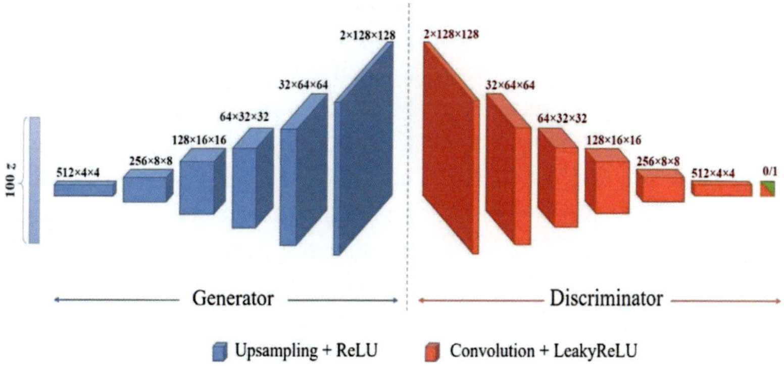

Figure 3.1. *Illustration of DCGAN general architecture.*

Source: Andrew Chang, Creative Commons License.

3.1.1. DCGAN Architecture

To optimize the DCGAN, several adjustments were made to the discriminator, generator, and the convergence of the GAN architecture. In this modified setup, pooling layers are not utilized at all (Bian et al., 2019). Neurons are not required to connect and combine their outputs to form pooling, and any convolutional classification strategy can be used for the discriminator if necessary. Batch normalization, also developed by the creators of DCGAN, helps stabilize the training process by normalizing the inputs at each layer. This normalization helps mitigate issues such as internal covariate shifts and ensures a more stable gradient flow during training. Convolutions and transposed convolutions are implemented within the context of a GAN (Suárez et al., 2017). These operations play a vital role in transforming and manipulating data, allowing the generator to create new samples and the discriminator to distinguish between real and fake samples. By incorporating these modifications and understanding the principles of convolutions and transposed convolutions, the performance and convergence of the GAN model can be enhanced. In a GAN, the generator and discriminator models operate together as a unified system. They are often referred to as adversaries because they engage in a game-like competition where there are no definitive winners or losers. The generator's objective is to produce synthetic images that can deceive the discriminator into believing they are real. Meanwhile, the discriminator's goal is to accurately distinguish between real and fake samples by examining the distinguishing features of each image. The interaction between the generator and discriminator is depicted in Figure 3.2, which showcases their interplay within the DCGAN architecture. In this architecture, convolutional and transposed convolutional layers are utilized instead of dense layers. Several design considerations come into play, such as incorporating batch normalization, selecting appropriate activation functions for different layers, carefully choosing the optimizer, and designing upscaling and downscaling layers in a specific way. The discriminator model essentially functions as a convolutional classification model, as its primary task is to classify the input images as real, or fake based on their distinguishing features (Chatterjee & Roy, 2021). This involves using convolutional layers to extract relevant features and making predictions based on these features. Overall, the GAN framework brings together the generator and discriminator models, allowing them to learn from each other and iteratively improve their performance. Through their competition and cooperation, GANs have proven to be highly effective in generating realistic and high-quality synthetic samples (Lu et al., 2019).

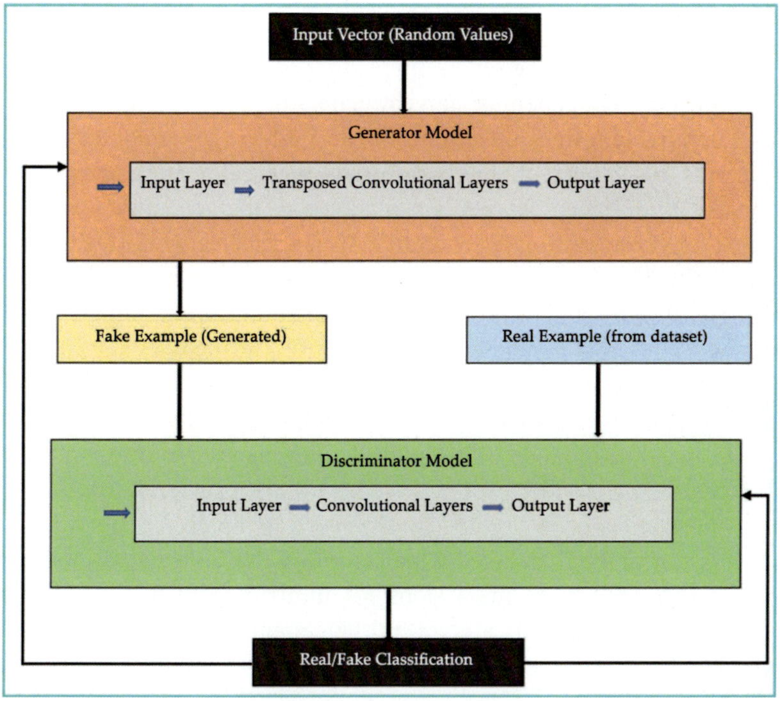

Figure 3.2. *Diagram of interaction between generator and discriminator in DC-GANs.*

Source: Arjovsky, Creative Commons License.

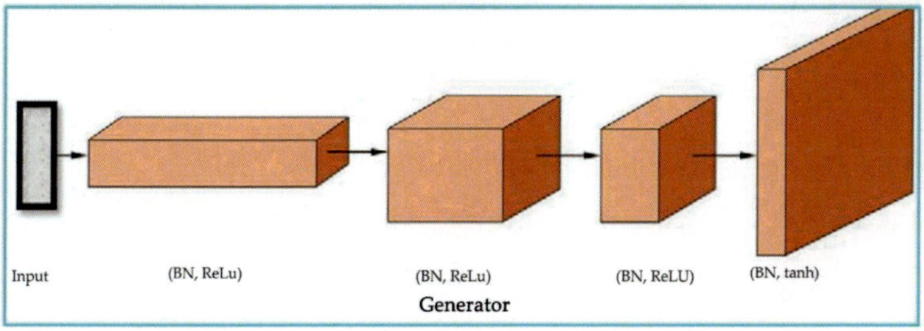

Figure 3.3. *Diagram of generator architecture in DCGANs.*

Source: Mehdi Mirza, Creative Commons License.

3.1.1.1. Generator

The initialization step and the requirements for constructing the DCGAN model differ significantly. The generator starts by generating initial images from random noise and iteratively refines them until the desired images are obtained. Figure 3.3 illustrates the general architecture of the generator, highlighting its key components. It presents a detailed visualization of the generator's architecture within the Deep Convolutional Generative Adversarial Network (DCGAN). The diagram emphasizes its core components, starting from the initial noise input layer, progressing through various convolutional and upsampling layers, and culminating in the final generated image output (Alrashedy et al., 2022). Each layer's structure and interconnections are meticulously displayed, providing a comprehensive view of how the generator synthesizes new data from random noise. This visualization aids in grasping the intricacies and importance of the generator within the broader DCGAN framework. It is evident from the figure that batch normalization is applied to all layers, and ReLU activation is used for all layers except the final layer, which employs the Tanh activation function. Figure 3.4 shows the three main steps for implementing the generator. The generator's main components are several layers and activation functions. The next section takes a closer overview of the generator's architecture (Horsley & Perez-Liebana, 2017).

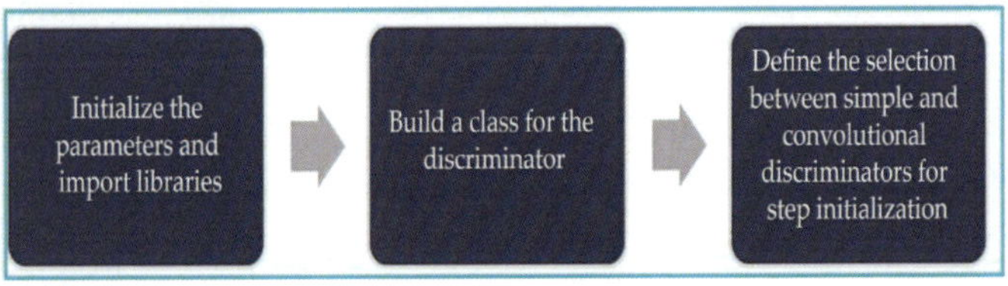

Figure 3.4. *Representation of generator implementation steps.*

Source: Bing Xu, Creative Commons License.

i. Linear Layer

   In a linear layer, the noise vector is passed through a layer, and the output of that layer is reshaped into a four-dimensional tensor.

ii. Batch Normalization Layer

   This layer stabilizes learning by normalizing inputs to zero mean and unit variance. This prevents training issues such as the vanishing gradient problem and allows the gradient to flow through the network (Kora Venu & Ravula, 2020).

iii. 2D Convolutional Layer

The generator sends the matrix through a convolutional layer with the same padding as the generator upsample. This allows the generator to learn from the upsampled data (Viola et al., 2021).

iv. ReLU Layer

Research in DCGAN recommends using ReLU for the generator rather than leaky ReLU because it allows the model to train quickly and fill the distribution's color space compared to leaky ReLU.

v. Tanh Activation

Research recommends using the tanh activation function for the generator, most likely due to tanh function properties, which allow the model to converge more quickly (Sindhura et al., 2021).

3.1.1.2. Discriminator

For the discriminator, a similar distinction is observed in terms of step initialization and model construction as is with the generator. The discriminator utilizes batch normalization in all layers, applies the Tanh activation function in the first layer, and employs the leaky ReLU activation function in the remaining layers. Figure 3.5 provides a general overview of the discriminator architecture. It offers an encompassing look at the discriminator's architecture within the Deep Convolutional Generative Adversarial Network (DCGAN). The visual representation meticulously outlines the structure, starting with the input image and traversing through a series of convolutional layers, downsampling stages, and finally converging to a single output node determining the authenticity of the given image (Choi & Han, 2022).

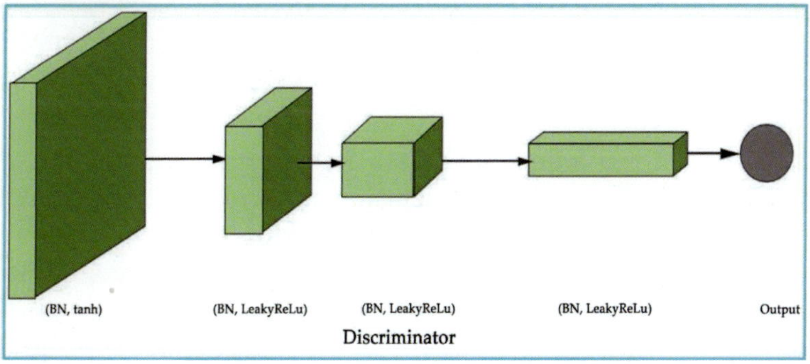

Figure 3.5. *Illustration of discriminator architecture in DCGANs.*

Source: Mehdi Ghayoum, Creative Commons License.

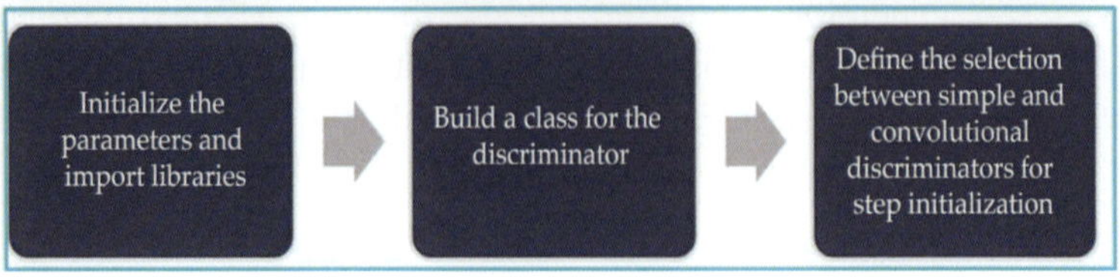

Figure 3.6. *Representation of discriminator implementation steps.*

Source: Aaron Courville, Creative Commons License.

The diagram underscores the integral role of the discriminator in evaluating and distinguishing between genuine and generated images, offering viewers a clear insight into its operation within the DCGAN system. Figure 3.6 illustrates the three main steps in implementing a discriminator in DCGAN. The discriminator has several components, including an activation function and a dropout layer (Schonfeld et al., 2020).

i. **Concat Layer**

This layer combines fake and real images into a single batch for feeding the discriminator. However, this step can be performed separately to obtain the generator loss.

ii. **Convolutional Layer**

This layer uses stride convolution to downsample the image and learn filters simultaneously (Abe et al., 2017).

iii. **Leaky ReLU**

According to research papers, leaky ReLU is better for discriminators than the max-out function used in the original GAN work because it simplifies training.

iv. **Dropout**

Dropout is a training-only task that helps prevent overfitting. The model tends to memorize actual image data, and training can fail at this point because the generator can no longer fool the discriminator (Rajeev & Natarajan, 2023).

v. **Batch Normalization**

The use of batch normalization is discussed in the paper. It is used at the end of each discriminator block except for the first one. According to the paper, applying batch normalization across all blocks can cause sample oscillation, leading to model instability (Kalayeh & Shah, 2019).

vi. **Fully Connected Layer**

This layer is called a fully connected layer because it applies a reshaped vector from the 2D batch normalization and linear layers.

vii. Sigmoid Activation

Because the discriminator deals with binary classifications, a sigmoid activation function makes the most sense for its output. Some additional tips and tricks come from practicing with different types of data using DCGAN (Mahmoud & Guo, 2019).

3.1.2. DCGAN Applications

DCGANs have shown impressive results in various applications as are discussed in the next section (He et al., 2021).

3.1.2.1. Image Generation

DCGANs have been widely used for generating high-quality images of different categories, such as human faces, animals, and natural landscapes. This has potential applications in fields, such as graphic design, gaming, and art.

3.1.2.2. Data Augmentation

DCGANs can be used to generate new training data, augmenting the size of the original dataset. This can help improve the performance of machine learning models, especially in scenarios where there is limited available data (Zhang et al., 2021).

3.1.2.3. Style Transfer

DCGANs can be used to transfer the style of one image to another, creating a new image that combines the content of one image with the style of another. This has applications in fields, such as art and design (Achicanoy et al., 2021).

3.1.2.4. Super-resolution

DCGANs can be used to enhance the resolution of images, resulting in high-quality images with more detail. This has applications in fields, such as medical imaging and surveillance.

3.1.2.5. Anomaly Detection

DCGANs can be trained to detect anomalies in images, such as defects in manufacturing processes or abnormalities in medical images. This can help improve the accuracy and efficiency of quality control processes. Overall,

DCGANs have shown great potential in various applications that require the generation or manipulation of images, and they continue to be an active area of research (Sabuhi et al., 2021).

3.1.3. DCGAN Issues

Despite the success of DCGANs in generating realistic images, several issues can arise during training (Shah et al., 2024).

3.1.3.1. Mode Collapse

Mode collapse is a common issue in GANs, including DCGANs. When mode collapse occurs, the generator produces a limited diversity of samples, often just replicating a few modes of the real data distribution. As a result, the generator fails to capture the true underlying data distribution. Mode collapse typically happens when the generator starts to produce samples that can easily fool the discriminator. Once the generator finds these "tricks," it keeps generating the same or very similar samples, since these are already enough to trick the discriminator (Saad et al., 2022).

3.1.3.2. Instability during Training

Training DCGANs can indeed be unstable. This instability is often due to the adversarial nature of GANs wherein the generator and the discriminator are competing against each other, and the continual adjustments each one makes in response to the other's actions can lead to oscillations and divergence.

3.1.3.3. Sensitivity to Initialization

DCGANs, like other types of GANs, can be sensitive to the initialization of the model weights. The random initialization of the network parameters can have a significant impact on the training dynamics and the performance of the network. Poor initialization can lead to issues, such as vanishing/exploding gradients, getting stuck in poor local minima, or mode collapse (Xu et al., 2020).

3.1.3.4. Vanishing Gradients

In DCGANs, as in many deep learning models, the issue of vanishing gradients can be encountered. This problem is characterized by the gradients of the loss function becoming increasingly smaller as they backpropagate through the layers of the network. The earlier layers of the network receive very small gradient updates, slowing down the learning process or causing it to halt altogether.

3.1.3.5. Overfitting

Overfitting in DCGANs can occur when the generator learns to recreate the training data too perfectly and fails to generalize to unseen examples. In other words, it is memorizing the training data instead of learning the underlying distribution, resulting in the generation of images that lack diversity and appear almost identical to the training examples (Webster et al., 2019).

3.1.3.6. Computational Complexity

Computational complexity is a significant issue in DCGANs, mainly due to the depth of the model and the extensive amount of computation needed during the training process. This complexity can lead to slow training times and high computational resource requirements, especially when dealing with large datasets or high-resolution images.

3.1.3.7. Hyperparameter Tuning

Hyperparameter tuning is an inherent issue in DCGANs, as with any machine learning model. Hyperparameters in DCGANs include the learning rate, the number of layers in the discriminator and generator, the number of units in each layer, the type of optimizer, batch size, and the type and scale of initialization, among others. The quality of the generated samples and the stability of the training process greatly depend on the correct setting of these hyperparameters. However, finding the right values can be a time-consuming and computationally expensive process (Dinakaran et al., (2021).

Practice Problem

Explain the architecture and training process of Deep Convolutional GANs (DC-GANs). Discuss their advantages over traditional GAN architectures.

Solution to Practice Problem

Deep Convolutional GANs (DCGANs) utilize convolutional neural networks (CNNs) in both the generator and discriminator models. The generator typically consists of transposed convolutional layers followed by batch normalization and ReLU activation functions. DCGANs offer advantages such as stable training dynamics, faster convergence, and the ability to generate high-resolution images with improved quality.

3.2. CONDITIONAL GENERATIVE ADVERSARIAL NETWORKS (CGANS)

Learning objectives

- Understand the architecture of cGANs
- Comprehend the applications and issues of cGANs

Conditional Generative Adversarial Networks (cGANs) are a type of GAN that allows the generation of data that satisfies specific conditions. Unlike traditional GANs, which generate random data, cGANs use a conditional vector to control the output. This conditional vector is typically a class label or a set of attributes that define the desired output. cGANs consist of two neural networks: a generator and a discriminator. The generator takes a noise vector and a conditional vector as inputs and generates an output that attempts to match the conditional vector. The discriminator, on the other hand, takes the generated output and the corresponding conditional vector or real data and tries to distinguish between the two. cGANs have a wide range of applications, including image-to-image translation, text-to-image synthesis, and image editing.

For instance, given an input image of a face with a specific attribute, such as glasses, a cGAN can generate an output image with the same face but without glasses. Another application is converting an image from one domain to another, such as changing a daytime image to a nighttime image. One of the significant advantages of cGANs is their ability to generate data that meets specific conditions, making them useful for various tasks, such as data augmentation, image restoration, and style transfer. However, cGANs also face several challenges, including mode collapse and instability during training. Addressing these issues requires careful selection of the architecture and hyperparameters, as well as appropriate training strategies, such as minimizing the Jensen-Shannon divergence between the generated and real distributions. Overall, cGANs have shown promising results in various applications, and their ability to generate specific data makes them a valuable addition to the GAN family (Hayatbini et al., 2019).

Remember

Conditional GANs (cGANs) condition the generation process on additional information, enabling controlled generation of specific data samples based on input conditions such as class labels or attributes.

3.2.1. cGAN Architecture

This section discusses the major components of the cGAN architecture, including the generator, discriminator, and general architecture. This discussion demonstrates the connection between the previous sections and compares it to a standard GAN (Chan & Spaeth, 2020).

3.2.1.1. cGAN Generator

The generator in cGAN uses labels or tags to provide additional information. The labels are represented as "y," and "z" is used as a random number to represent the initial noise data, which leads the generator to produce the output x'|y. The generator takes in the label and a vector of random numbers as input, and the output includes samples that are intended to be as convincing as possible in terms of how well they match their labels: G(z, y) = x′|y. Figure 3.7 presents the foundational architecture of the generator in a cGAN. This architecture, distinct from traditional GANs, incorporates conditional information, allowing for directed generation processes. The illustration emphasizes how the conditional data is introduced into the generator and how it interacts with the latent variables to produce outputs that align with specific conditions. Such a visualization underscores the unique capability of cGANs to generate targeted content based on specific criteria or labels. The output of the generator is not simply x', but fake samples that try to match the label y as closely as possible. These outputs denoted as x', are then sent to the discriminator along with the label y (Ma et al., 2021).

3.2.1.2. cGAN Discriminator

The discriminator in cGAN takes in two types of inputs:

a) Real training dataset samples labeled with their respective labels: (x, y),

b) Fake samples generated by the generator along with the label: (x'|y, y) (Sun et al., 2023).

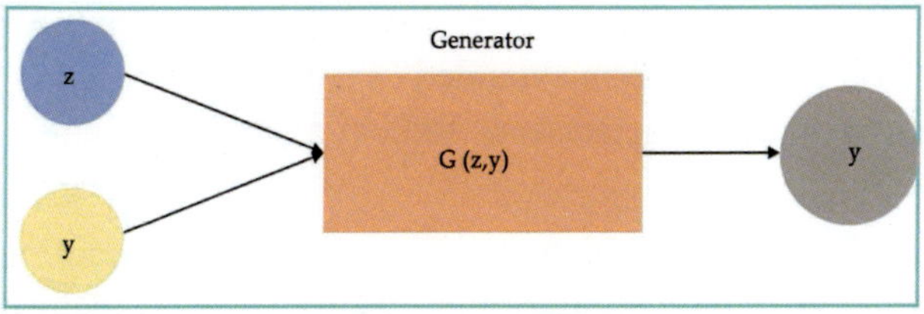

Figure 3.7. *Diagram of general cGAN generator structure.*

Source: Luke Metz, Creative Commons License.

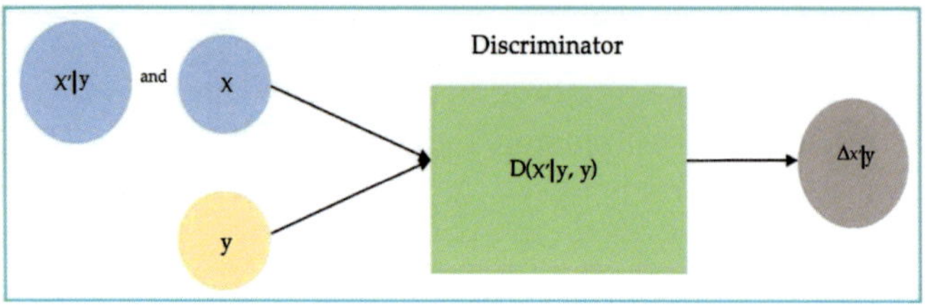

Figure 3.8. *Diagram of general cGAN discriminator structure.*

Source: Luke Metz, Creative Commons License.

The output from the discriminator is a single probability indicating whether the input example is a true example-label pair. The aim is to distinguish between fake example-label pairs generated by the generator and real example-label pairs from the training data set. Figure 3.8 showcases the typical architecture of the discriminator within a cGAN. This structure is designed to evaluate the authenticity of input samples while considering the conditional context. The depiction likely emphasizes how the conditional information is seamlessly integrated into the discriminator, influencing its decision-making process. By doing so, the cGAN discriminator can distinguish between genuine and generated samples more effectively in a conditional setting. This visualization helps elucidate the nuanced differences between traditional GAN discriminators and their conditional counterparts (Huang et al., 2020).

3.2.1.3. General Architecture

Figure 3.9 presents a comparative high-level architectural diagram of both traditional GAN and cGAN. Briefly, one can discern the differences and similarities between the two structures. In the cGAN side of the diagram, it is evident that the label y is fed into both the generator and the discriminator, emphasizing the conditional nature of its operation. By comparing these models side by side, the visualization clearly illustrates how the incorporation of conditionality in cGANs offers an extended capability compared to the standard GAN, enabling a more targeted and context-aware generation of samples (Bittner et al., 2019).

This side-by-side representation serves as an efficient tool for understanding the advancements and modifications brought by cGAN in the realm of generative models. The discriminator is trained to accept only true matching pairs, and as a result, it develops the ability to recognize mismatched pairs.

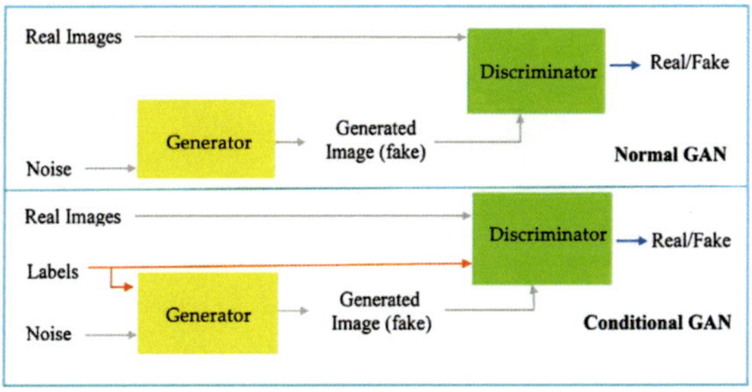

Figure 3.9. *Diagram of cGAN architecture.*

Source: Mehdi Ghayoum, Creative Commons License.

The cGAN discriminator is fed both fake labeled samples (x'|y, y) generated by the generator and real labeled samples (x, y), and it learns to determine whether a particular example-label pair is real or fake. To optimally train a conditional GAN, both the generator and discriminator must be trained simultaneously (Pang & Liu, 2020):

a) The generator is trained to generate data that will "fool" the discriminator into categorizing it as real.

b) The discriminator is trained to recognize the "real" category of labeled data provided by the generator.

The goal is to minimize the loss of the discriminator when it is fed batches of real and fake labeled data. If implemented correctly, these strategies will result in a generator that produces convincingly realistic data corresponding to the input labels, and a discriminator that has learned powerful feature representations for each label characteristic of the training data (Tavolara et al., 2019).

3.2.2. cGAN Applications

cGANs have a wide range of applications in various fields (Senaras et al., 2018).

3.2.2.1. Image and Video Editing

cGANs can be used to edit or transform images and videos in various ways. For example, cGANs can be trained to colorize grayscale images or convert low-resolution images to high-resolution ones.

3.2.2.2. Data Augmentation

cGANs can be used to generate synthetic data to augment existing datasets, which can be useful in tasks, such as image classification, object detection, and segmentation (Woldesellasse & Tesfamariam, 2023).

3.2.2.3. Text-to-image Synthesis

cGANs can be used to generate images from textual descriptions, which can be useful in fields, such as advertising and e-commerce.

3.2.2.4. Face Recognition

cGANs can be trained to generate face images for different poses, lighting conditions, and expressions, which can be useful in face recognition applications (Deng et al., 2019).

3.2.2.5. Fashion and Interior Design

cGANs can be trained to generate new designs of clothes or furniture, which can be useful for the fashion and interior design industries.

3.2.2.6. Medical Imaging

cGANs can be used to generate synthetic medical images that can be useful in medical diagnosis and treatment planning (Singh & Raza, 2021).

3.2.2.7. Speech Synthesis

cGANs can be trained to generate realistic speech from textual input, which can be useful in text-to-speech applications.

3.2.3. cGAN Issues

cGANs have some issues that can affect their performance. Here are some common problems and possible solutions (Ahsan et al., 2022).

3.2.3.1. Mode Collapse

Mode collapse is a leading problem in training GANs, and it affects cGANs as well. In the context of GANs, mode collapse refers to the situation where the generator produces limited diversity in its outputs, often generating very similar or even identical samples, regardless of the variation in the input noise vector.

This happens when the generator finds a particular point in the space that can fool the discriminator and, therefore, keeps producing similar samples around that point. When mode collapse occurs in a cGAN, the generator starts ignoring the provided conditional input, and instead of generating different outputs for different conditions, it produces the same output irrespective of the condition.

3.2.3.2. Lack of Diversity

Lack of diversity, or mode collapse, is a common issue when training cGANs. This happens when the generator produces the same or similar outputs regardless of changes in the input noise vector and the conditional input. This lack of diversity in the generated samples greatly reduces the utility of the model, as it is unable to cover the broad range of data that should be possible given the different conditional inputs (Majid & Ali, 2023).

3.2.3.3. Difficulty in Training

Training cGANs can indeed be challenging, due to reasons similar to those for standard GANs. These challenges include balancing the generator and discriminator during training, mode collapse, and vanishing gradients.

3.2.3.4. Sensitivity to Input Noise

In cGANs, sensitivity to input noise is a commonly encountered issue. This issue arises because the generator of a cGAN receives both a random noise vector and some conditional input. The random noise is intended to enable the generator to produce diverse outputs given the same conditional input, but if the generator becomes too sensitive to this noise, it can lead to unpredictable and low-quality results (Lauks et al., 1983).

3.2.3.5. Overfitting

Overfitting in cGANs is a common problem where the generator learns to produce outputs that are too like the training data and fails to generalize well to new inputs. This could result in a lack of diversity in generated samples and an inability to generate realistic samples for unseen conditional inputs (Eken, 2021).

3.3. CYCLIC GENERATIVE ADVERSARIAL NETWORK (CYCLEGAN)

Learning objectives

- Understand the architecture of CycleGAN
- Comprehend the issues and applications of CycleGAN

CycleGAN is a technique used for training models to translate from one domain to another without the need for paired examples. The models are trained using samples from both the source and target domains, which can be unrelated. To enhance the stability of the generator models and guide the process of sample generation, cycle consistency is incorporated into the CycleGAN architecture. This consistency ensures that a sample generated by the first generator is fed into the second generator and vice versa. CycleGAN is a type of GAN that allows unsupervised learning of image-to-image translation models, making it a powerful tool for various applications, such as style transfer, image colorization, and domain adaptation. CycleGAN does not require paired training data, and it learns to translate images from one domain to another through cycle consistency loss. This ensures that the translated images stay close to the original images in the source domain while also maintaining consistency in both directions. CycleGAN has been used in various applications, including artistic style transfer, image-to-image translation, voice conversion, and domain adaptation. It has also been utilized for text-to-image synthesis. The general architecture of CycleGAN consists of two parts, each with two generators and two discriminators. Its potential for creative expression and problem-solving is vast, and its applications are numerous. This section will review the architecture, issues, and applications of CycleGAN (Babu & Dubey, 2021).

Remember

CycleGANs aim to learn mappings between two different domains without paired data, allowing for unpaired image-to-image translation tasks such as style transfer and domain adaptation.

3.3.1. CycleGAN Architecture

Image-to-image translation challenges aim to find a mapping between input and output images using a training set of pre-aligned image pairs. Traditionally, creating an image-to-image translation model necessitated a training set of paired instances. Numerous instances of an input image X (such as summer landscapes) and the corresponding image with the desired change that could serve as the expected output image Y (for instance, winter landscapes) would be used (Almahairi et al., 2018). However, for many tasks, paired training data is not available, and typically, a significant number of paired samples are needed when training a model for image-to-image translation. The need for a paired training dataset is one of the limitations, as compiling these databases is a challenging and time-consuming task. Some of these datasets are difficult, expensive, or even impossible to create. For instance, capturing photographs of artworks created by deceased artists or taking photos under different settings and lighting conditions can be challenging (Harms et al., 2019). Moreover, often, datasets simply do not exist, especially in the case of great paintings. As a result, people seek alternative training methods when they aim to train an image-to-image translation system without using paired samples. CycleGAN is a training model technique proven effective for unpaired image-to-image translation. One of the most intriguing aspects of CycleGAN is that it can be trained without paired data. CycleGAN is based on the GAN architecture, which has been extended, and the training is done on two generator models and two discriminator models simultaneously. One generator's output is used to generate images for another domain, while the other generator's output is used to generate images for the first domain. Both generators use images from their respective domains. Then, discriminator models are used to determine the likelihood that the images truly represent something that exists, and the generator models are accordingly adjusted. This extension may be sufficient on its own to generate realistic images in each domain; however, it is not enough to generate translations of the provided input images. CycleGAN promotes cycle consistency by introducing a new loss that computes the difference between the second generator's output and the original image and vice versa. This loss also computes the difference between the first generator's output and the original image. This enhances the stability of the generator models and directs the process of producing images in the new domain toward image translation. This also makes the image-creation process more efficient. For example, for swapping photos from summer to winter and vice versa, which present very different scenery, CycleGAN can be used (Yang et al., 2020).

a) **Collection 1:** Photos of summer landscapes.

b) **Collection 2:** Photos of winter landscapes.

The architecture will consist of two GANs, each with its own discriminator and generator models, resulting in a total of four models. The first GAN will be responsible for converting summer images into winter images, while the second GAN will perform the opposite task of converting winter images into summer images.

a) **GAN 1:** Translates photos from collection 1 (summer images) to collection 2 (winter images).

b) **GAN 2:** Translates photos from collection 2 (winter images) to collection 1 (summer images).

Figure 3.10 illustrates the distinction between paired and unpaired training data. In the paired setup, training examples {xi, yi } exist where a direct correspondence between xi and yi is evident. On the other hand, unpaired images originate from different scenes, resulting in pairs X and Y that are distinct from each other. The general design of a Cycle GAN can be divided into three main parts (Oh et al., 2020).

Figure 3.10. *Illustration of the distinction between paired and unpaired data.*

Source: Ian J. Goodfellow, Creative Commons License.

The first part is the generator models, which are conditional models that generate a new image based on the input image. The second part is the discriminator models, which determine the likelihood that the generated image came from the target image collection. Both the generator and discriminator models are trained using adversarial loss, like traditional GAN models. However, these models alone are not enough to translate the input image to the target domain. To achieve this, cycle consistency loss is introduced, which compares the input image with the output image produced by the Cycle GAN using methods like the L1 norm or the sum of absolute differences in pixel values. There are two GANs used in the Cycle GAN architecture to calculate cycle consistency loss and update the generator models with each new round of training. For instance, GAN 1 takes a photo of a summer scene and converts it into a winter landscape. The resulting image is passed through GAN 2, which transforms it back to a summer landscape image. The difference in appearance between the input image and the output image from GAN 2 is used to modify the generator models to minimize the appearance difference. The same procedure is repeated in reverse to achieve a backward cycle consistency loss from generator 2 to generator 1 and to compare the original winter image with the generated photo (Sim et al., 2020).

3.3.2. CycleGAN Applications

CycleGAN has been deployed in various contexts, including style transfer, object transformation, season translation, photograph generation from paintings, and photo enhancement. During the style transfer process, the network converts data, which could be any photograph, into other artworks, such as a Van Gogh painting. The process by which a network changes the class of an object from one to another is referred to as object transfiguration. This section reviews some of these applications (Bargshady et al., 2022).

3.3.2.1. Artistic Style Transfer

CycleGAN can be used to transfer the style of an artist from one image to another. This has applications in the fields of art and design.

3.3.2.2. Image-to-image Translation

CycleGAN can be used to translate images from one domain to another. For example, it can be used to translate images of horses to images of zebras.

3.3.2.3. Medical Image Analysis

CycleGAN can be used to translate images from one modality to another. This has applications in medical image analysis, where images from one modality can be translated into another to aid in diagnosis (Zhou et al., 2020).

3.3.2.4. Video Stabilization

CycleGAN can be used to stabilize videos by translating frames from one domain to another.

3.3.2.5. Virtual Try-on

CycleGAN can be used to generate images of people wearing clothes that they have not worn. This has applications in the fashion industry.

3.3.2.6. Colorization

CycleGAN can be used to translate black-and-white images to colored images.

3.3.2.7. 3D Shape Synthesis

CycleGAN can be used to generate 3D shapes from 2D images.

3.3.2.8. Domain Adaptation

CycleGAN can be used to adapt models trained on one dataset to perform well on another dataset. Overall, CycleGAN has the potential to revolutionize many fields by providing a simple yet effective way to translate images from one domain to another without the need for paired training data. Here are some other main applications presented in some reference research papers (Soto et al., 2020).

3.3.2.9. Style Transfer

The process by which an artist modifies the artistic qualities of one work of art, such as a painting, to another form, such as a photograph, is referred to as "style transfer." Many artists' styles, such as those of Monet, Van Gogh, Cezanne, and Ukiyo-e, have been applied to landscape photographs to demonstrate how CycleGAN works. Figure 3.11 shows how the style transfer transforms the input image (on the left) into a different artist's style (on the right) (Tmenova et al., 2019).

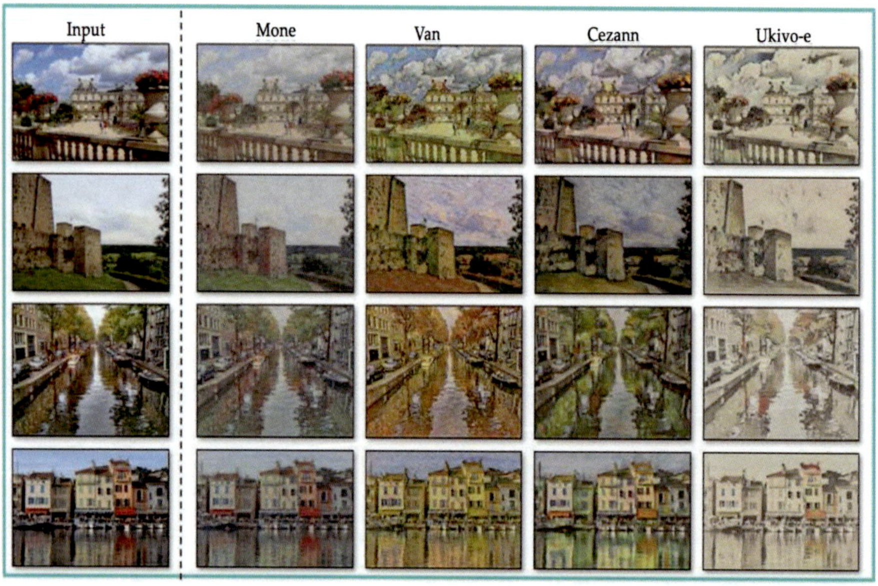

Figure 3.11. *Representation of the style transformation of input image.*

Source: Sherjil Ozair, Creative Commons License.

3.3.2.10. Season Transfer

The process of transforming a photograph taken during one season, such as summer, to make it appear as though it was taken during another season, such as winter, is known as "season transfer." CycleGAN is demonstrated by cycling through photographs of winter landscapes, summer landscapes, and back-to-winter landscapes. Figure 3.12 illustrates these processes (Paudel & Sah, 2021).

Figure 3.12. *Illustration of season transfer.*

Source: Soumith Chintala, Creative Commons License.

3.3.3. CycleGAN Issues

Several issues can arise when using CycleGAN.

3.3.3.1. Lack of Diversity in Generated Images

One of the most common issues with CycleGAN, and GANs in general, is the lack of diversity in the generated images, a problem also known as mode collapse. In this scenario, the generator produces very similar outputs for different inputs, which means that the model is not effectively learning to represent the full range of the target data distribution (Kim & Byun, 2020).

3.3.3.2. Poor Image Quality

Another common issue with CycleGAN is that the generated images may be of poor quality. This can be due to a variety of reasons, such as the model not being able to fully capture the details of the input images, the presence of noise in the training data, or the model overfitting the training data (Cho et al., 2020).

3.3.3.3. Unbalanced Image Domains

In some cases, the two image domains that are to be translated by CycleGAN might be unbalanced. That is, there may be significantly more images in one domain than the other, or the complexity of images in one domain may be much higher than that of the other domain. This can lead to the model overfitting to the larger or more complex domain, resulting in poor translation performance for the smaller or less complex domain.

3.3.3.4. Difficulty in Choosing Hyperparameters

Selecting hyperparameters in CycleGAN can be tricky because they significantly impact the model's performance and training stability. These include the learning rate, number of generator/discriminator layers, batch size, and lambda value for cycle consistency loss.

3.3.3.5. Long Training Times

Training a CycleGAN can be computationally intensive and may require a large amount of data and processing power. This can make it difficult to iterate quickly on the model and experiment with different settings. CycleGAN involves training two generative adversarial networks simultaneously, which can be computationally expensive and result in long training times (Sandfort et al., 2019).

3.3.3.6. Mode Collapse

One common problem in GANs is mode collapse, where the generator starts producing the same outputs (or a small set of outputs) for different inputs. This is a significant issue because it means the network is not learning to represent the full complexity of the target data distribution.

3.3.3.7. Overfitting

The model performs well on the training data but poorly on the test data. CycleGAN, like other deep learning models, can overfit if not properly regularized. Overfitting means the model learns the training data too well, including its noise and outliers, resulting in poor performance on unseen data.

3.3.3.8. Gradient Vanishing/Exploding

In CycleGANs, the vanishing/exploding gradient problem can occur during backpropagation, making the network hard to train. This is when gradient values become so large (exploding gradients) or so small (vanishing gradients) that they hinder the model's learning process (Gautam et al., 2022).

3.3.3.9. Unbalanced Data

CycleGAN is designed for unpaired image-to-image translation, which inherently tackles some unbalanced data issues. However, if there is a severe imbalance within each domain or between domains, the model may perform poorly.

3.3.3.10. Image Artifacts

CycleGANs can sometimes produce images with noticeable artifacts or irregularities, affecting the quality of the generated images.

3.3.3.11. Lack of Diversity

Lack of diversity (or mode collapse) is a common issue in GANs, where the generator starts to produce limited or identical outputs regardless of varying inputs (Nerrienet et al., 2023).

3.4. SEMI-SUPERVISED GENERATIVE ADVERSARIAL NETWORK (SGAN)

Learning objectives

- Understand the architecture of SGAN
- Comprehend the issues and applications of SGAN

The Semi-Supervised Generative Adversarial Network (SGAN) is an extension of GAN that uses both labeled and unlabeled data to improve the training of generative models. Semi-supervised learning plays a crucial role, given the cost and availability of labeled data. Its networks combine supervised learning loss with unsupervised loss and can work with any neural network architecture, including feedforward and recurrent networks (Balakrishnan et al., 2021). The goal of semi-supervised learning is to generalize from a small subset of labeled data. Discriminators are trained on both labeled and unlabeled data to distinguish between real and fake data and to categorize the labeled training images into the appropriate groups. The labeled data is used to train both the discriminator and the generator models, and then the unlabeled data is used to further train the generator model. By doing so, SGAN can generate high-quality data that is more diverse and better reflects the underlying distribution of the training data. It has been shown to outperform traditional supervised and unsupervised learning methods in many tasks (Das et al., 2021). However, SGAN also faces challenges, such as selecting the labeled data and balancing the supervised and unsupervised loss functions. The discriminator is trained to not only distinguish between real and fake data but also to classify the labeled data into their respective classes. The generator is trained to generate data that not only tricks the discriminator but also produces realistic samples that belong to the labeled classes. SGAN has found applications in various fields, such as image and speech recognition, natural language processing, and even drug discovery. It has shown promising results in improving the quality and quantity of generated data, which can benefit various industries. Figure 3.13 provides a visual representation of the overarching architecture of the SGAN. Typically, an SGAN incorporates both unsupervised and supervised learning elements, allowing it to make use of both labeled and unlabeled data (Dogan & Keles, 2020).

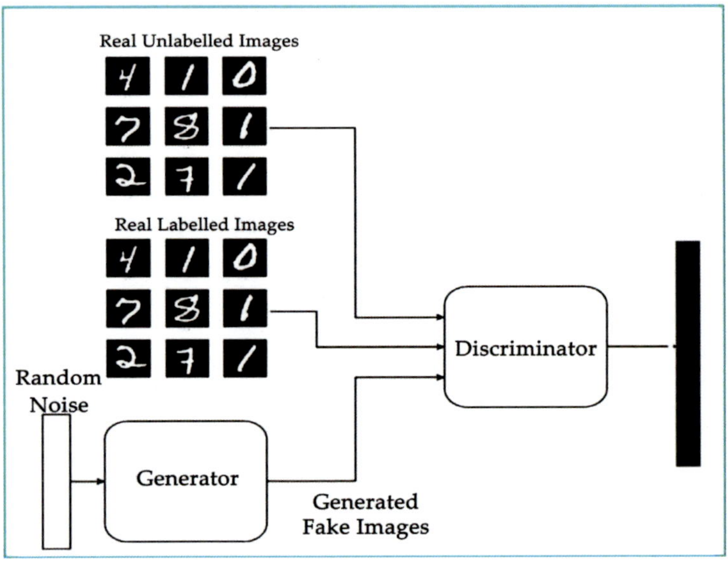

Figure 3.13. *Diagram of SGAN architecture.*

Source: Mehdi Ghayoum, Creative Commons License.

The diagram exhibits the interplay between the generator, which produces synthetic data samples, and the discriminator, which classifies these samples either as real or fake while also assigning class labels to real data. By learning from a combination of both types of data, SGANs aim to optimize generative capabilities and classification accuracy simultaneously (Sajun & Zualkernan, 2022).

3.4.1. SGAN Architecture

Deep supervised learning methods have recently achieved significant success in both research and industry, but their success heavily depends on the availability of large amounts of labeled data. However, labeled data is more expensive to collect than unlabeled data in most applications. This problem motivates the use of semi-supervised learning, which can be trained to perform well with a small amount of labeled data (Olut et al., 2018). Semi-supervised learning is a well-known machine learning method where only a portion of the data in a set is labeled. In this approach, the discriminator uses three types of data: labeled training, unlabeled training, and generator-generated fake data. This is effective because discriminators are trained on both labeled and unlabeled data. What the discriminator learns about images without labels should help it describe the features of images with labels. In practice, this means that the discriminator has a SoftMax output that minimizes the cross-entropy (Kothari & Alahi, 2023). Semi-supervised learning attempts to generalize from a small subset of labeled data points to classify previously unseen examples effectively.

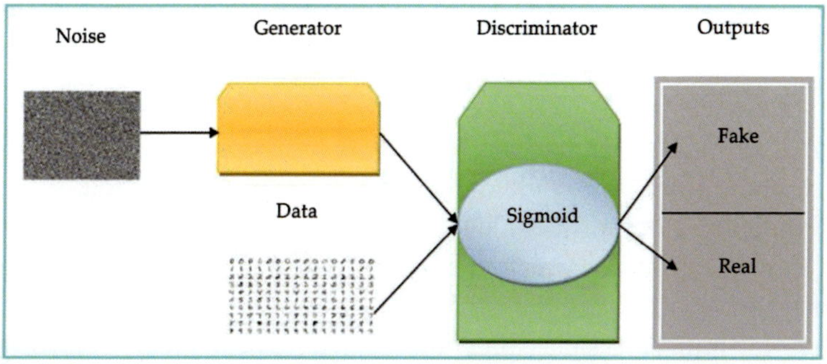

Figure 3.14. *Illustration of general GAN architecture.*

Source: Alec Radford, Creative Commons License.

It accomplishes this by internalizing hidden data structures and requiring that labeled and unlabeled data come from the same distribution. Figure 3.14 shows the entire regular GAN, including input data (both noise and real data), generator, discriminator, and outputs. Figure 3.15 presents the general architecture of the SGAN. Central to the visualization is the network's unique dual-input design: one for noise and the other two for labeled and unlabeled data. The generator module takes in random noise and crafts synthetic data samples. Simultaneously, the discriminator receives both labeled and unlabeled data samples, effectively discerning real from fake and, for labeled samples, classifying them into their respective categories. Figures 3.15 and 3.14 show the general architecture of a semi-supervised GAN, with the main differences being in the input data (labeled and unlabeled data) and the activation function in the discriminator (Zhong et al., 2022).

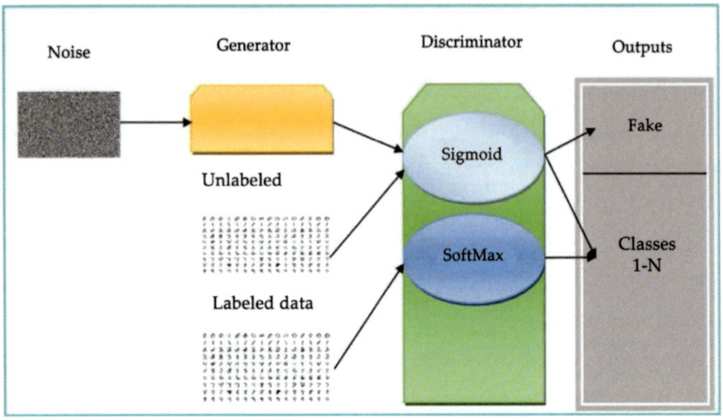

Figure 3.15. *Illustration of Semi-Supervised GAN architecture.*

Source: Mehdi Mirza, Creative Commons License.

The semi-supervised GAN has a similar structure to a regular GAN, but instead of determining which of the N+1 classes come from the training dataset, and which come from the generator, its discriminator is a multiclass classifier. The discriminator's output includes the probability of an image being real or fake and the probability of it belonging to one of the N classes. So, instead of binary classification in a regular GAN, the discriminator in a semi-supervised GAN performs multi-class classification (Chavdarova & Fleuret, 2018).

3.4.2. SGAN Applications

The SGAN has shown great potential in real-world applications due to its benefits. For instance, GONet is a system that addresses the problem of traversability estimation for robots, and researchers have used SGANs to solve the issue of semantic image segmentation. Inspired by these findings, SGANs have been applied to the detection of road patches in images. Semi-supervised learning has also been used to address the problem of cross-modal information retrieval. Researchers have used SGANs to tackle novel problems that lack reasonable solutions as well as to conduct spoofing attacks on speaker recognition systems. In many cases, SGANs are useful when there is a shortage of labeled data available. Overall, semi-supervised learning GANs have numerous applications in various fields, and their potential for further use continues to be explored (Tobias et al., 2021).

3.4.2.1. Image Classification

Semi-supervised GANs can be used to improve image classification by using both labeled and unlabeled data.

3.4.2.2. Object Detection

These GANs can be used to detect and identify objects in images with the help of labeled and unlabeled data.

3.4.2.3. Natural Language Processing

Semi-supervised GANs can be used for tasks, such as text classification, machine translation, and sentiment analysis (Thirumagal & Saruladha, 2021).

3.4.2.4. Healthcare

These GANs can be used for medical image analysis, such as identifying tumors in MRI scans, with the help of labeled and unlabeled data.

3.4.2.5. Fraud Detection

Semi-supervised GANs can be used to detect fraud in financial transactions by using labeled and unlabeled data.

3.4.2.6. Autonomous Vehicles

These GANs can be used for object detection and recognition in autonomous vehicles with the help of labeled and unlabeled data (Rossi et al., 2021).

3.4.2.7. Recommender Systems

Semi-supervised GANs can improve recommender systems by using labeled and unlabeled data to understand user preferences better.

3.4.2.8. Gaming

These GANs can generate new game levels, characters, and game assets in gaming.

3.4.2.9. Virtual Reality

Semi-supervised GANs can be used to generate realistic virtual environments by using both labeled and unlabeled data (Veneva et al., 2022).

3.4.2.10. Advertising

These GANs can be used for targeted advertising by analyzing user behavior and preferences with the help of labeled and unlabeled data.

3.4.3. SGAN Issues

Semi-supervised learning with GANs is a relatively new area of research, and there are several issues that researchers are working to overcome (Saxena & Cao, 2021).

3.4.3.1. Lack of Labeled Data

SGANs attempt to address the problem of scarce labeled data in machine learning. Collecting a large amount of labeled data is often time-consuming, costly, and, in some cases, practically impossible. However, unlabeled data is typically abundant and more easily accessible. Here are some problems associated with the lack of labeled data in SGANs.

a) **Model performance:** Models trained with less labeled data might not perform well due to high variance, which can lead to overfitting. The model may learn to perform very well on the training data but fail to generalize well to unseen data.

b) **Data representation:** With insufficient labeled data, the model might not learn an accurate representation of the true data distribution. This can lead to generating outputs that do not accurately represent the target domain (Livny et al., 2010).

3.4.3.2. Difficulty in Finding the Right Balance between Labeled and Unlabeled Data

SGANs leverage both labeled and unlabeled data during the training process. However, finding the right balance between these two data types can pose a significant challenge for several reasons:

a) **Importance of unlabeled data:** Unlabeled data is typically used to improve the generator's performance in creating realistic examples. However, if too much emphasis is placed on the unlabeled data, the model might not learn enough about the structure of the labeled data to make accurate predictions.

b) **Influence of labeled data:** Conversely, if too much weight is given to the labeled data, the model could be overfit to this data and fail to generalize well to unseen examples. It might also not generate diverse enough examples as it focuses too much on replicating the labeled examples (Ren et al., 2023).

3.4.3.3. Mode Collapse

Mode collapse is a common issue in GANs and so in the SGANs. When mode collapse occurs, the generator produces a limited variety of samples, often focusing on a few modes of data distribution and ignoring others. As a result, the diversity of generated samples is significantly reduced.

3.4.3.4. Difficulty in Training

Semi-supervised learning with GANs can be challenging to train, as it involves optimizing two networks simultaneously. Training GANs, including SGANs, can be challenging due to the nature of their adversarial learning paradigm. This difficulty is often amplified in the semi-supervised setting due to the additional complexity of handling both labeled and unlabeled data. Specific issues might include the instability of the training process, the vanishing gradients problem, and the difficulty of achieving an equilibrium between the generator and the discriminator.

3.4.3.5. Stability Issues

GANs can be unstable, leading to poor training performance and results. Training GANs, including SGANs, often face issues of instability. This often arises from the adversarial nature of GAN training, where the generator and the discriminator are in a constant push-pull dynamic. In many cases, one model may dominate the other, leading to poor performance. For instance, a too-strong discriminator can lead to vanishing gradients for the generator, causing it to stop learning (Jabbar et al., 2021).

3.5. LEAST SQUARES GENERATIVE ADVERSARIAL NETWORK (LSGAN)

Learning objectives

- Understand the architecture of LSGAN
- Comprehend the applications and issues of LSGAN

LSGAN, or Least Squares GAN, is a type of generative adversarial network that uses the least squares loss function in its discriminator. This aims to improve the stability of GAN training and has demonstrated better results in some applications compared to standard GANs. The standard GAN loss function, which utilizes binary cross-entropy, can lead to issues like vanishing gradients and mode collapse, where the generator produces a limited range of samples failing to cover the complete distribution of the real data. LSGANs address this issue by training the generator and discriminator to minimize the least squares loss instead. This encourages the generator to produce more diverse samples and contributes to smoother and more stable training. LSGANs have been successfully applied to various tasks, such as image synthesis, text-to-image translation, and video prediction. They have been shown to produce high-quality samples with better visual fidelity and diversity. However, LSGANs can be computationally expensive to train due to the quadratic optimization problem inherent in the least squares loss function. Techniques like mini-batch discrimination and spectral normalization have been proposed to mitigate this issue. Overall, LSGANs hold promising potential to enhance the capabilities of generative models for various applications. This chapter provides an overview of LSGAN and coding examples for further practice. Figure 3.16 illustrates the general architecture of an LSGAN (Mao et al., 2017).

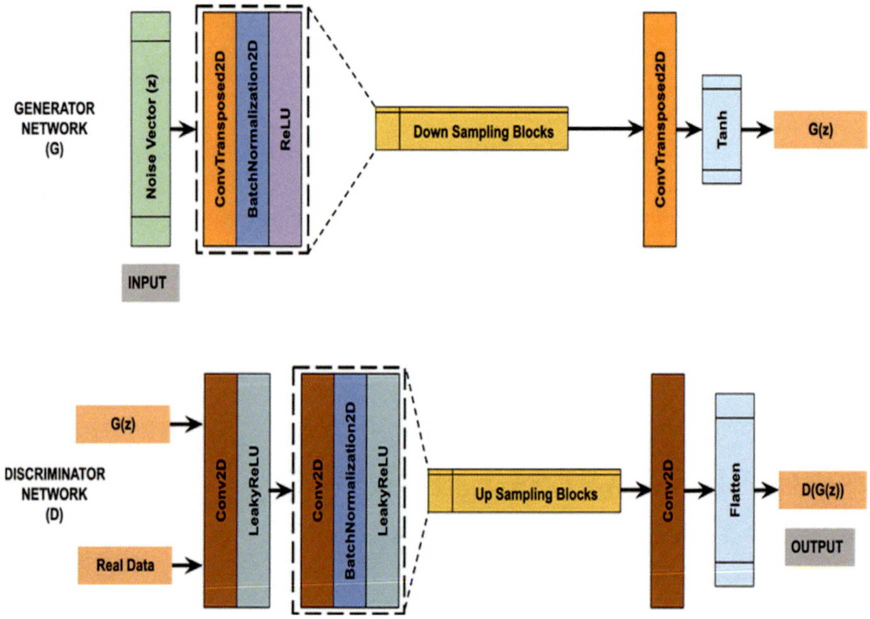

Figure 3.16. *Representation of general LSGAN architecture.*

Source: Bing Xu, Creative Commons License.

3.5.1. LSGAN Architecture

In a standard GAN, the generator and discriminator are trained using the binary cross-entropy loss function. The discriminator's goal is to classify the input images as real or fake, while the generator aims to create images that can trick the discriminator into believing they are real. Conversely, LSGANs employ a least squares loss function for both the generator and the discriminator. The discriminator is trained to assign high values to real images and low values to fake ones, while the generator strives to produce images that receive high values from the discriminator. This loss function encourages the generator to produce samples that are closer to the real data, and the discriminator can distinguish between real and fake samples using a more relaxed boundary, making the training process smoother and more stable. As a result, LSGANs have demonstrated the ability to produce high-quality samples with superior visual fidelity and diversity compared to standard GANs (Kieu et al., 2021).

a) Loss functions for discriminator in GAN (LD_{GAN}) and LSGAN (LD_{LSGAN}):

$$L(G,D) = \mathrm{E}x \sim pdata(x)\left[\log D(x)\right] + \mathrm{E}z \sim pz(z)\left[\log\left(1 - D(G(z))\right)\right]$$

where:

i. E is the expectation.

ii. D(x) is the discriminator's output for real data.

iii. G(z) is the generator's output from noise z.

iv. D(G(z)) is the discriminator's output for fake data.

$$LD_{LSGAN} = \mathrm{E}\left[\left(D(x)-1\right)^2\right] + \mathrm{E}\left[D(G(z))^2\right]$$

b) Loss functions for the generator in GAN (LG_{GAN}) and LSGAN (LG_{LSGAN}): The generator's loss for a traditional GAN is:

$$L_G = \mathrm{E}\left[\log\left(1 - D(G(z))\right)\right]$$

However, in practice, it is common to use (Yue et al., 2021):

$$L_G = \mathrm{E}\left[\log\left(D(G(z))\right)\right]$$

$$LG_{LSGAN} = 1/2\left(\mathrm{E}\left[\left(D(G(z))-1\right)^2\right]\right)$$

3.5.2. LSGAN Applications

LSGAN is a type of GAN that employs a least squares loss function instead of the traditional cross-entropy loss function. This modification results in more stable training and enables the generation of sharper images. LSGAN has been utilized across various domains, including image synthesis, video synthesis, and style transfer. In image synthesis, LSGAN is used for generating high-quality images in numerous applications, such as face generation, object generation, and image inpainting (Ataş, 2023). It has also demonstrated impressive results in generating high-quality 3D models, expanding its use to the creation of 3D objects. In the field of video synthesis, LSGAN has shown its effectiveness in generating high-quality videos. It has found various applications, such as video prediction, video super-resolution, and video style transfer. Moreover, LSGAN has been instrumental in generating realistic human motion and 3D pose estimation from 2D images. In the realm of style transfer, LSGAN has been deployed to generate images that capture the style of one image and the content of another. This technique has found applications in various domains like art, fashion, and design. In addition to visual applications, LSGAN has shown promise in natural language processing, where it has been used for tasks like text generation, translation, and summarization. It has also been applied in speech processing for tasks like speech recognition and synthesis. Furthermore, LSGAN has been beneficial in the field of drug discovery, where it has been used to generate new molecular structures with desirable properties. It has shown the potential to accelerate the drug discovery process by generating diverse and novel molecules that can be synthesized and tested in the lab. In summary, LSGAN has proven its effectiveness across a wide array of applications and shows great promise as a tool for generating high-quality images, videos, and data (Bin, 2023).

3.5.2.1. Some Experimental Results

DCGAN serves as a foundation upon which the least-square loss is implemented to form the LSGAN. The images produced by LSGANs surpass those generated by the baseline methods, namely DCGANs, and EBGANs.

3.5.2.2. Stability Comparison on Gaussian Mixture Distribution Dataset

In this dataset, a simple architecture consisting of three fully connected layers is used for both the generator and the discriminator. The mode collapse issue for standard GANs begins at step 15k, where they only generate samples following a single valid data distribution mode. Conversely, LSGANs can effectively learn the Gaussian mixture distribution, avoiding the mode collapse issue and generating samples with greater diversity (Ruan et al., 2023).

3.5.3. LSGAN Issues

One of the main issues with LSGANs is the instability during training. While the objective function of LSGANs is less prone to mode collapse than traditional GANs, the optimization process can still be difficult to converge. This can result in the generator producing poor-quality images or the discriminator failing to accurately distinguish real and fake samples. Additionally, LSGANs can suffer from gradient vanishing or exploding, which can hinder the learning process. Another challenge is the selection of hyperparameters, such as the learning rate, batch size, and number of layers, which can significantly impact the performance of the LSGAN. Some of the issues with LSGAN and their possible solutions are discussed in the following subsections (Dewi et al., 2021).

3.5.3.1. Mode Collapse

While LSGAN already improves stability over the standard GAN loss; it can still suffer from mode collapse and can benefit from some solutions. Mode collapse is a common issue in GANs, including LSGANs, where the generator starts producing a limited range of samples, failing to cover the full diversity of the real data. This often occurs when the generator discovers that certain outputs are more likely to fool the discriminator, leading it to produce these outputs repeatedly. Consequently, the GAN fails to generate a diverse set of samples, limiting its usefulness (Tomar & Gupta, 2023).

3.5.3.2. Gradient Vanishing/Exploding

Gradient vanishing or exploding is a common problem in deep learning models, including LSGANs. The issue arises during backpropagation, where the gradients of the loss function either become too small (vanish) or too large (explode). When gradients vanish, the weights of the earlier layers in the network are not updated effectively during training, making it difficult for the network to learn. When gradients explode, the weights of the earlier layers can fluctuate wildly, leading to instability in the model's training process.

3.5.3.3. Unstable Training

GANs can be difficult to train due to their adversarial nature, often leading to unstable training dynamics. Unstable training in LSGANs could manifest as:

a) **Mode collapse:** This is where the generator starts to collapse to produce the same or very similar outputs (one mode of the data distribution), instead of generating diverse samples from the data distribution.

b) **Oscillations:** This is where the generator's and discriminator's losses fail to converge and instead oscillate indefinitely.

c) **Vanishing/Exploding gradients:** As discussed earlier, these problems can also lead to unstable training (Sisson & Moncayo, 2023).

3.5.3.4. Evaluation Metrics

In GANs and their variants like LSGANs, evaluating the quality and diversity of the generated samples can be quite challenging. Here are some issues and solutions related to this:

a) **Lack of ground truth:** Unlike in supervised learning, where there is a clear ground truth for comparison, in generative models like LSGANs, the objective is to generate samples that are similar to the real data distribution, and there is no clear-cut ground truth.

b) **Quality vs. Diversity:** A key challenge is evaluating both the quality (how realistic individual samples look) and diversity (how much the samples cover the whole data distribution) of the generated samples. A model can generate very high-quality samples that lack diversity (e.g., by always generating the same realistic-looking image) or highly diverse but low-quality samples.

c) **Subjective evaluation:** Traditional metrics often involve human evaluation, which can be highly subjective and non-scalable (Lagan et al., 2020).

3.5.3.5. Limited Training Data

Training GANs, including LSGANs, requires substantial amounts of data. Limited data could lead to issues, such as overfitting, poor generalization, and lack of diversity in the generated samples. When the available training data is scarce, the model might not be able to learn the underlying distribution effectively, resulting in generated outputs that are not diverse or realistic.

3.6. WASSERSTEIN GENERATIVE ADVERSARIAL NETWORKS (WGAN)

Learning objectives

- Understand the architecture of WGANs
- Comprehend the issues and applications of WGANs

The Wasserstein Generative Adversarial Network (WGAN), proposed in 2017, aims to improve learning stability, solve issues such as mode collapse, and generate meaningful learning curves that can be used for debugging and hyperparameter searches. WGAN is a type of GAN that uses Wasserstein distance as a loss function instead of the traditional binary cross-entropy loss.

The WGAN architecture was proposed in a paper titled "Wasserstein GAN" by Martin Arjovsky, Soumith Chintala, and Léon Bottou, which was published in 2017. The Wasserstein distance, also known as the Earth-Mover (EM) distance, is a measure of the distance between two probability distributions. It provides a more stable and meaningful training signal for the generator in GANs compared to binary cross-entropy loss, which suffers from mode collapse and instability issues. In WGAN, the discriminator is not limited to outputting a probability between 0 and 1; instead, it outputs a scalar value representing the estimated Wasserstein distance between the generated and real distributions. The generator is trained to minimize this distance, while the discriminator is trained to maximize it. This creates a more informative feedback signal for the generator, which encourages it to generate samples that are closer to the real data distribution. WGAN has been successfully applied to various tasks, such as image generation, super-resolution, and style transfer. Its stability and ability to generate high-quality samples make it a popular choice for generative modeling tasks. However, WGAN also has its own set of challenges and limitations. One of the main issues is the difficulty in tuning the hyperparameters, such as the number of critic updates per generator update and the Lipschitz constant of the discriminator. Additionally, the weight clipping method used to enforce the Lipschitz constraint can lead to gradient vanishing or exploding problems, which can affect the training stability. Overall, WGAN is a powerful and promising approach for generative modeling, but it requires careful tuning and implementation to overcome its challenges and achieve good results. This chapter reviews this approach's architecture and provides some coding examples for learning about the MNIST and Fashion MNIST datasets (Arjovsky et al., 2017).

Did You Know?

Wasserstein GANs (WGANs) introduce Wasserstein distance as the metric for measuring the difference between the generated and real data distributions, leading to more stable training dynamics and improved convergence properties compared to traditional GANs.

3.6.1. WGAN Architecture

WGAN is an extension of GAN that aims to make the training process more stable and less affected by the model's architecture and hyperparameter settings. Stable training involves finding and maintaining a balance between the capabilities of the generator and the discriminator. WGAN achieves this by modifying or replacing the discriminator with a critic that rates how real or fake an image is based on mathematical reasoning that minimizes the difference between the data's distribution in the training dataset and the generated examples. The EM distance is used to measure this difference. To convert GAN and DCGAN architectures to WGAN, several modifications are made, including using a linear activation function instead of a sigmoid in the critic's output layer, training the critic and generator models with Wasserstein loss, and setting a range of critic model weights after each mini-batch update. For example, consider the moving boxes problem shown in Figure 3.17, where two boxes must be moved to minimize transport costs. In P1, moving box A from position 2 to position 3 costs 1, and moving box B from position 6 to position 5 costs 1, resulting in a total cost of 2. In P2, moving box B from position 2 to position 5 costs 3, while moving box A from position 6 to position 3 costs 3, resulting in a total cost of 6. Although the outputs are the same in both P1 and P2 (box A in position 3 and box B in position 5), the total cost is different. The Wasserstein distance used in WGAN provides the minimum cost, like P1, whereas normal GAN does not guarantee this (Bhatia & Dahyot, 2019). The Wasserstein distance formula is:

$$W(p_r, p_g) = \inf_{\gamma \sim \Pi(p_r, p_g)} \mathbb{E}_{(x,y)\sim\gamma}\left[\|x - y\|\right]$$

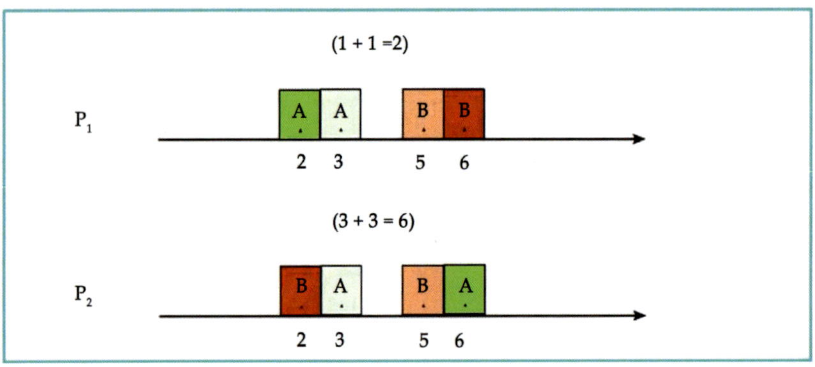

Figure 3.17. *Example of moving boxes in WGAN.*

Source: Alec Radford, Creative Commons License.

In the above equation, $\prod(\mathbf{p}_r, \mathbf{p}_g)$, is the set of all possible combinations of two probability distributions pr and pg. The joint distribution $\gamma \in \prod(\mathbf{p}_r, \mathbf{p}_g)$, describes one plan for moving, just like in the example above, and the γ (**x, y**), shows how much it should be moved from point x to point y (the point x has the same probability distribution as point y). When x is used as the starting point, and y is used as the destination, the traveling distance is x y − and the cost (the total measure of movement) is γ (**x, y**) (Dörner et al., 2020) :

$$\sum_{x,y}\gamma(x,y)\|x-y\| = \mathbb{E}_{x,y-\gamma}\|x-y\|$$

In WGAN, the EM distance is used to find the cheapest way to move from one distribution to another. The "inf" in the definition of the Wasserstein distance stands for "infinity" or "greatest lower bound," indicating that only the lowest cost matters. Moreover, instead of using a discriminator to classify whether an image is real or fake, the WGAN replaces the discriminator with a critic that assigns a score to an image based on its realism. The amount of generator loss has a significant impact on the WGAN's convergence. The following are the average loss values for a small batch (Wu et al., 2020).

$$\textbf{Critic Loss} = [\text{average critic score on real images}] - [\text{average critic score on fake images}]$$

$$\textbf{Generator Loss} = -[\text{average critic score on fake images}]$$

To calculate the Wasserstein loss by this formula:

$$\textbf{Wasserstein Loss} = \text{label} \times \text{average critic score}$$

or

$$\textbf{Wasserstein Loss (real images)} = +1 \times \text{average predicted score}$$

$$\textbf{Wasserstein Loss (fake images)} = -1 \times \text{average predicted score}$$

In WGAN, a lower critic loss indicates a higher output quality. For instance, if there are 30 real images and 40 fake images, the loss is −10, but if there are 20 real images and 40 fake images, the loss is −20, which is lower, and the output quality is higher. These values depend on the ratio of real to fake images.

Figures 3.18 and 3.19 illustrate the differences between the general architecture of GAN and WGAN. To identify the key differences between the two figures, explore numbers 1–3. The network designs for GAN and WGAN are nearly identical, with the exception that WGAN uses a critic instead of a discriminator, and the critic's output function is not a sigmoid. The only other significant difference is the cost function used for the discriminator/ critic and generator (Ye et al., 2018).

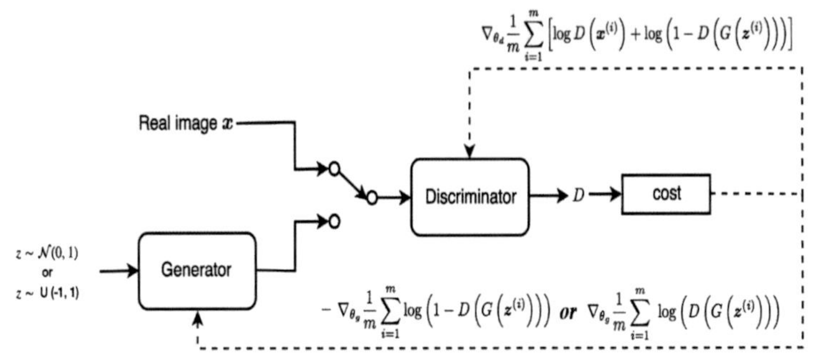

Figure 3.18. *Illustration of normal GAN architecture.*

Source: Soumith Chintala, Creative Commons License.

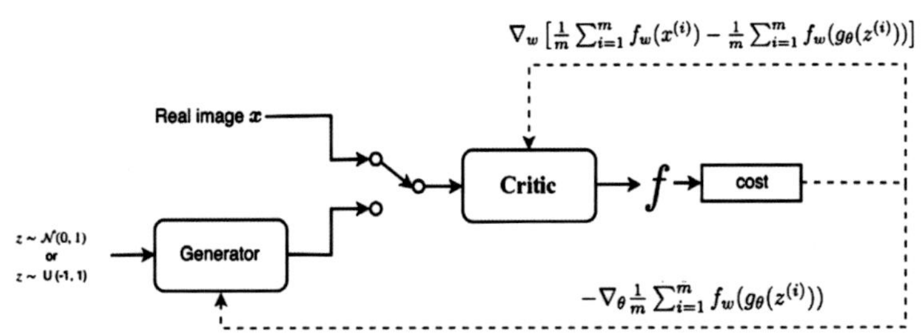

Figure 3.19. *Illustration of WGAN architecture.*

Source: Luke Metz, Creative Commons License.

The implementation of WGAN differs in several ways, including:

a) Using a linear activation function in the critic model's output layer instead of a sigmoid

b) Assigning −1 labels to real images and 1 to fake images instead of 0 and 1

c) Training the critic and generator models with Wasserstein loss

d) Limiting the weights of critic models to a certain range after each mini-batch update

e) Updating the critic model more frequently than the generator model

f) Using a small learning rate (Gong et al., 2019).

3.6.2. WGAN Applications

WGAN has been successfully applied in a wide range of applications.

3.6.2.1. Image Synthesis

WGAN has shown promising results in generating high-quality images, especially in domains where GANs have struggled, such as medical imaging (Shamsolmoali et al., 2021).

3.6.2.2. Style Transfer

WGAN has been used for style transfer tasks, where it can preserve the content of an image while transferring the style from another image.

3.6.2.3. Super-resolution

WGAN has been applied to super-resolution tasks, where it can generate high-resolution images from low-resolution inputs.

3.6.2.4. Data Augmentation

WGAN can be used for data augmentation in various applications, such as in the medical domain, where there may be limited data available.

3.6.2.5. Anomaly Detection

WGAN has been used for anomaly detection in various fields, such as in detecting fraud in financial transactions or identifying anomalies in medical images (Han et al., 2021).

3.6.2.6. Speech Synthesis

WGAN has shown promising results in synthesizing human-like speech.

3.6.2.7. Music Generation

WGAN has also been applied to music generation tasks, where it can generate novel and diverse music compositions.

3.6.2.8. Video Generation

WGAN has been used for video generation tasks, such as generating realistic video sequences from still images or generating novel video sequences. Overall, WGAN has shown promising results in a wide range of applications and has the potential to be used in various fields to generate high-quality and diverse data.

3.6.3. WGAN Issues

Several WGAN issues make it challenging to use in any capacity. One of the main issues with traditional GANs is that the loss function used to train them is not very informative and can be difficult to optimize. The WGAN was introduced as a way to address this issue. However, it also has its own set of issues that need to be addressed (Jin et al., 2019).

3.6.3.1. Vanishing Gradients

WGANs were specifically designed to address the vanishing gradients problem found in traditional GANs. This issue arises when the discriminator becomes too powerful and the generator struggles to learn due to minimal gradient feedback. WGANs solve this issue by replacing the standard GAN loss function with the Wasserstein loss function. This function provides smooth and meaningful gradients almost everywhere, even when the discriminator is very confident about its decisions. Thus, the generator always has useful feedback to learn from, mitigating the vanishing gradient problem. The Wasserstein loss also reduces the risk of mode collapse, which is another common issue in GANs. Moreover, the WGAN model implements a Lipschitz constraint by weight clipping or GP, ensuring the function does not become too steep and keeping the gradients manageable, further contributing to solving the vanishing gradients problem (Neves et al., 2021).

3.6.3.2. Hyperparameter Tuning

In WGANs, hyperparameters play a crucial role in balancing the learning of the generator and the discriminator and can influence the quality and diversity of the generated samples. However, choosing optimal hyperparameters can be tricky and time-consuming. One common issue in WGAN is the need to tune the weight clipping parameter or the GP lambda, which helps enforce the Lipschitz constraint. If these parameters are set incorrectly, they can lead to undesired behaviors, such as discriminator saturation or inadequate learning of the generator. A common solution to this issue is using a systematic approach like grid search or random search to find the best hyperparameters. Additionally, modern approaches like Bayesian Optimization or Automated Machine Learning (AutoML) tools can be used for hyperparameter optimization. It is also beneficial to leverage the research community's findings. For instance, in WGANs, it is often recommended to use RMSProp or Adam as the optimizer, and it is often suggested to use more discriminator updates per generator update than in traditional GANs. Also, monitoring the Wasserstein distance during training can provide a more reliable metric for tracking GAN training than traditional GAN loss. However, as the specifics can vary greatly based on the dataset and the problem at hand, the most effective strategy is often a combination of leveraging existing research and conducting careful experimentation (Santos & Carvalho, 2020).

3.6.3.3. Evaluation of Results

Evaluation of GANs, including WGANs, is challenging because they do not optimize a well-defined likelihood function. This makes it hard to compare the performance of different models or even different runs of the same model. One of the common issues is that traditional metrics, such as accuracy or loss value, may not directly translate into the quality or diversity of the generated samples. This is especially true for WGANs, where the discriminator (called the critic in WGAN terminology) is trained to estimate the Wasserstein distance between the real and generated distributions, rather than to classify samples as real or fake.

3.6.3.4. Computational Resources

WGANs, like other GAN architectures, can be computationally intensive, requiring a significant amount of processing power and memory. The requirement to train two networks (the generator and the discriminator) simultaneously, the use of deep convolutional layers, and the need for large numbers of training iterations all contribute to the high computational cost. Moreover, WGANs employ a technique known as weight clipping or GP to ensure that the discriminator (or critic) follows the Lipschitz constraint. This technique involves additional computations, further adding to the computational burden. To mitigate this issue, several strategies can be adopted (Wan et al., 2022).

a) **Hardware acceleration:** The use of Graphics Processing Units (GPUs) or Tensor Processing Units (TPUs) can dramatically speed up the training process as these devices are designed for high-performance computation, which is required for training deep learning models.

b) **Efficient coding practices:** Techniques, such as batch processing, in-place operations, and reduced precision calculations, can help to optimize memory usage and computational efficiency.

c) **Model simplification:** If feasible, reducing the complexity of the generator and discriminator networks can save computational resources. This might involve using fewer layers or reducing the dimensionality of the latent space.

d) **Distributed training:** Leveraging distributed computing resources can help to scale the training process across multiple devices or machines, thus shortening the overall training time.

e) **Transfer learning:** Instead of training the model from scratch, a pre-trained model can be used and fine-tuned on the specific task, which can save a significant amount of computational resources (Pei et al., 2022).

SUMMARY

- This chapter explores various architectures and variations of GANs, each designed to address specific challenges or cater to applications. These include Deep Convolutional GANs (DCGANs), Conditional GANs (cGANs), CycleGANs, Semi-Supervised GANs (SGANs), Least Squares GANs (LSGANs), and Wasserstein GANs (WGANs).
- DCGANs utilize convolutional neural networks (CNNs) in both the generator and discriminator models. They are well-suited for generating high-resolution images and have stable training dynamics.
- cGANs condition the generation process on additional information, such as class labels or auxiliary features. This enables the controlled generation of specific data samples based on input conditions.
- CycleGANs aim to learn mappings between two different domains without paired data. They employ cycle consistency loss to ensure that the translated samples maintain their original characteristics.
- LSGANs utilize a least squares loss function instead of binary cross-entropy for training the discriminator. This leads to more stable training dynamics and improved convergence properties.
- WGANs introduce Wasserstein distance as the metric for measuring the difference between the generated and real data distributions. They address mode collapse and training instability issues inherent in traditional GANs.
- Each type of GAN discussed in this chapter offers unique advantages and is tailored to specific use cases or challenges in generative modeling.

MULTIPLE CHOICE QUESTIONS

1. What type of neural network architecture is commonly used in Deep Convolutional GANs (DCGANs)?

a) Recurrent Neural Networks (RNNs)

b) Multilayer Perceptrons (MLPs)

c) Convolutional Neural Networks (CNNs)

d) Generative Adversarial Networks (GANs)

2. Conditional GANs (cGANs) condition the generation process on:

a) Random noise vectors

b) Additional information such as class labels

c) Feedback from the discriminator

d) Gradient updates

3. Which type of GAN is designed to learn mappings between two different domains without paired data?

a) Deep Convolutional GANs (DCGANs)

b) Conditional GANs (cGANs)

c) CycleGANs

d) Self-Attention GANs (SGANs)

4. What type of GAN incorporates self-attention mechanisms to capture long-range dependencies in the data?

a) Deep Convolutional GANs (DCGANs)

b) Conditional GANs (cGANs)

c) CycleGANs

d) Self-Attention GANs (SGANs)

5. Which type of GAN utilizes a least squares loss function instead of binary cross-entropy for training the discriminator?

a) Conditional GANs (cGANs)

b) Least Squares GANs (LSGANs)

c) Wasserstein GANs (WGANs)

d) Self-Attention GANs (SGANs)

REVIEW QUESTIONS

1. What are Deep Convolutional GANs (DCGANs), and what advantages do they offer over traditional GAN architectures?
2. How do Conditional GANs (cGANs) differ from traditional GANs, and what are some practical applications of cGANs?
3. Explain the concept of CycleGANs and their significance in unpaired image-to-image translation tasks.
4. Describe the key characteristics and benefits of Least-squares GANs (LSGANs) in comparison to traditional GANs.
5. What is the main idea behind Wasserstein GANs (WGANs), and how do they address training instability issues?

Answers to Multiple Questions

1. (c) 2. (b) 3. (c) 4. (d) 5. (b)

REFERENCES

1. Abe, K., Iwana, B. K., Holmer, V. G., & Uchida, S. (2017). Font creation using class discriminative deep convolutional generative adversarial networks. In *2017 4th IAPR Asian Conference on Pattern Recognition (ACPR)* (Vol. 3, pp. 232–237). IEEE. https://doi.org/10.1109/ACPR.2017.62.
2. Achicanoy, H., Chaves, D., & Trujillo, M. (2021). Stylegans and transfer learning for generating synthetic images in industrial applications. *Symmetry, 13*(8), 1497. https://doi.org/10.3390/sym13081497.
3. Ahsan, R., Shi, W., Ma, X., & Lee Croft, W. (2022). A comparative analysis ofCGAN basedoversamplingforanomalydetection.*IETCyber Physical Systems: Theory & Applications, 7*(1), 40–50. https://doi.org/10.1049/cps.2020.0167.
4. Almahairi, A., Rajeshwar, S., Sordoni, A., Bachman, P., & Courville, A. (2018). Augmented cyclegan: Learning many-to-many mappings from unpaired data. In *International conference on machine learning*. PMLR. (Vol. 2, pp. 195–204). https://arxiv.org/abs/1802.10151
5. Alrashedy, H. H. N., Almansour, A. F., Ibrahim, D. M., & Hammoudeh, M. A. A. (2022). BrainGAN: brain MRI image generation and classification framework using GAN architectures and CNN models. *Sensors, 22*(11), 4297. https://doi.org/10.3390/s22114297.
6. Arjovsky, M., Chintala, S., & Bottou, L. (2017). Wasserstein generative adversarial networks. In *International conference on machine learning*. PMLR. (Vol. 2, pp. 214–223). http://proceedings.mlr.press/v70/arjovsky17a.html (accessed on 27 June 2024).
7. Ataş, İ. (2023). Comparison of deep convolution and least squares GANs for diabetic retinopathy image synthesis. *Neural Computing and Applications, 35*(19), 14431–14448. https://doi.org/10.1007/s00521-023-06654-0.
8. Babu, K. K., & Dubey, S. R. (2021). CSGAN: Cyclic-synthesized generative adversarial networks for image-to-image transformation. *Expert Systems with Applications, 169*, 114431. https://doi.org/10.1016/j.eswa.2020.114431.
9. Balakrishnan, V., Champion, D., Barr, E., Kramer, M., Sengar, R., & Bailes, M. (2021). Pulsar candidate identification using semi-supervised generative adversarial networks. *Monthly Notices of the Royal Astronomical Society, 505*(1), 1180–1194. https://doi.org/10.1093/mnras/stab1434.

10. Bargshady, G., Zhou, X., Barua, P. D., Gururajan, R., Li, Y., & Acharya, U. R. (2022). Application of CycleGAN and transfer learning techniques for automated detection of COVID-19 using X-ray images. *Pattern Recognition Letters, 153*, 67–74. https://doi.org/10.1016/j.patrec.2022.07.015.
11. Bhatia, S., & Dahyot, R. (2019). Using WGAN for improving imbalanced classification performance. In *CEUR Workshop Proceedings* (Vol. 2563, pp. 365–375). CEUR. https://ceur-ws.org/Vol-2563/aics_34.pdf
12. Bian, Y., Wang, J., Jun, J. J., & Xie, X. Q. (2019). Deep convolutional generative adversarial network (dcGAN) models for screening and design of small molecules targeting cannabinoid receptors. *Molecular pharmaceutics, 16*(11), 4451–4460. https://doi.org/10.1021/acs.molpharmaceut.9b00691.
13. Bin, W. (2023). Application of improved image restoration algorithm and depth generation in English intelligent translation teaching system. *Soft Computing, 7*(2), 1–11. https://doi.org/10.1007/s00500-023-06349-w.
14. Bittner, K., Körner, M., Fraundorfer, F., & Reinartz, P. (2019). Multi-task cgan for simultaneous spaceborne dsm refinement and roof-type classification. *Remote Sensing, 11*(11), 1262. https://doi.org/10.3390/rs11111262.
15. Chan, Y. H. E., & Spaeth, A. B. (2020). Architectural visualization with conditional generative adversarial networks (cGAN). In *Proceedings of the 38th eCAADe Conference* (Vol. 2, pp. 299–308). http://papers.cumincad.org/data/works/att/ecaade2020_131.pdf (accessed on 27 June 2024).
16. Chatterjee, A., & Roy, S. (2021). A fusion-based approach to generate and classify synthetic cancer cell image using dcgan and cnn architecture. In *Analyzing Data Through Probabilistic Modeling in Statistics*. IGI global. (Vol. 2, pp. 184–203). https://doi.org/10.4018/978-1-7998-6475-0.ch010.
17. Chavdarova, T., & Fleuret, F. (2018). Sgan: An alternative training of generative adversarial networks. In *Proceedings of the IEEE conference on computer vision and pattern recognition* (Vol. 3, pp. 9407–9415). https://doi.org/10.1109/CVPR.2018.00982.
18. Cho, S. W., Baek, N. R., Koo, J. H., Arsalan, M., & Park, K. R. (2020). Semantic segmentation with low light images by modified CycleGAN-based image enhancement. *IEEE Access, 8*, 93561–93585. https://doi.org/10.1109/ACCESS.2020.2994975.
19. Choi, J., & Han, B. (2022). Mcl-gan: Generative adversarial networks with multiple specialized discriminators. *Advances in Neural Information Processing Systems, 35*, 29597–29609. https://proceedings.neurips.cc/

paper_files/paper/2022/file/beac6bfb7eac3d651307c16ac747df01-Paper-Conference.pdf

20. Das, A., Devarampati, V. K., & Nair, M. S. (2021). NAS-SGAN: A semi-supervised generative adversarial network model for atypia scoring of breast cancer histopathological images. *IEEE Journal of Biomedical and Health Informatics, 26*(5), 2276–2287.
21. Deng, J., Pang, G., Zhang, Z., Pang, Z., Yang, H., & Yang, G. (2019). cGAN based facial expression recognition for human-robot interaction. *IEEE Access, 7*, 9848–9859.
22. Dewi, C., Chen, R. C., Liu, Y. T., & Yu, H. (2021). Various generative adversarial networks model for synthetic prohibitory sign image generation. *Applied Sciences, 11*(7), 2913.
23. Dinakaran, R., & Zhang, L. (2021). Object detection using deep convolutional generative adversarial networks embedded single shot detector with hyper-parameter optimization. In *2021 IEEE Symposium Series on Computational Intelligence (SSCI)* (Vol. 3, pp. 1–6). IEEE.
24. Dogan, Y., & Keles, H. Y. (2020). Semi-supervised image attribute editing using generative adversarial networks. *Neurocomputing, 401*, 338–352.
25. Dörner, S., Henninger, M., Cammerer, S., & ten Brink, S. (2020). WGAN-based autoencoder training over-the-air. In *2020 IEEE 21st International Workshop on Signal Processing Advances in Wireless Communications (SPAWC)* (Vol. 4, pp. 1–5). IEEE.
26. Durgadevi, M. (2021). Generative adversarial network (GAN): A general review on different variants of GAN and applications. In *2021 6th International Conference on Communication and Electronics Systems (ICCES)* (Vol. 1, pp. 1–8). IEEE.
27. Eken, E. (2021). Determining overfitting and underfitting in generative adversarial networks using Fréchet distance. *Turkish Journal of Electrical Engineering and Computer Sciences, 29*(3), 1524–1538.
28. Gao, F., Yang, Y., Wang, J., Sun, J., Yang, E., & Zhou, H. (2018). A deep convolutional generative adversarial network (DCGANs)-based semi-supervised method for object recognition in synthetic aperture radar (SAR) images. *Remote Sensing, 10*(6), 846.
29. Gautam, A., Sit, M., & Demir, I. (2022). Realistic river image synthesis using deep generative adversarial networks. *Frontiers in Water, 4*, 784441.
30. Gong, X., Chang, S., Jiang, Y., & Wang, Z. (2019). AutoGAN: Neural architecture search for generative adversarial networks. In *Proceedings of the IEEE/CVF International Conference on Computer Vision* (Vol. 4, pp. 3224–3234).

31. Gui, J., Sun, Z., Wen, Y., Tao, D., & Ye, J. (2021). A review on generative adversarial networks: Algorithms, theory, and applications. *IEEE Transactions on Knowledge and Data Engineering, 35*(4), 3313–3332.
32. Han, X., Chen, X., & Liu, L. P. (2021). GAN ensemble for anomaly detection. In *Proceedings of the AAAI Conference on Artificial Intelligence* (Vol. 35, pp. 4090–4097).
33. Harms, J., Lei, Y., Wang, T., Zhang, R., Zhou, J., Tang, X., & Yang, X. (2019). Paired cycle-GAN-based image correction for quantitative cone-beam computed tomography. *Medical Physics, 46*(9), 3998–4009.
34. Hayatbini, N., Kong, B., Hsu, K. L., Nguyen, P., Sorooshian, S., Stephens, G., & Ganguly, S. (2019). Conditional generative adversarial networks (cGANs) for near real-time precipitation estimation from multispectral GOES-16 satellite imageries—PERSIANN-cGAN. *Remote Sensing, 11*(19), 2193.
35. He, Y., Tang, H., Ren, Y., & Kumar, A. (2021). A semi-supervised fault diagnosis method for axial piston pump bearings based on DCGAN. *Measurement Science and Technology, 32*(12), 125104.
36. Horsley, L., & Perez-Liebana, D. (2017). Building an automatic sprite generator with deep convolutional generative adversarial networks. In *2017 IEEE Conference on Computational Intelligence and Games (CIG)* (Vol. 2, pp. 134–141). IEEE.
37. Huang, J., Le, Z., Ma, Y., Fan, F., Zhang, H., & Yang, L. (2020). MGMDcGAN: Medical image fusion using multi-generator multi-discriminator conditional generative adversarial network. *IEEE Access, 8*, 55145–55157.
38. Jabbar, A., Li, X., & Omar, B. (2021). A survey on generative adversarial networks: Variants, applications, and training. *ACM Computing Surveys (CSUR), 54*(8), 1–49.
39. Jin, Q., Lin, R., & Yang, F. (2019). E-WACGAN: Enhanced generative model of signaling data based on WGAN-GP and ACGAN. *IEEE Systems Journal, 14*(3), 3289–3300.
40. Kalayeh, M. M., & Shah, M. (2019). Training faster by separating modes of variation in batch-normalized models. *IEEE Transactions on Pattern Analysis and Machine Intelligence, 42*(6), 1483–1500.
41. Kieu, M., Berlincioni, L., Galteri, L., Bertini, M., Bagdanov, A. D., & Del Bimbo, A. (2021). Robust pedestrian detection in thermal imagery using synthesized images. In *2020 25th International Conference on Pattern Recognition (ICPR)* (Vol. 4, pp. 8804–8811). IEEE.

42. Kim, D., & Byun, J. (2020). Data augmentation using CycleGAN for overcoming the imbalance problem in petrophysical facies classification. In *SEG International Exposition and Annual Meeting* (Vol. 4, pp. 546–550). SEG.
43. Kora Venu, S., & Ravula, S. (2020). Evaluation of deep convolutional generative adversarial networks for data augmentation of chest x-ray images. *Future Internet, 13*(1), 8.
44. Kothari, P., & Alahi, A. (2023). Safety-compliant generative adversarial networks for human trajectory forecasting. *IEEE Transactions on Intelligent Transportation Systems, 24*(4), 4251–4261.
45. Lagan, S., Aquino, P., Emerson, M. R., Fortuna, K., Walker, R., & Torous, J. (2020). Actionable health app evaluation: Translating expert frameworks into objective metrics. *NPJ Digital Medicine, 3*(1), 100.
46. Lauks, I., Chan, P., & Babic, D. (1983). The extended gate chemically sensitive field effect transistor as multi-species microprobe. *Sensors and Actuators, 4*, 291–298.
47. Livny, A., Sgan-Cohen, H. D., Junadi, S., & Marcenes, W. (2010). Traumatic dental injuries and related factors among sixth grade schoolchildren in four Palestinian towns. *Dental Traumatology, 26*(5), 422–426.
48. Lu, S., Sirojan, T., Phung, B. T., Zhang, D., & Ambikairajah, E. (2019). DA-DCGAN: An effective methodology for DC series arc fault diagnosis in photovoltaic systems. *IEEE Access, 7*, 45831–45840.
49. Ma, Y., Zhong, G., Liu, W., Wang, Y., Jiang, P., & Zhang, R. (2021). ML-CGAN: Conditional generative adversarial network with a meta-learner structure for high-quality image generation with few training data. *Cognitive Computation, 13*, 418–430.
50. Mahmoud, M. A., & Guo, P. (2019). A novel method for traffic sign recognition based on DCGAN and MLP with PILAE algorithm. *IEEE Access, 7*, 74602–74611.
51. Majid, H., & Ali, K. H. (2023). Automatic diagnosis of coronavirus using conditional generative adversarial network (CGAN). *Iraqi Journal of Science, 10*(45), 4542–4556.
52. Mao, X., Li, Q., Xie, H., Lau, R. Y., Wang, Z., & Paul Smolley, S. (2017). Least squares generative adversarial networks. In *Proceedings of the IEEE International Conference on Computer Vision* (Vol. 2, pp. 2794–2802).
53. Nerrienet, N., Peyret, R., Sockeel, M., & Sockeel, S. (2023). Standardized CycleGAN training for unsupervised stain adaptation in invasive carcinoma classification for breast histopathology. *Journal of Medical Imaging, 10*(6), 067502–067502.

54. Neves, D. T., Naik, M. G., & Proença, A. (2021). SGAIN, WSGAIN-CP and WSGAIN-GP: Novel GAN methods for missing data imputation. In *International Conference on Computational Science* (Vol. 5, pp. 98–113). Cham: Springer International Publishing.
55. Oh, G., Sim, B., Chung, H., Sunwoo, L., & Ye, J. C. (2020). Unpaired deep learning for accelerated MRI using optimal transport driven CycleGAN. *IEEE Transactions on Computational Imaging, 6*, 1285–1296.
56. Olut, S., Sahin, Y. H., Demir, U., & Unal, G. (2018). Generative adversarial training for MRA image synthesis using multi-contrast MRI. In *PRedictive Intelligence in MEdicine: First International Workshop, PRIME 2018, Held in Conjunction with MICCAI 2018, Granada, Spain, September 16, 2018, Proceedings* (Vol. 4, pp. 147–154). Cham: Springer International Publishing.
57. Pang, Y., & Liu, Y. (2020). Conditional generative adversarial networks (CGAN) for aircraft trajectory prediction considering weather effects. In *AIAA SciTech 2020 Forum* (Vol. 2, pp. 1853–1855).
58. Paudel, B. H., & Sah, R. K. (2021). Landscape image season transfer using generative adversarial networks. In *Proceedings of 10th IOE Graduate Conference* (Vol. 10, pp. 2350–8906).
59. Pei, X., Su, S., Jiang, L., Chu, C., Gong, L., & Yuan, Y. (2022). Research on rolling bearing fault diagnosis method based on generative adversarial and transfer learning. *Processes, 10*(8), 1443.
60. Rajeev, C., & Natarajan, K. (2023). Data augmentation in classifying chest radiograph images (CXR) using DCGAN-CNN. In *GANs for Data Augmentation in Healthcare* (Vol. 3, pp. 91–110). Cham: Springer International Publishing.
61. Ren, Z., Li, Q., Cao, K., Li, M. M., Zhou, Y., & Wang, K. (2023). Model performance and interpretability of semi-supervised generative adversarial networks to predict oncogenic variants with unlabeled data. *BMC Bioinformatics, 24*(1), 43.
62. Rossi, L., Ajmar, A., Paolanti, M., & Pierdicca, R. (2021). Vehicle trajectory prediction and generation using LSTM models and GANs. *PLOS ONE, 16*(7), 253868.
63. Ruan, D., Chen, X., Gühmann, C., & Yan, J. (2023). Improvement of generative adversarial network and its application in bearing fault diagnosis: A review. *Lubricants, 11*(2), 74.
64. Saad, M. M., Rehmani, M. H., & O'Reilly, R. (2022). Addressing the intra-class mode collapse problem using adaptive input image normalization in GAN-based X-ray images. In *2022 44th Annual International Conference*

of the IEEE Engineering in Medicine & Biology Society (EMBC) (Vol. 1, pp. 2049–2052). IEEE.

65. Sabuhi, M., Zhou, M., Bezemer, C. P., & Musilek, P. (2021). Applications of generative adversarial networks in anomaly detection: A systematic literature review. *IEEE Access, 9*, 161003–161029.
66. Sajun, A. R., & Zualkernan, I. (2022). Survey on implementations of generative adversarial networks for semi-supervised learning. *Applied Sciences, 12*(3), 1718.
67. Sandfort, V., Yan, K., Pickhardt, P. J., & Summers, R. M. (2019). Data augmentation using generative adversarial networks (CycleGAN) to improve generalizability in CT segmentation tasks. *Scientific Reports, 9*(1), 16884.
68. Santos, A., & Carvalho, D. R. (2020). Generating synthetic 2019-nCoV samples with WGAN to increase the precision of an ensemble classifier. *Euromerican Journal of Applied Computing, 10*(2), 369–375.
69. Saxena, D., & Cao, J. (2021). Generative adversarial networks (GANs) challenges, solutions, and future directions. *ACM Computing Surveys (CSUR), 54*(3), 1–42.
70. Schonfeld, E., Schiele, B., & Khoreva, A. (2020). A u-net based discriminator for generative adversarial networks. In *Proceedings of the IEEE/CVF Conference on Computer Vision and Pattern Recognition* (Vol. 1, pp. 8207–8216).
71. Senaras, C., Niazi, M. K. K., Sahiner, B., Pennell, M. P., Tozbikian, G., Lozanski, G., & Gurcan, M. N. (2018). Optimized generation of high-resolution phantom images using cGAN: Application to quantification of Ki67 breast cancer images. *PLOS ONE, 13*(5), 196846.
72. Shah, D., Ullah Khan, M. A., & Abrar, M. (2024). Reliable breast cancer diagnosis with deep learning: DCGAN-driven mammogram synthesis and validity assessment. *Applied Computational Intelligence and Soft Computing, 2024. 7*(5), 987–990.
73. Shamsolmoali, P., Zareapoor, M., Granger, E., Zhou, H., Wang, R., Celebi, M. E., & Yang, J. (2021). Image synthesis with adversarial networks: A comprehensive survey and case studies. *Information Fusion, 72*, 126–146.
74. Sim, B., Oh, G., Kim, J., Jung, C., & Ye, J. C. (2020). Optimal transport driven CycleGAN for unsupervised learning in inverse problems. *SIAM Journal on Imaging Sciences, 13*(4), 2281–2306.
75. Sindhura, D. N., Pai, R. M., Bhat, S. N., & MM, M. P. (2021). Synthetic vertebral column fracture image generation by deep convolution generative

adversarial networks. In *2021 IEEE International Conference on Electronics, Computing and Communication Technologies (CONECCT)* (Vol. 2, pp. 1–4). IEEE.

76. Singh, N. K., & Raza, K. (2021). Medical image generation using generative adversarial networks: A review. *Health Informatics: A Computational Perspective in Healthcare, 8*(2), 77–96.

77. Sisson, N., & Moncayo, H. (2023). Machine learning based architecture for generation of synthetic flight test data. In *AIAA SCITECH 2023 Forum* (Vol. 3, pp. 1814–1816).

78. Soto, P. J., Costa, G. A. O. P., Feitosa, R. Q., Happ, P. N., Ortega, M. X., Noa, J., & Heipke, C. (2020). Domain adaptation with CycleGAN for change detection in the Amazon forest. *ISPRS Archives, 43*(B3), 1635–1643.

79. Suárez, P. L., Sappa, A. D., & Vintimilla, B. X. (2017). Infrared image colorization based on a triplet DCGAN architecture. In *Proceedings of the IEEE Conference on Computer Vision and Pattern Recognition Workshops* (Vol. 2, pp. 18–23).

80. Sun, Z., Zhang, H., Bai, J., Liu, M., & Hu, Z. (2023). A discriminatively deep fusion approach with improved conditional GAN (im-cGAN) for facial expression recognition. *Pattern Recognition, 135*, 109157.

81. Tavolara, T. E., Niazi, M. K. K., Arole, V., Chen, W., Frankel, W., & Gurcan, M. N. (2019). A modular cGAN classification framework: Application to colorectal tumor detection. *Scientific Reports, 9*(1), 18969.

82. Thirumagal, E., & Saruladha, K. (2021). GAN models in natural language processing and image translation. In *Generative Adversarial Networks for Image-to-Image Translation* (Vol. 4, pp. 17–57). Academic Press.

83. Tmenova, O., Martin, R., & Duong, L. (2019). CycleGAN for style transfer in X-ray angiography. *International Journal of Computer Assisted Radiology and Surgery, 14*, 1785–1794.

84. Tobias, G., Sgan-Cohen, H., Spanier, A. B., & Mann, J. (2021). Perceptions and attitudes toward the use of a mobile health app for remote monitoring of gingivitis and willingness to pay for mobile health apps (part 3): Mixed methods study. *JMIR Formative Research, 5*(10), 26125.

85. Tomar, S., & Gupta, A. (2023). A review on mode collapse reducing GANs with GAN's algorithm and theory. *GANs for Data Augmentation in Healthcare, 8*, 21–40.

86. Veneva, E., Belcheva, A., & Raycheva, R. (2022). Virtual reality induced analgesia and dental pain. In *Treatments, Mechanisms, and Adverse*

Reactions of Anesthetics and Analgesics (Vol. 3, pp. 575–581). Academic Press.

87. Viola, J., Chen, Y., & Wang, J. (2021). FaultFace: Deep convolutional generative adversarial network (DCGAN) based ball-bearing failure detection method. *Information Sciences, 542*, 195–211.
88. Wan, Y., Qu, Y., Gao, L., & Xiang, Y. (2022). Privacy-preserving blockchain-enabled federated learning for B5G-driven edge computing. *Computer Networks, 204*, 108671.
89. Wang, Y., Yu, B., Wang, L., Zu, C., Lalush, D. S., Lin, W., & Zhou, L. (2018). 3D conditional generative adversarial networks for high-quality PET image estimation at low dose. *NeuroImage, 174*, 550–562.
90. Webster, R., Rabin, J., Simon, L., & Jurie, F. (2019). Detecting overfitting of deep generative networks via latent recovery. In *Proceedings of the IEEE/CVF Conference on Computer Vision and Pattern Recognition* (Vol. 1, pp. 11273–11282).
91. Woldesellasse, H., & Tesfamariam, S. (2023). Data augmentation using conditional generative adversarial network (cGAN): Application for prediction of corrosion pit depth and testing using neural network. *Journal of Pipeline Science and Engineering, 3*(1), 100091.
92. Wu, C. H., Chang, H. T., & Amjad, A. (2020). Eye in-painting using WGAN-GP for face images with mosaic. In *2020 International Conference on Image, Video Processing and Artificial Intelligence*. SPIE. (Vol. 11584, pp. 146–149).
93. Xu, Z., Guo, Y., & Saleh, J. H. (2020). Tackling small data challenges in visual fire detection: A deep convolutional generative adversarial network approach. *IEEE Access, 9*, 3936–3946.
94. Yang, H., Sun, J., Carass, A., Zhao, C., Lee, J., Prince, J. L., & Xu, Z. (2020). Unsupervised MR-to-CT synthesis using structure-constrained CycleGAN. *IEEE Transactions on Medical Imaging, 39*(12), 4249–4261.
95. Ye, S., Jiang, T., Qin, S., Zou, W., & Deng, C. (2018). Speech enhancement based on a new architecture of Wasserstein generative adversarial networks. In *2018 11th International Symposium on Chinese Spoken Language Processing (ISCSLP)*. IEEE. (Vol. 3, pp. 399–403).
96. Yue, Y., Liu, H., Meng, X., Li, Y., & Du, Y. (2021). Generation of high-precision ground penetrating radar images using improved least square generative adversarial networks. *Remote Sensing, 13*(22), 4590.
97. Zhang, L., Duan, L., Hong, X., Liu, X., & Zhang, X. (2021). Imbalanced data enhancement method based on improved DCGAN and its application. *Journal of Intelligent & Fuzzy Systems, 41*(2), 3485–3498.

98. Zhong, D., Lyu, S., Shivakumara, P., Yin, B., Wu, J., Pal, U., & Lu, Y. (2022). Sgbanet: Semantic GAN and balanced attention network for arbitrarily oriented scene text recognition. In *European Conference on Computer Vision*. Cham: Springer Nature Switzerland. (Vol. 3, pp. 464–480).

99. Zhou, L., Schaefferkoetter, J. D., Tham, I. W., Huang, G., & Yan, J. (2020). Supervised learning with CycleGAN for low-dose FDG PET image denoising. *Medical Image Analysis, 65*, 101770.

CHAPTER 4

TRAINING GENERATIVE ADVERSARIAL NETWORKS (GANS)

LEARNING OBJECTIVES

At the end of this chapter, readers will be able to:

1. Understand how to prepare the environment for training GANs.
2. Comprehend the process of implementing the generator for training GANs.
3. Gain insight into how to implement the discriminator in GANs.
4. Comprehend key concepts such as loss function, model construction, and generated data samples in the training stage of GANs.
5. Understand common challenges while implementing GANs.

INTRODUCTORY EXAMPLE

A company named "TechGen Innovations" specializes in computer vision solutions. TechGen Innovations utilizes the training of Generative Adversarial Networks (GANs) to generate synthetic data for training computer vision models. By employing GAN training techniques, TechGen Innovations enhances the diversity and quantity of its training datasets, leading to more robust and accurate computer vision algorithms. This enables the company to develop advanced solutions for image recognition, object detection, and video analysis, catering to various industries such as automotive, healthcare, and security.

UNIT INTRODUCTION

This chapter will explore the implementation of GANs in more detail. The first chapter of this book offered a detailed overview, elaborating the extensive range of capabilities and remarkable achievements of GANs in various domains, including video, image, speech, and text generation. In this chapter, the fundamental implementation of GANs will be explored. It will start with a basic code that creates a straight line using the equation $y = x$. This method will provide a thorough grasp of the components and mechanisms of GANs and their utilization in 1D GAN. Upon completing this chapter, readers will develop a more profound comprehension of GANs and the extensive scope of their remarkable capabilities (Saxena & Cao, 2021).

Did You Know?

Training Generative Adversarial Networks (GANs) requires iteratively changing the parameters of the generator and discriminator using mini batches. The implementation of this adversarial training technique facilitates the enhancement of both models' ability to generate more authentic data samples and progressively enhance their performance.

4.1. PREPARING THE ENVIRONMENT

Learning objectives

- Comprehend the hardware and software requirements for implementing GANs.
- Gain insight into the modules and libraries required for implementing GANs.

Properly setting up the environment is crucial before implementing a GAN. One of the critical steps in this process involves selecting the appropriate hardware and software components necessary for the successful implementation of GANs. The hardware requirements depend on the scale and intricacy of the model, as well as the total size of the dataset. Large-scale applications of GANs often demand substantial computational resources (Xu et al., 2020).

4.1.1. Hardware Requirements

Modern computers with a fast CPU and a specialized graphics processing unit (GPU) are essential for successfully implementing GANs. These specifications offer sufficient processing power to train relatively modest models with minimal datasets. However, when working with larger models or datasets, it may be imperative to use a high-performance computer or a multi-GPU system. Obtaining a top-tier GPU with ample memory and a high processing speed would significantly enhance the GAN's ability to efficiently handle and train on extensive datasets (Alqahtani et al., 2021). When doing GAN training in an educational environment, it is crucial to meticulously evaluate the memory demands. These models may need substantial memory resources, leading to slower training or potential memory issues. To address these challenges, it is crucial to ensure that the training system for GANs has sufficient memory capacity. Improving the hardware, such as upgrading the CPU and expanding the RAM, may greatly accelerate the training time. It is advisable to use a minimum of 8GB of RAM, but having a larger RAM is consistently helpful. If the necessary hardware is not easily accessible, cloud-based systems can be utilized (Shrivastava et al., 2021). Platforms like Google Cloud, Amazon Web Services, and Microsoft Azure offer access to GPUs and other necessary resources for training GANs. In addition, several internet services, like Paperspace, FloydHub, and Google Colab, provide complimentary access to GPUs for a certain duration. These venues are excellent for delving into GANs or engaging in small-scale initiatives. The training process of a GAN is usually time-consuming, ranging from several hours to many days or more. The length of the training process is contingent upon several aspects, including the magnitude and intricacy of the dataset, the structure of the GAN, the hardware employed for training, the optimizer, and the selection of hyperparameters. Further information about these specific issues will be provided in subsequent sections throughout this chapter (Hanif et al., 2019).

4.1.2. Software Requirements

After completing the hardware configuration for GAN training, it is crucial to consider the necessary software requirements. The prerequisites for executing the GAN model are categorized into the programming language and the necessary libraries. The selection of programming languages and libraries can significantly impact the efficiency and simplicity of implementation. Python, R, MATLAB, and C++ are often used programming languages in academic settings for developing GANs. Proficiency in the programming language alone is insufficient. It is crucial to possess a profound comprehension of pertinent deep-learning frameworks like PyTorch, MXNet, Keras, and TensorFlow. When choosing libraries for GAN implementation, it is essential to consider the programming language and the individual project needs. Several factors must be considered, including the characteristics of the data and the desired result. This book utilizes Python and Keras framework, which are included in the TensorFlow library (Rizvi et al., 2021).

a) To effectively construct a GAN model, it is crucial to verify that all essential libraries, involving TensorFlow and any supplementary dependencies, are correctly installed.

b) Ensure that all the requisite packages, modules, and libraries are imported into the coding environment.

c) Verify that the imported modules and libraries are prepared for usage (He et al., 2020).

4.1.3. Importing Required Modules and Libraries

In Python, the package manager pip may be utilized to install the necessary libraries. Figure 4.1 depicts the step-by-step process of installing a library with pip package management (Fei et al., 2022).

```
pip install [library name]
```

Figure 4.1. *Illustration of the library installation syntax in Python.*

Source: Sanaa Kaddoura, Creative Commons License.

```
# A module to transform data to NumPy arrays and create random noise
import numpy as np
from tensorflow.keras.models import Sequential
# Layers to be used in generator and discriminator
from tensorflow.keras.layers import Dense, LeakyReLU
# A module to plot generated data
import matplotlib.pyplot as plt
```

Figure 4.2. *Representation of importing libraries and modules.*

Source: Ian Goodfellow, Creative Commons License.

To effectively construct a 1D GAN, it is crucial to employ essential libraries for numerical calculation, data visualization, analysis, and manipulation. By integrating these libraries, users may obtain the necessary tools and functionalities needed to smoothly incorporate the GAN model. Figure 4.2 provides an elaborate illustration of the procedure for importing these libraries into a Python environment. Ensuring the presence of a dataset of superior quality is crucial for the efficient training of a GAN. The effectiveness of a GAN model in generating realistic data is highly reliant on the information included within the dataset. By establishing a pair of independent variables with identical values dispersed evenly throughout a specific interval, it becomes possible to create a straight-line equation y = x. The test data can undergo an analogous procedure. Data quality is essential for evaluating the output's quality and guaranteeing consistency during the training phase. This chapter involves the preparation of the dataset y = x using the NumPy linespace function. The dataset comprises 1000 distinct values ranging from -1 to 1. The data is structured as a NumPy array. The dataset comprises a singular array encompassing a compilation of x and y sequences. The input arrays are arranged horizontally, using a column-wise technique (Yadav et al., 2023).

This section will examine the essential procedures for preparing the dataset y = x to train the GAN model. Figure 4.4 depicts the initial stage of generating a variable x, with 1000 values ranging from -1 to 1, as indicated in lines 2 and 4. Moreover, in line 6, giving a value to the variable y, which is equal to x, is evident. An essential stage in this method entails combining the two variables by horizontally concatenating them into a unified array. The process is illustrated in lines 1 to 6 of the code shown in Figure 4.4 (Rahman & Amyot, 2014).

X-Data	Y-Data
0.325325	0.325325
0.62963	0.62963
-0.173173	-0.173173

Figure 4.3. *Visualization of first five rows in the dataset.*

Source: Karras, Creative Commons License.

```
# Create variable X
X_train = np.linspace(-1, 1, 1000)
# Reshape X variable
X_train =X_train.reshape(-1, 1)
# Create variable Y such that y=x
y_train = X_train
```

Figure 4.4. *Representation of creating the dataset.*

Source: Reem Nassar, Creative Commons License.

Practice Problem

Outline the procedures required to set up the environment for training Generative Adversarial Networks (GANs). Enumerate the essential libraries and frameworks needed, and elucidate the steps to assure the availability of GPU for enhanced training.

Solution to Practice Problem

The process of creating the environment for training GANs involves the installation of libraries such as TensorFlow or PyTorch, assuring the availability of a GPU for faster training, and configuring the development environment. Essential libraries and frameworks comprise TensorFlow, Keras, PyTorch, and NumPy. GPU availability may be guaranteed by verifying the hardware prerequisites and installing the appropriate drivers and CUDA libraries.

4.2. IMPLEMENTING THE GENERATOR

Learning objectives

- Understand the process of training the generator.

The generator yields a pair of points, x, and y, with identical values. The implementation utilizes a network of deep neural networks including fully linked layers. This network has been taught to understand the underlying patterns that are visible in the training data shown in Figure 4.4. Following a productive training session, the generator is capable of readily generating new instances that smoothly blend with the preexisting training data. The generator initiates by subjecting a random noise vector to many stages of processing, resulting in the generation of two output points. The structure of the generator might differ based on the problem being addressed (Qu et al., 2020). Typically, the procedure involves employing several up-sampling and completely linked layers to enhance the resolution of the output.

The generator in the implemented one-dimensional model is constructed using a sequential Keras model. Initially, an input layer is employed to receive a random noise vector as its input. The noise dimension is configured to be 100. Commonly, 100 is often utilized in GAN implementation literature, while other possible values may also be used. The input is subsequently analyzed by a Dense layer with 16 units.

Subsequently, a LeakyReLU activation function is implemented, employing an alpha coefficient of 0.01 to proficiently manage negative input values. GANs can employ several activation functions such as ReLU, Sigmoid, Tanh, Linear, and LeakyReLU (Cohen et al., 2006). The choice of the activation function is contingent upon the problem being addressed. The final Dense layer is equipped with a Linear activation function and consists of two output units. The output layer of the generator employs a Linear activation function to provide continuous output values that are not constrained inside a certain range. Linear activation enables the output values to cover the whole range of real numbers, in contrast to activation functions like Sigmoid or Tanh which confine the output values inside a certain range. Generally, the input data is confined to the interval between -1 and 1. Nevertheless, it may be readily modified to suit any actual numerical value (Porubän et al., 2009).

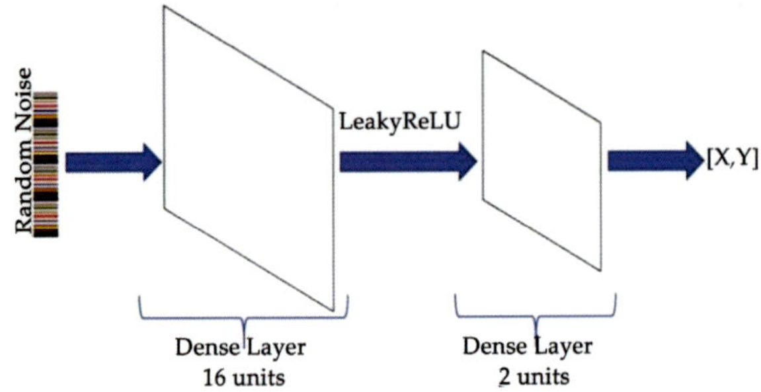

Figure 4.5. *Diagram of GAN Generator architecture.*

Source: Sana Kaddoura, Creative Commons License.

```
def build_generator(noise_dim):
    # Add layers one after one in the sequence
    model = Sequential()
    # First fully connected layer
    model.add(Dense(16, activation = 'relu'  kernel_initializer = 'he_uniform',
input_dim = noise_dim))
    # Add LeakyReLU activation function
    model.add(LeakyReLU(alpha=0.01))
    # Output layer with the shape of 2
    model.add(Dense(2, activation = 'linear'))
    return model
```

Figure 4.6. *Illustration of the Generator model.*

Source: Reem Nassar, Creative Commons License.

Thus, it is considered suitable to use a Linear activation function at the output layer of the generator in this situation. The comprehensive execution of the generator is depicted in Figure 4.5, showcasing the procedure of acquiring input noise and transmitting it across the layers to produce two locations where y is equal to x. The dense layer is shown as a two-dimensional (2D) block because of its ability to produce a 2D tensor. The batch size is denoted by the initial dimension, whereas the second dimension corresponds to the output units. In the next chapters, a two-dimensional block will be employed to symbolize the thick layer. Figure 4.6 illustrates the code implementation (Thibault & Consel, 1997).

4.3. IMPLEMENTING THE DISCRIMINATOR

Learning objectives

- Comprehend the process of implementing the discriminator in GANs.

The discriminator in GANs classifies produced data points as real or fake. The model is trained to determine if a group of points is real from the dataset or fake from the generator. Implementing the discriminator requires a fully connected deep neural network with binary classification output. To improve authenticity classification, the discriminator is trained on actual data. The discriminator uses several fully connected layers to extract attributes from incoming data and categorize it like a classifier. Typically, the discriminator can use ReLU or LeakyReLU activation functions. GAN discriminator uses the Keras toolkit sequential model. A 32-unit layer completes the connection.

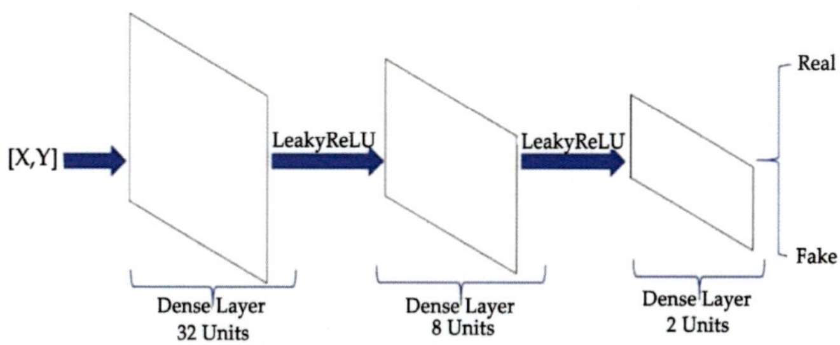

Figure 4.7. *Diagram of the GAN discriminator architecture.*

Source: Ian Goodfellow, Creative Commons License.

```
def build_discriminator():
    # Add layers one after one in the sequence
    model = Sequential()
    # First fully connected layer
    model.add(Dense(32, activation = 'relu', kernel_initializer = 'he_uniform', input_dim = 2))
    # Add LeakyReLU activation function
    model.add(LeakyReLU(alpha=0.01))
    # Second fully connected layer
    model.add(Dense(8, activation = 'relu', kernel_initializer = 'he_uniform'))
    # Add LeakyReLU activation function
    model.add(LeakyReLU(alpha=0.01))
   # Output layer with the shape of 2
    model.add(Dense(1, activation = 'sigmoid'))
    return model
```

Figure 4.8. *Representation of the discriminator model.*

Source: Reem Nassar, Creative Commons License.

The LeakyReLU activation function is then implemented with an alpha coefficient of 0.01. The output tensor from the fully connected layer is further reduced by passing it through an 08-unit fully connected layer. A 0.01-alpha LeakyReLU activation layer follows this layer. Finally, a Dense layer with a Sigmoid activation function and one unit is added to the model to achieve binary classification. Figure 4.6 shows the discriminator structure, whereas Figures 4.7 and 4.8 show the code implementation (Becerra et al., 2013).

4.4. TRAINING STAGE

Learning objectives

- Comprehend the stages in training of GANs.
- Understand the process of model construction before training the GAN model
- Understand the process of creating loss functions
- Comprehend common challenges while implementing GANs.

The GAN engages in a game of probability, where the generator and the discriminator compete against one another. A generator aims to produce x and y values that closely resemble genuine data. Concurrently, a discriminator diligently operates to distinguish between authentic x and y points and those that have been artificially produced. The discriminator and the generator participate in a competitive interaction, continuously attempting to surpass each other in a strategic game, to improve their abilities over time. The generator improves its ability to provide data points that can mislead the discriminator. The discriminator improves its ability to distinguish between genuine and falsely created points to accurately represent a linear pattern. The goal is to achieve a state where the generator can produce random points that can form a linear trajectory (Huang et al., 2021).

4.4.1. Model Construction

The GAN model must be built, and loss functions defined before training and altering the training loop. A Generative Adversarial Network (GAN) merges a generator and a discriminator to create an adversarial model. Positioning the discriminator above the generator allows fine-tuning of the adversarial model. GAN training methods include Adam Optimizer, RMSprop, SGD, and Adagrad. RMSprop and Adagrad can be used instead of the Adam Optimizer if the Stochastic Gradient Descent (SGD) has convergence issues (Bridle, 1989). Generative Adversarial Networks (GANs) are trained using two loss functions: one for the generator model and one for the discriminator model. Generators aim to minimize loss, whereas discriminators aim to enhance it. The discriminator model can use hinge loss or binary cross-entropy loss, whereas the generator uses the former. The Adam optimizer and binary cross-entropy loss function build the discriminator and adversarial models. The model creation code is shown in Figure 4.9. The discriminator is initially non-trainable in the adversarial model, especially the GAN, as indicated in line 9. During adversarial model training, only the generator will be modified (Hsiao, 2019).

```
1   def construct_models(noise_dim):
2       # Build the discriminator model
3       discriminator = build_discriminator()
4       # Compile the discriminator
5       discriminator.compile(loss = 'binary_crossentropy' , optimizer = 'adam', metrics = ['accuracy'])
6       # Build the generator model
7       generator = build_generator(noise_dim)
8       # Freeze the discriminator during generator training
9       discriminator.trainable = False
10      gan = Sequential()
11      # Pit the generator and discriminator against each other
12      gan.add(generator)
13      gan.add(discriminator)
14      # Compile the GAN model
15      gan.compile(loss = 'binary_crossentropy', optimizer = 'adam', metrics = ['accuracy'])
16      return generator, discriminator, gan
```

Figure 4.9. *Representation of model construction in GAN training.*

Source: Radford, Creative Commons License.

4.4.2. Loss Function

This section will examine the evolution of the loss functions employed during the training phase to compute the losses of both the generator and the discriminator. Figure 4.10 displays the comprehensive design for loss functions. The train_on_batch function, found in lines 4 and 8, is currently used to train a model on one batch of data and its related labels (Brophy et al., 2021). Subsequently, the model parameters undergo fine-tuning by considering the disparity between the anticipated and real labels. The loss function of the discriminator necessitates the input data X, which comprises a combination of real and fake data points, together with their related labels y. The loss of the generator function is determined by utilizing the noise created in conjunction with actual labels as its input (Minarno et al., 2023).

```
# Define discriminator loss function
def disc_loss(model, X, y):
    # Train the model on a batch of data and return the loss value
    return model.train_on_batch(X,y)
# Define generator loss function
def gen_loss(model, X, y):
    # Train the model on a batch of data and return loss value
    return model.train_on_batch(X,y)
```

Figure 4.10. *Illustration of loss function in GAN training.*

Source: Reem Nassar, Creative Commons License.

Remember

The selection of the loss function is essential in GAN training, since it dictates the optimization process of the models during training. The generator and discriminator employ distinct loss functions to direct their individual aims.

4.4.3. Plot Generated Data Samples

Before commencing the training of the GAN model, it is crucial to create a function that enables the visual representation of the produced points. This function will be utilized throughout the training phase to assess the model's efficacy by examining the quality of the produced points.

```
def print_generated_samples(batch_size, noise_dim):
    # Create test data
    X_test = np.random.uniform(low=-1, high =1, size=(batch_size//2, 1))
    y_test = X_test
    # Generate samples
    noise = np.random.normal(0, 1, (batch_size//2, noise_dim))
    gen_data = generator.predict(noise)
    # Plot generated data
    plt.scatter(X_test, y_test, color = 'red')
    plt.scatter(gen_data[:,0], gen_data[:,1], color = 'blue')
    plt.xlim(-1,1)
    plt.ylim(-1,1)
    plt.legend(["real data", "generated data"], loc = "lower right")
    plt.show()
```

Figure 4.11. *Representation of data visualization in GAN training.*

Source: Sanaa Kaddoura, Creative Commons License.

The code for viewing data is seen in Figure 4.11 (Livak, 1999). The scatter plot displays the plotted points, which include both generated and actual data, on lines 9 and 10. The graphic will display real samples in red and synthetic samples in blue. The function employed to render Figures 4.16–4.19, which are presented later in the text, is applied (Rosenfeld et al., 2022).

4.4.4. Training GAN

Epochs and batches are commonly employed in the training of GAN models. The number of epochs determines the duration for which the model may learn from the training data. Augmenting the number of epochs has the potential to enhance performance, while it also carries the danger of overfitting. Conversely, the batch size plays a crucial role in defining the amount of training data utilized to update the weights of the model, hence impacting the speed and stability of the training process (Hardy et al., 2019). Increasing the size of the dataset often results in improved performance but at the cost of increased computational resources and processing time. During each period, the generator and discriminator take turns training by using a group of actual and created data points. The method is iterated across numerous epochs, precisely 600, to optimize the weights and get the required level of performance. The determination of the number of batches per epoch and the number of epochs depends upon several criteria, such as the data size, model complexity, and desired performance level. The performance of the model may be influenced by several elements, including its complexity, which encompasses the number of layers and nodes it possesses (Nguyen et al., 2017). Utilizing a more advanced model can yield superior outcomes but with a potential vulnerability to overfitting. The training phase is deemed finished when the generator is capable of producing samples that closely resemble actual data points in both y and x dimensions. In this instance, the generator effectively outsmarts the discriminator with remarkable precision (Schonfeld et al., 2020). Mapping the coordinates on a two-dimensional axis enables a graphical depiction of the model's performance, illustrating the evolution of epochs. Figures 4.12, 4.13, and 4.14 depict several phases of the training process, showcasing the training of the discriminator, the training of the generator, and the training loop. Here is an overview of the training process (Che et al., 2020):

a) Generate a random sample of normally distributed noise, as shown in line 5 of Figure 4.14.

b) Employ the generator to generate artificial data points from this noise, using the procedure shown in line 7 of Figure 4.14.

c) Acquire a set of actual data points from the training data; refer to line 11 in Figure 4.14.

d) In line 13, assign a label of 0.9 to genuine data samples. In line 15 of Figure 4.14, label the generated data samples as zeros.

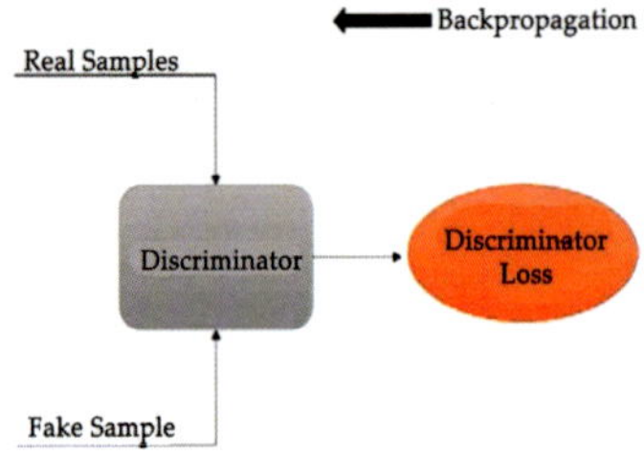

Figure 4.12. *Diagram of training stage in the discriminator.*

Source: Gulrajani, Creative Commons License.

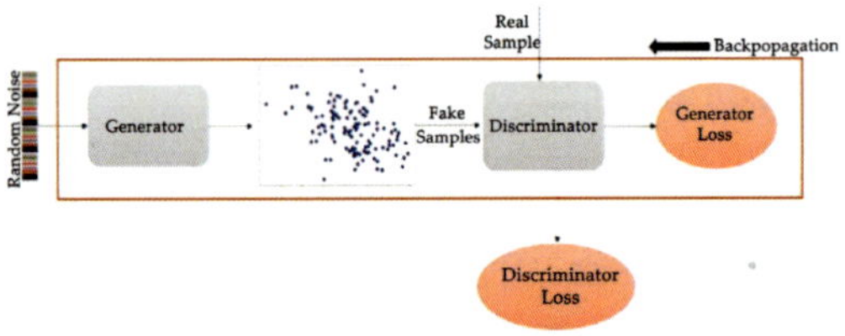

Figure 4.13. *Diagram of training stage in the generator.*

Source: Chintala, Creative Commons License.

e) Train the discriminator and compute the loss for both the generated and actual data, utilizing their respective accurate labels as indicated in lines 16 and 19 of Figure 4.14. Figure 4.12 illustrates the training procedure of the discriminator (Chang et al., 2020).

f) Create an extra set of random data samples at line 23 of Figure 4.14.

g) Train the Generative Adversarial Network (GAN) model using the freshly produced data samples. Assign labels of value 1 to trick the discriminator, as indicated in line 27 of Figure 4.14. The architecture employed for training the generator is depicted in Figure 4.13.

h) Iterate through steps 1 to 7 for numerous epochs to improve the efficiency of both the generator and discriminator (Tran et al., 2021).

To begin the training process, the initial step involves invoking the function for training and constructing the models (Esmaeilpour et al., 2022). The provided code snippet initiates the training process as seen in Figure 4.15. When dealing with this image, it is important to carefully consider the batch size and number of epochs, since these factors have a substantial influence on the training process.

```
def training(generator, discriminator, gan, noise_dim, epochs, batch_size):
    # Enumerate over epochs
    for e in range(epochs):
    # Random normal array for generator input
    noise = np.random.normal(0, 1, (batch_size, noise_dim))
    # Create fake data points by the generator
    fake_samples = generator.predict(noise)
    # Stack X and Y variable horizontally to build the dataset
    real_data = np.hstack((X_train, y_train))
    # Get random real data points from the training data
    real_data = real_data[np.random.randint(0, real_data.shape[0], size = batch_size)]
    # Create real labels
    real_labels = np.ones((batch_size, 1))*0.9
    # Generate fake labels generated data points as zeros
    fake_labels = np.zeros((batch_size, 1))
    # Calculate the loss of real data points
    discriminator_loss_real = disc_loss(discriminator, real_data, real_labels)
    # Calculate the loss of generated data points
    discriminator_loss_fake = disc_loss(discriminator, fake_samples, fake_labels)
    # Compute total discriminator loss
    discriminator_loss = 0.5 * np.add(discriminator_loss_real, discriminator_loss_fake)
    # Generate random points as input for the generator
    x_gan = np.random.normal(0, 1, (batch_size, noise_dim))
    # Generate real labels for GAN
    y_gan = np.ones((batch_size, 1))
    #calculate the generator loss
    gan_loss = gen_loss(gan, x_gan, y_gan)
    # Print the progress
    if e % 10 == 0 or e == epochs-1:
        print('Epoch: ', e, ' Generator Loss: ', gan_loss , ' Discriminator Loss: ', discriminator_loss)
        print_generated_samples(batch_size, noise_dim)
```

Figure 4.14. *Representation of the GAN training process.*

Source: Hermosilla, Creative Commons License.

As previously stated, the performance of the model during training is significantly influenced by the number of training iterations, which are also referred to as epochs (Tran et al., 2018). As time increases, the data points that are produced become increasingly similar to the training data, resulting in a more realistic representation. This is a direct result of the generator's superior capability to outwit the discriminator. The inclusion of several images serves to emphasize the correlation between the growing number of epochs and the resulting data points. The progression of the obtained data points is illustrated in Figures 4.16–4.19. Figures 4.16 and 4.19 demonstrate an improvement in the generator's ability to trick the discriminator. Comparing the blue line (created data points) with the red line (actual data points) reveals the extent of the development that has been achieved (Hou et al., 2022).

Remember

GAN training presents difficulties stemming from problems including mode collapse, training instabilities, and disappearing gradients. Conducting experiments using various training strategies and regularization methods is crucial for overcoming these problems and attaining consistent training results.

```
# Construct the models
generator, discriminator, gan = construct_models(100)
# Train GAN
training(generator, discriminator, gan, 100, 600, 128)
```

Figure 4.15. *Code for calling the training function.*

Source: Karras, Creative Commons License.

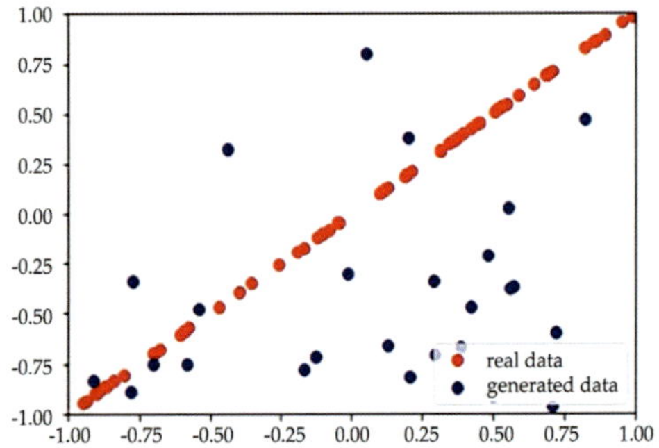

Figure 4.16. *Graph of generated points at epoch 0.*

Source: A, Courville, Creative Commons License.

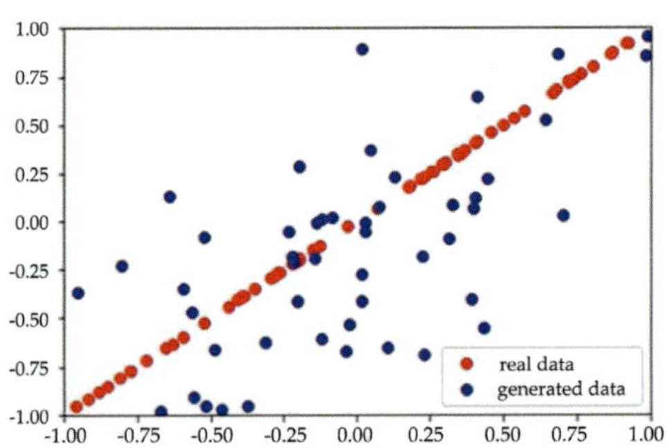

Figure 4.17. *Graph of generated points at epoch 200.*

Source: Ahmed, Creative Commons License.

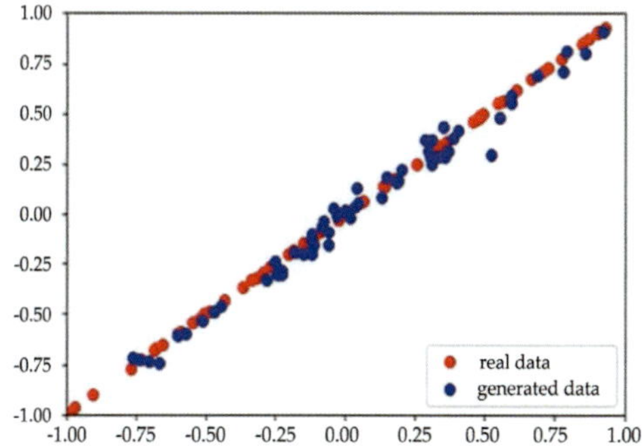

***Figure 4.18.** Graph of generated points at epoch 400.*

Source: D. Amodei, Creative Commons License.

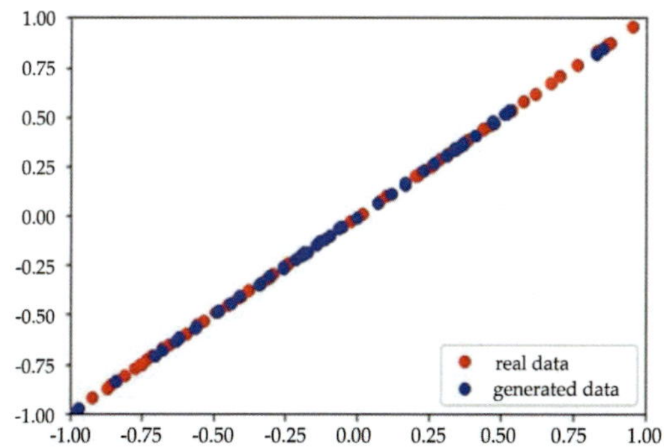

***Figure 4.19.** Graph of generated points at epoch 600.*

Source: V. Dumollin, Creative Commons License.

4.4.5. Common Challenges While Implementing GANs

During the creation and training of a GAN model, one may encounter a range of obstacles and errors. A problem that may occur is model collapse, which refers to the generator's output being constrained and unable to include the complete range of variety within the data (Sampath et al., 2021). An inherent problem that frequently occurs during the training of a model is instability, characterized by the discriminator and generator oscillating rather than converging to a stable solution. Furthermore, the vanishing gradient problem poses a hindrance to model training when the gradients diminish to an insufficient magnitude throughout the training procedure (Frid-Adar et al., 2018). A frequent obstacle that develops is the phenomenon of overfitting, in which the model gets excessively intricate and ends up remembering the training data. By meticulously selecting the model architecture, optimizing hyperparameters, and employing efficient regularization algorithms, it is possible to overcome these obstacles (Mescheder et al., 2018).

SUMMARY

- This chapter explores the intricacies of training Generative Adversarial Networks (GANs), a popular type of deep learning model used to generate realistic data samples. The training of GANs involves several crucial components, including environment setup, generator and discriminator model development, and training execution.
- Establishing the development environment entails establishing the essential libraries and frameworks such as TensorFlow or PyTorch, and ensuring the presence of a GPU for accelerated training.
- The chapter also discusses the structure of the generator and discriminator models in a GAN. Moreover, this chapter highlights the training phase of GANs, which encompasses the construction of the model, the formulation of a loss function, and the generation of data samples. Additionally, it addresses the typical difficulties that emerge with the implementation of GANs. Developers with a profound comprehension of training GANs may proficiently employ these models to provide varied and authentic data samples for a broad spectrum of applications and domains.

MULTIPLE CHOICE QUESTIONS

1. **What is the purpose of preparing the environment in training Generative Adversarial Networks (GANs)?**
   a) Selecting the dataset for training
   b) Installing necessary libraries and frameworks
   c) Designing the architecture of the generator
   d) Defining the loss function for the discriminator
2. **Which component of a Generative Adversarial Network (GAN) is responsible for generating synthetic data samples?**
   a) Discriminator
   b) Trainer
   c) Generator
   d) Validator
3. **What is the role of the discriminator in training a GAN?**
   a) Generate synthetic data samples
   b) Classify data samples as real or fake

c) Optimize the loss function of the generator
d) Determine the architecture of the neural network

4. Which loss function is commonly used for training the discriminator in a GAN?

a) Mean Squared Error (MSE) loss
b) Cross-Entropy loss
c) Huber loss
d) Mean Absolute Error (MAE) loss

5. What is the primary objective of the generator in a GAN during training?

a) Maximize the discriminator's loss
b) Minimize the discriminator's loss
c) Maximize the generator's loss
d) Minimize the generator's loss

REVIEW QUESTIONS

1. What are the main steps involved in preparing the environment for training Generative Adversarial Networks (GANs)?
2. Describe the role of the generator and discriminator in a GAN.
3. What is the primary objective of training the discriminator in a GAN?
4. Explain the significance of the loss function in training Generative Adversarial Networks.
5. How does the training process of GANs typically proceed?
6. What are some common loss functions used in training the generator and discriminator in GANs?
7. How does Adam optimization contribute to stabilizing training and improving convergence in GANs?

Answers to Multiple Questions

1. (b) 2. (c) 3. (b) 4. (b) 5. (b)

REFERENCES

1. Alqahtani, H., Kavakli-Thorne, M., & Kumar, G. (2021). Applications of generative adversarial networks (GANs): An updated review. *Archives of Computational Methods in Engineering, 28*, 525–552.
2. Becerra, F. E., Fan, J., & Migdall, A. (2013). Implementation of generalized quantum measurements for unambiguous discrimination of multiple non-orthogonal coherent states. *Nature Communications, 4*(1), 2028.
3. Bridle, J. (1989). Training stochastic model recognition algorithms as networks can lead to maximum mutual information estimation of parameters. *Advances in Neural Information Processing Systems, 2*, 32–36.
4. Brophy, E., De Vos, M., Boylan, G., & Ward, T. (2021). Multivariate generative adversarial networks and their loss functions for synthesis of multichannel ECGs. *IEEE Access, 9*, 158936–158945.
5. Chang, Q., Qu, H., Zhang, Y., Sabuncu, M., Chen, C., Zhang, T., & Metaxas, D. N. (2020). Synthetic learning: Learn from distributed asynchronized discriminator GAN without sharing medical image data. In *Proceedings of the IEEE/CVF Conference on Computer Vision and Pattern Recognition* (Vol. 3, pp. 13856–13866).
6. Che, T., Zhang, R., Sohl-Dickstein, J., Larochelle, H., Paull, L., Cao, Y., & Bengio, Y. (2020). Your GAN is secretly an energy-based model and you should use discriminator driven latent sampling. *Advances in Neural Information Processing Systems, 33*, 12275–12287.
7. Cohen, A., Donadio, S., Garzaran, M. J., Herrmann, C., Kiselyov, O., & Padua, D. (2006). In search of a program generator to implement generic transformations for high-performance computing. *Science of Computer Programming, 62*(1), 25–46.
8. Esmaeilpour, M., Chaalia, N., Abusitta, A., Devailly, F. X., Maazoun, W., & Cardinal, P. (2022). Bi-discriminator GAN for tabular data synthesis. *Pattern Recognition Letters, 159*, 204–210.
9. Fei, Y., Liao, W., Zhang, S., Yin, P., Han, B., Zhao, P., & Lu, X. (2022). Integrated schematic design method for shear wall structures: A practical application of generative adversarial networks. *Buildings, 12*(9), 1295.
10. Frid-Adar, M., Klang, E., Amitai, M., Goldberger, J., & Greenspan, H. (2018). Synthetic data augmentation using GAN for improved liver lesion classification. In *2018 IEEE 15th International Symposium on Biomedical Imaging (ISBI 2018)*. IEEE. (Vol. 2, pp. 289–293).
11. Hardy, C., Le Merrer, E., & Sericola, B. (2019). MD-GAN: Multi-discriminator generative adversarial networks for distributed datasets. In

2019 IEEE International Parallel and Distributed Processing Symposium (IPDPS). IEEE. (Vol. 2, pp. 866–877).

12. He, C., Huang, S., Cheng, R., Tan, K. C., & Jin, Y. (2020). Evolutionary multiobjective optimization driven by generative adversarial networks (GANs). *IEEE Transactions on Cybernetics, 51*(6), 3129–3142.
13. Hou, L., Cao, Q., Shen, H., Pan, S., Li, X., & Cheng, X. (2022). Conditional GANs with auxiliary discriminative classifier. In *International Conference on Machine Learning*. PMLR. (Vol. 1, pp. 8888–8902).
14. Hsiao, Y. H. (2019). Signal discrimination using category-preserving bag-of-words model for condition monitoring. *Neural Computing and Applications, 31*(12), 8615–-8630.
15. Huang, K., Wang, Z. A., Song, C., Xu, K., Li, H., Wang, Z., & Fan, H. (2021). Quantum generative adversarial networks with multiple superconducting qubits. *npj Quantum Information, 7*(1), 165.
16. Livak, K. J. (1999). Allelic discrimination using fluorogenic probes and the 5′ nuclease assay. *Genetic Analysis: Biomolecular Engineering, 14*(5–6), 143–149.
17. Mescheder, L., Geiger, A., & Nowozin, S. (2018). Which training methods for GANs do actually converge? In *International Conference on Machine Learning*. PMLR. (Vol. 2, pp. 3481–3490).
18. Minarno, A. E., Antoko, T. D., & Azhar, Y. (2023). Generation of batik patterns using generative adversarial network with content loss weighting. *International Journal on Advanced Science, Engineering & Information Technology, 13*(1), 97–100.
19. Nguyen, T., Le, T., Vu, H., & Phung, D. (2017). Dual discriminator generative adversarial nets. *Advances in Neural Information Processing Systems, 30*, 98–100.
20. Porubän, J., Forgáč, M., & Sabo, M. (2009). Annotation based parser generator. In *2009 International Multiconference on Computer Science and Information Technology*. IEEE. (Vol. 1, pp. 707–714).
21. Qu, K., Gong, T., & Shao, J. (2020). Design and implementation of system generator based on rule engine. *Procedia Computer Science, 166*, 517–522.
22. Rahman, A., & Amyot, D. (2014). A DSL for importing models in a requirements management system. In *2014 IEEE 4th International Model-Driven Requirements Engineering Workshop (MoDRE)*. IEEE. (Vol. 2, pp. 37–46).

23. Rizvi, S. K. J., Azad, M. A., & Fraz, M. M. (2021). Spectrum of advancements and developments in multidisciplinary domains for generative adversarial networks (GANs). *Archives of Computational Methods in Engineering, 28*(7), 4503–4521.
24. Rosenfeld, B., Simeone, O., & Rajendran, B. (2022). Spiking generative adversarial networks with a neural network discriminator: Local training, Bayesian models, and continual meta-learning. *IEEE Transactions on Computers, 71*(11), 2778–2791.
25. Sampath, V., Maurtua, I., Aguilar Martin, J. J., & Gutierrez, A. (2021). A survey on generative adversarial networks for imbalance problems in computer vision tasks. *Journal of Big Data, 8*, 1–59.
26. Saxena, D., & Cao, J. (2021). Generative adversarial networks (GANs) challenges, solutions, and future directions. *ACM Computing Surveys (CSUR), 54*(3), 1–42.
27. Schonfeld, E., Schiele, B., & Khoreva, A. (2020). A U-net based discriminator for generative adversarial networks. In *Proceedings of the IEEE/CVF Conference on Computer Vision and Pattern Recognition* (Vol. 1, pp. 8207–8216).
28. Shrivastava, N., Hanif, M. A., Mittal, S., Sarangi, S. R., & Shafique, M. (2021). A survey of hardware architectures for generative adversarial networks. *Journal of Systems Architecture, 118*, 102227.
29. Thibault, S., & Consel, C. (1997). A framework for application generator design. *ACM SIGSOFT Software Engineering Notes, 22*(3), 131–135.
30. Tran, N. T., Bui, T. A., & Cheung, N. M. (2018). Dist-GAN: An improved GAN using distance constraints. In *Proceedings of the European Conference on Computer Vision (ECCV)* (Vol. 2, pp. 370–385).
31. Tran, N. T., Tran, V. H., Nguyen, N. B., Nguyen, T. K., & Cheung, N. M. (2021). On data augmentation for GAN training. *IEEE Transactions on Image Processing, 30*, 1882–1897.
32. Xu, H., Li, C., Rahaman, M. M., Yao, Y., Li, Z., Zhang, J., & Teng, Y. (2020). An enhanced framework of generative adversarial networks (EF-GANs) for environmental microorganism image augmentation with limited rotation-invariant training data. *IEEE Access, 8*, 187455–187469.
33. Yadav, P., Kaur, R., & Hariharan, U. (2023). A study on customized face generator using generative adversarial networks (GANs). In *2023 7th International Conference on Electronics, Materials Engineering & Nano-Technology (IEMENTech)*. IEEE. (Vol. 1, pp. 1–6).

CHAPTER 5

SECURITY ISSUES IN GENERATIVE ADVERSARIAL NETWORKS

LEARNING OBJECTIVES

At the end of this chapter, readers will be able to:

1. Understand the security concerns associated with GANs.
2. Gain insight into the safety features of GAN network.
3. Identify potential security attacks that can be launched using GANs, such as password cracking, malware hiding, and facial manipulation.

INTRODUCTORY EXAMPLE

Within the field of cybersecurity, "SecureNet Solutions" is widely recognized as a prominent provider of cutting-edge threat detection and mitigation services. Utilizing state-of-the-art technologies, such as Generative Adversarial Networks (GANs), SecureNet Solutions strives to protect organizations from ever-changing cyber threats and malicious activities.

SecureNet Solutions has recently experienced a significant increase in highly advanced malware attacks that specifically target their clients' networks. Conventional methods of detecting signatures were found to be ineffective against these new threats, which has led to a demand for creative solutions.

Through the utilization of GANs, SecureNet Solutions has created an innovative malware detection system that can generate synthetic malware samples to effectively train detection algorithms. The system's ability to continuously learn and evolve its detection capabilities allows it to rapidly adjust to emerging threats as they arise.

By incorporating advanced GAN-based techniques, SecureNet Solutions has bolstered their cybersecurity capabilities, offering clients heightened defense against malicious attacks and safeguarding the integrity and safety of their digital assets.

UNIT INTRODUCTION

The frequency, intensity, and relevance of cyber-attacks are increasing, whether they occur when data is at rest or in transit. The Internet has evolved from a mere curiosity to an essential element in the lives of nearly all individuals who utilize or are impacted by contemporary technology daily. Hackers promptly discerned the importance of the information available on the Internet and society's reliance on network connectivity and communication. The Internet of Things (IoT) is the upcoming stage in contemporary networking, involving the creation and usage of production and detecting equipment. By 2030, an astonishing 50 billion gadgets are projected to be integrated into the current system, creating a multitude of new possibilities and opportunities for manipulation. Cyber-attacks continuously endanger the financial stability of individuals. Dutta et al. state that devices and systems can undergo catastrophic failures that can significantly disrupt users' daily lives. Sophisticated intrusions are being developed utilizing intricate algorithms to avoid detection systems that are insufficiently adjusted to the increasing complexity of threats. Adversaries possess the capacity to preserve, scrutinize, and exchange data relating to the operator's digital presence. The combination of these hazards, along with a deficiency in strong detection measures, exposes sensitive data to potential harm. Halting these assaults on networks and systems is an essential objective in the realm of cybersecurity (Kathole et al., 2023).

Although safety systems have made significant progress and become more resistant to a broader variety of threats, there are still certain unattended vulnerabilities that might be exploited for possible assaults. Hence, it is wise to contemplate the measures a defense could employ to protect oneself against an attack, even in the absence of any awareness of its existence. Recognition systems are employed to safeguard systems against identified dangers. This review has been sparked by several cases lacking sufficient protection (Dutta et al., 2019):

a) **Weather Network Ransomware:** In April 2019, during a severe storm in the southern United States, an attack by ransomware caused the cable station to be non-functional for over an hour. As a result, the lack of critical data had the potential to result in the loss of possessions and even lives.

b) **Capital One Fissure:** In July 2019, a significant data breach occurred where personal identity information, such as birthdays and Social Security numbers, was stolen by hackers from several thousand credit card applicants.

c) **Texas Ransomware:** In August of 2019, a cyber-attack impacted the computer systems of 22 small towns in Texas. Consequently, the government's ability to issue birth and death information was hindered.

As machine learning (ML) emerged, researchers began leveraging its capabilities to strengthen safety systems. ML is a method where a computer program enhances its performance through accumulated experience. With increased time for data-driven training, more data can be collected to better align with the stated objectives. Here is a visual representation of the basic GAN architecture (Khalil et al., 2020).

GANs appear to be a highly effective technique to train a neural network to replicate a specific attack. GANs can generate synthetic data by learning from real-world data. This generated data can be used to explore different scenarios and uncover potential charges that may not have been previously known. It allows for investigation using data that a user would not typically provide during training. The GANs approach proves highly effective in system security, as it accurately handles the constant emergence of new and unforeseen data threats (Pan et al., 2019). With the utilization of GANs, designers can predict and counter future threats, enhancing security measures to proactively defend against potential attacks. In addition, hackers could potentially exploit this technique to create additional vulnerabilities. This study aims to examine the security measures provided and the potential risks associated with the use of GANs. Studying the application of GANs for safety is truly captivating. This chapter aims to provide a comprehensive overview of the development and utilization of GANs in enhancing security measures. Special emphasis is placed on utilizing GANs to identify and combat potential threats to systems (Zareapoor et al., 2019).

5.1. GANS NETWORK SAFETY

Learning objectives

- Understand how effectively one can work on the safety of GAN network
- Comprehend cyber interruption and malware detection in GANs.

This section will provide a comprehensive overview of the existing research on GANs and the security concerns that arise in today's network environment.

5.1.1. Generative Adversarial Network

In 2014, Ian Good fellow pioneered the notion of Generative Adversarial Networks (GANs). Figure 5.1 illustrates a dual-network architecture comprising a producer and a discriminator. The network is trained using an adversarial approach, where the producer model G attempts to mimic the data distribution by utilizing a random noise vector that is fed into the discriminator model D. The model undergoes evaluation and produces a probability value to ascertain if the information originated from G or a credible source. The objective is to strengthen the authenticity of the data, increasing the likelihood that D will perceive it as originating from the genuine dataset (Huang et al., 2017).

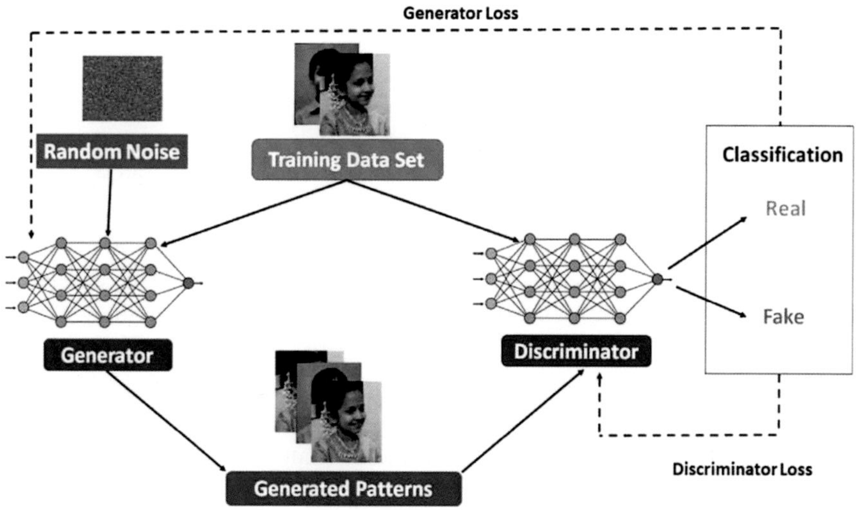

Figure 5.1. *Illustration of the system architecture of GAN.*

Source: Roshani Raut, Creative Commons License.

5.1.2. GANs in Safety

This section will provide an in-depth review of GANS network safety and explore strategies for optimizing its effectiveness (Tanner et al., 2015).

5.1.2.1. Obscuring Delicate Information

Many businesses and government agencies have valuable data that academics are unable to access due to restrictions. As an example, healthcare institutions hold a significant amount of sensitive patient data. In addition, banks take measures to safeguard their customers' statements and financial information. Sharing protected data with scientists or analysts would undoubtedly offer valuable insights and support future studies. Research in artificial intelligence (AI) has shown that a well-trained GAN can generate new information that accurately represents the original. Consequently, while the GANs may safeguard the actual data, the generated data likely maintains comparable patterns and visions to the original data. The gathered data exhibits a striking resemblance to the characteristics of the initial dataset. This information should be further analyzed to ensure its security. Mirjalili et al. (2014), also mentioned that a computerized analysis could potentially be employed for age or gender-based profiling, which could challenge the relevance of biostatistics in certain assertions. They introduced a novel auto-encoder model that utilizes an enhanced GAN to convert a given facial image into a format suitable for facial recognition while avoiding gender classification (Sun et al., 2024).

5.1.3. Cyber Interruption and Malware Detection

Cyber disruptions are applied to intentionally disturb and cause harm to computer systems by bypassing their security mechanisms or generating an adverse working environment. Cyber intrusions can result in several outcomes, including the illegal disclosure of information, modification of data, and loss of valuable data. An Intrusion Detection System (IDS) will continuously monitor the system and instantly notify the user in case of any potentially dangerous activity. Researchers have conducted studies on several IDSs utilizing statistical learning and neural networks. Chen et al. (2012) emphasized the potential efficacy of a GAN-based model for implementing an IDS. GANs are utilized in intrusion detection due to their profound comprehension of typical data (Jeffrey et al., 2024).

Chen et al. (2012), proposed a GAN-based model that incorporates a modified loss function and many intermediate layers to enhance the discriminator's decision-making accuracy. Researchers have employed GANs to identify malware. Malware refers to malicious software specifically designed to inflict harm against a computer system. It is crucial to acknowledge that malware can be employed for objectives beyond invasions. Anderson et al. proposed a new method known as adversarial-tuned field formation. Burks (2010) recently conducted a comprehensive examination of the performance of GANs and variational autoencoder (VAE) representations in the domain of malware recognition. Their research uncovered a substantial enhancement in efficiency when GANs were employed. In addition, a multitude of scientists have suggested inventive defensive methodologies and algorithms to effectively mitigate various attacks that rely on GANs (Gómez et al., 2022).

Samangouei et al. (2017), developed Defense-GAN, a generative adversarial network that demonstrates exceptional proficiency in creating images that are free from any disturbances or distortions. The suggested GAN can mitigate a wide range of attack strategies and improve the effectiveness of current defense measures. Most of the defensive techniques currently employed are customized to suit individual models. Given the remarkable generating capabilities of GANs, Defense-GAN can be employed in conjunction with any classifier and for diverse attack situations (Murray & Rawat, 2021).

5.1.4. Security Examination

Cyber-physical production schemes (CPPSs) are a cutting-edge security architecture that seamlessly combines electronic and physical security levels.

This kind of system holds great importance from both an economic and social standpoint. CPPS involves the integration of networks, computation, and physical operations within separate but interconnected subsystems. Examining the security of cyber and human systems across different domains is a crucial area of study (Dumagpi & Jeong, 2020). Chhetri and colleagues introduced the GAN-Sec scheme, a security analysis model that utilizes the GAN algorithm. GAN-Sec conducts safety analysis by analyzing the signal and energy flow within a system. GANs can be used to assess the satisfaction of fundamental security measures such as privacy, access, and integrity. The authors utilized an additive manufacturing system as a case study to showcase the efficacy of GAN-Sec, as illustrated in Table 5.1. The results suggest that the proposed model can analyze security breaches that result from side-channel incidents. In addition, GAN-Sec can help evaluate the effectiveness of a model in detecting and addressing integrity and availability attacks (Zhou et al., 2021).

Practice Problem

Describe a scenario where GANs are used to hide malware within legitimate software images. Discuss the potential risks and implications of using GANs for malware hiding attacks and strategies for detecting hidden malware.

Solution to Practice Problem

In a scenario where GANs are used to hide malware within legitimate software images, attackers can train GAN models to embed malware in benign software images. These GAN-generated images appear normal to security scanners but contain hidden malware payloads that can be executed upon installation. Detecting hidden malware requires advanced analysis techniques, such as behavioral monitoring and anomaly detection, to identify suspicious behavior and patterns indicative of malware activity.

Table 5.1. *Analysis of GAN Security Issues*

Purpose of Work	Challenges
Obscuring delicate information	Examine the security concerns
Cyber interruption and malware recognition	Concentrate on cyber and malware attacks, not detection.
Safe image steganography	Image processing dominates, but security is lacking.
Neural cryptography	Focus on small dataset machine learning and encryption.
Security analysis	Only analysis is done; no topic is chosen.

Source: Roshani Raut, Creative Commons License.

5.2. SECURITY ATTACKS IN GANS

Learning objectives

- Understand the threat of cracking passwords in GANs
- Comprehend how GAN may be used to deceive image recognition system.

Using a pre-existing dataset, the discriminator is assigned the task of distinguishing between genuine and malicious communication. This attack is directed through an Intrusion Detection System (IDS), and the output of the IDS is then passed through the discriminator, effectively emulating the behavior of the IDS. Lin et al. (2019), achieved impressive results, significantly reducing malware detection rates from 70% down to less than 1% (Hu & Pang, 2021).

Lin et al. (2019) employed a comparable approach to address the issue of denial of service (DoS) attacks. The author selectively modified the aspects of the attack that were unrelated to the DoS incident, while keeping the effective components unchanged. The writers were able to reduce the accurate favorable rates by half, bringing it down to 47.6%. The lack of accurately classified datasets has hindered the progress of malware research (Navidan et al., 2021).

Singh et al. (2019) suggested using ACGANs to enhance existing malware images by incorporating additional labeled datasets, thereby addressing this issue. AC-GANs have significantly enhanced the reliability and resilience of training. Thanks to an increasing number of samples for training, the augmentation technique has significantly enhanced malware databases.

Exploring various aspects of cyber security vulnerability to adversarial GAN attacks can provide valuable insights into the nature of such attacks. The concepts discussed here can also be applied to other fields, broadening the understanding of adversarial GAN charge (Yeh et al., 2021).

5.2.1. Cracking Passphrases

Modern password-cracking methods involve generating millions of hashes using a vast word list and then comparing them to the target password hashes to crack them. These word collections typically consist of commonly used or previously employed passwords, but they are not comprehensive. The effectiveness of this method is constrained by the length of the word list, which can limit the ability to crack passwords (Nam et al., 2020).

When used in conjunction with HashCat, PassGAN can accurately predict a significantly higher number of unique passwords compared to HashCat alone, with an increase ranging from 51 to 73%. These figures are quite alarming, as

PassGAN can generate an incredibly large number of password guesses (Garg & Ahuja, 2019).

5.2.2. Hiding Malware

In the realm of cyber security, a GAN can serve the purpose of generating data and cleverly bypassing detection systems. The article "Generating Argumentative Malware Illustrations for Black-Box Occurrences Using GAN" delves deeply into this subject matter (Kim et al., 2018). It has the potential to be used for developing malware that can bypass ML-based detection systems. The concept is like a conventional GAN, where the Black Box detector acts as the discriminator. The generator is given a mix of random noise and malware samples, while the discriminator is provided with harmless instances to assist the generator in recognizing what is classified as "not malware" (Zhang et al., 2021).

5.2.3. Forging Facial Detection

The final portion of the GAN applications section delves into one of the most common uses of GANs: picture creation and modification. With its advanced capabilities, a GAN can effectively trick existing image recognition platforms and produce incredibly realistic counterfeit images.

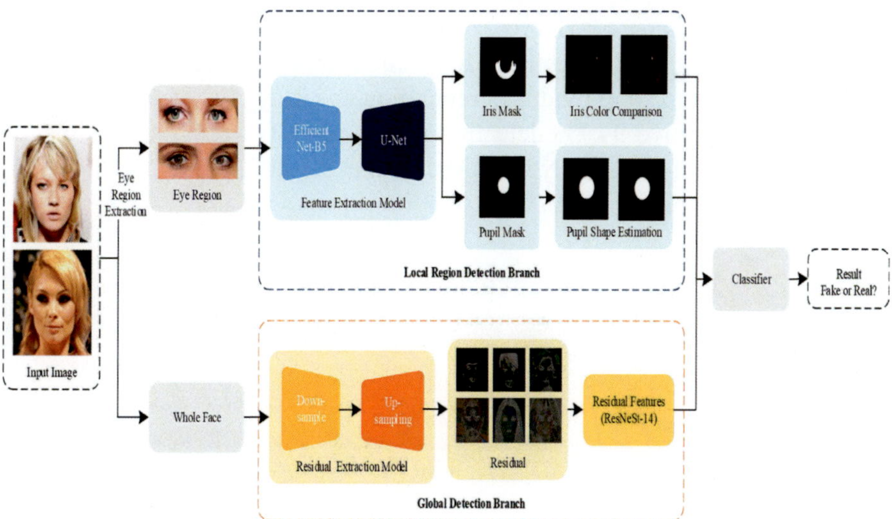

Figure 5.2. Schematic of GAN generated fake face detection method.

Source: Roshani Raut, Creative Commons License.

Although this chapter does not specifically focus on cyber security, it has significant implications for the industry (Peng et al., 2019). Using this advanced technology could potentially generate manipulated images and videos of public figures, individuals of importance, and even yourself. If the rapid production of realistic false images and movies becomes widespread, it poses a significant threat to both national and individual security. In today's era, the belief in seeing alone has diminished, leading to the urgent need for the swift advancement of detection systems that can effectively differentiate between authentic and deceptive (Jia et al., 2022).

5.2.4. Detection and Response

The final topic discussed in this chapter is detection and response. Unfortunately, there is no easy solution or quick fix that can be utilized. It is necessary to educate the public and raise awareness to address this problem. Understanding the inner workings of a GAN and being prepared for any potential adversarial situations is crucial for effectively identifying and reacting to them. GANs are set to become increasingly important for those involved in the field of machine learning-based cyber security (Randhawa et al., 2021). When it comes to detecting and responding to GAN attacks, it is crucial to develop systems with GANs and not rely solely on the assumption that ML detection is foolproof. DeepFD is a solution that has been developed to address the challenges posed by GAN-generated images. The researchers at DeepFD have created a system that can detect and flag potentially harmful GAN-generated images, which could pose a threat to an individual's reputation or safety. The DeepFD method achieves an impressive 94.7% detection rate in identifying fabricated images generated by cutting-edge GAN networks (Qui et al., 2021).

SUMMARY

- This chapter explores cutting-edge research on a range of topics, including image steganography, neural cryptography, and malware generation. The aim is to enhance the system's ability to defend itself against attacks, showcasing the potential for combining neural networks and cybersecurity.
- Furthermore, the chapter delves into various GAN variants that academics have employed to address critical security issues. This paper explores the advancements of GANs in enhancing surveillance for security protocols and establishing robust intrusion detection systems. It also delves into the applications of GANs in secure image steganography, neural cryptography, and security analysis.
- In addition, GANs are used to improve the performance of malware and intrusion attacks. The effectiveness of GANs is demonstrated by their capacity to produce fresh and unexplored data that could potentially reveal vulnerabilities in defensive systems. Computer systems have been trained by researchers to generate attacks that are challenging to detect and easily bypass detection measures.
- Creating GANs to assess the security strength of products offered by businesses is certainly a valuable endeavor. GANs have the potential to generate tests for a wide variety of known and unknown threats, leading to significant improvements in computers, computer-based products, and Internet of Things devices. Currently, the utilization of GANs in security is still in its early stages, but it is expected to rapidly progress soon.

MULTIPLE CHOICE QUESTIONS

1. What are some security concerns associated with GAN networks?

a) Network latency

b) Cyber interruptions and malware detection

c) Data encryption

d) Hardware compatibility

2. Which of the following is not a security attack in GANs?

a) Cracking passwords

b) Hiding malware

c) Generating synthetic data for training

d) Forging facial detection

3. **How can GANs be exploited in the context of cybersecurity?**
   a) By generating realistic synthetic data for training intrusion detection systems
   b) By enhancing network performance
   c) By optimizing hardware utilization
   d) By improving data encryption techniques
4. **What is one potential application of GANs in cybersecurity?**
   a) Generating synthetic data for training intrusion detection systems
   b) Enhancing network latency
   c) Optimizing hardware utilization
   d) Improving data compression algorithms
5. **Which security concern is not typically associated with GANs?**
   a) Cyber interruptions
   b) Malware detection
   c) Data encryption
   d) Password cracking

REVIEW QUESTIONS

1. What are some of the security concerns associated with GAN networks, and how do they impact their deployment in security-sensitive applications?
2. Explain the concept of cyber interruptions in the context of GANs. What are some potential threats posed by cyber interruptions, and how can they be mitigated?
3. Discuss the security attacks that can be launched using GANs, such as cracking passwords, hiding malware, and forging facial detection. What are the implications of these attacks in various domains?
4. How can GANs be exploited for malicious purposes in the field of cybersecurity? Provide examples of how GAN-generated data can be used to bypass security measures or deceive security systems.
5. What are some potential applications of GANs in cybersecurity, and how do they address security challenges? Explain how GANs can be used for tasks such as intrusion detection, malware detection, and vulnerability assessment.

Answers to Multiple Questions

1. (b) 2. (c) 3. (a) 4. (a) 5. (c)

REFERENCES

1. Burk, D. L. (2010). Copyright and paratext in computer gaming. *Emerging Ethical Issues of Life in Virtual Worlds, 4*(4), 33–53.
2. Chen, Z., Roussopoulos, M., Liang, Z., Zhang, Y., Chen, Z., & Delis, A. (2012). Malware characteristics and threats on the internet ecosystem. *Journal of Systems and Software, 85*(7), 1650–1672.
3. Dumagpi, J. K., & Jeong, Y. J. (2020). Evaluating GAN-based image augmentation for threat detection in large-scale x-ray security images. *Applied Sciences, 11*(1), 36.
4. Dutta, I. K., Ghosh, B., & Bayoumi, M. (2019). Lightweight cryptography for internet of insecure things: A survey. In *2019 IEEE 9th Annual Computing and Communication Workshop and Conference (CCWC)*. IEEE. (Vol. 2, pp. 0475–0481).
5. Garg, V., & Ahuja, L. (2019). Password guessing using deep learning. In *2019 2nd International Conference on Power Energy, Environment and Intelligent Control (PEEIC)*. IEEE. (Vol. 1, pp. 38–40).
6. Gómez, Á. L. P., Maimó, L. F., Celdrán, A. H., & Clemente, F. J. G. (2022). Malware detection in industrial scenarios using machine learning and deep learning techniques. *Advances in Malware and Data-Driven Network Security, 7*(3), 74–93.
7. Hu, H., & Pang, J. (2021). Membership inference attacks against GANs by leveraging over-representation regions. In *Proceedings of the 2021 ACM SIGSAC Conference on Computer and Communications Security* (Vol. 3, pp. 2387–2389).
8. Huang, X., Li, Y., Poursaeed, O., Hopcroft, J., & Belongie, S. (2017). Stacked generative adversarial networks. In *Proceedings of the IEEE Conference on Computer Vision and Pattern Recognition* (pp. 5077–5086).
9. Jeffrey, N., Tan, Q., & Villar, J. R. (2024). A hybrid methodology for anomaly detection in cyber–Physical systems. *Neurocomputing, 568*, 127068.
10. Jia, S., Ma, C., Yao, T., Yin, B., Ding, S., & Yang, X. (2022). Exploring frequency adversarial attacks for face forgery detection. In *Proceedings of the IEEE/CVF Conference on Computer Vision and Pattern Recognition* (Vol. 1, pp. 4103–4112).

11. Kathole, A. B., Vhatkar, K. N., Raut, R., Patil, S. D., & Jadhav, A. (2023). Security issues in generative adversarial networks. In *Generative Adversarial Networks and Deep Learning*. Chapman and Hall/CRC. (Vol. 2, pp. 67–78).
12. Khalil, K., Elgazzar, K., Abdelgawad, A., & Bayoumi, M. (2020). A security approach for CoAP-based internet of things resource discovery. In *2020 IEEE 6th World Forum on Internet of Things (WF-IoT)*. IEEE. (Vol. 3, pp. 1–6).
13. Kim, J. Y., Bu, S. J., & Cho, S. B. (2018). Zero-day malware detection using transferred generative adversarial networks based on deep autoencoders. *Information Sciences, 460*, 83–102.
14. Lin, C. H., Chang, C. C., Chen, Y. S., Juan, D. C., Wei, W., & Chen, H. T. (2019). Coco-GAN: Generation by parts via conditional coordinating. In *Proceedings of the IEEE/CVF International Conference on Computer Vision* (pp. 4512–4521).
15. Mirjalili, S., Mirjalili, S. M., & Lewis, A. (2014). Grey wolf optimizer. *Advances in Engineering Software, 69*, 46–61.
16. Murray, A., & Rawat, D. B. (2021). Network hazard flow for multi-tiered discriminator analysis enhancement with systems-theoretic process analysis. In *2021 IEEE Global Humanitarian Technology Conference (GHTC)*. IEEE. (Vol. 2, pp. 55–61).
17. Nam, S., Jeon, S., & Moon, J. (2020). Generating optimized guessing candidates toward better password cracking from multi-dictionaries using relativistic GAN. *Applied Sciences, 10*(20), 7306.
18. Navidan, H., Moshiri, P. F., Nabati, M., Shahbazian, R., Ghorashi, S. A., Shah-Mansouri, V., & Windridge, D. (2021). Generative adversarial networks (GANs) in networking: A comprehensive survey & evaluation. *Computer Networks, 194*, 108149.
19. Pan, Z., Yu, W., Yi, X., Khan, A., Yuan, F., & Zheng, Y. (2019). Recent progress on generative adversarial networks (GANs): A survey. *IEEE Access, 7*, 36322–36333.
20. Peng, F., Zhang, L. B., & Long, M. (2019). FD-GAN: Face de-morphing generative adversarial network for restoring accomplice's facial image. *IEEE Access, 7*, 75122–75131.
21. Qui, C. P. X., Quang, D. H., Duy, P. T., & Pham, V. H. (2021). Strengthening IDS against evasion attacks with GAN-based adversarial samples in SDN-enabled network. In *2021 RIVF International Conference on Computing and Communication Technologies (RIVF)*. IEEE. (Vol. 3, pp. 1–6).

22. Randhawa, R. H., Aslam, N., Alauthman, M., Rafiq, H., & Comeau, F. (2021). Security hardening of botnet detectors using generative adversarial networks. *IEEE Access, 9*, 78276–78292.
23. Samangouei, P., Patel, V. M., & Chellappa, R. (2017). Facial attributes for active authentication on mobile devices. *Image and Vision Computing, 58*, 181–192.
24. Singh, A., Dutta, D., & Saha, A. (2019). MIGAN: malware image synthesis using GANs. In *Proceedings of the AAAI Conference on Artificial Intelligence* (Vol. 33, pp. 10033–10034).
25. Sun, Z., Shen, Y., Zhou, Q., Zhang, H., Chen, Z., Cox, D., & Gan, C. (2024). Principle-driven self-alignment of language models from scratch with minimal human supervision. *Advances in Neural Information Processing Systems, 36*, 987–990.
26. Tanner, C., Gans, D., White, J., Nath, R., & Pohl, J. (2015). Electronic health records and patient safety. *Applied Clinical Informatics, 6*(01), 136–147.
27. Yeh, C. Y., Chen, H. W., Shuai, H. H., Yang, D. N., & Chen, M. S. (2021). Attack as the best defense: Nullifying image-to-image translation GANs via limit-aware adversarial attack. In *Proceedings of the IEEE/CVF International Conference on Computer Vision* (Vol. 2, pp. 16188–16197).
28. Zareapoor, M., Celebi, M. E., & Yang, J. (2019). Diverse adversarial network for image super-resolution. *Signal Processing: Image Communication, 74*, 191–200.
29. Zhang, Y., Li, H., Zheng, Y., Yao, S., & Jiang, J. (2021). Enhanced DNNs for malware classification with GAN-based adversarial training. *Journal of Computer Virology and Hacking Techniques, 17*, 153–163.
30. Zhou, Q., Zuley, M., Guo, Y., Yang, L., Nair, B., Vargo, A., & Wu, S. (2021). A machine and human reader study on AI diagnosis model safety under attacks of adversarial images. *Nature Communications, 12*(1), 7281.

CHAPTER 6

IMAGE EDITING USING GANS

LEARNING OBJECTIVES

At the end of this chapter, readers will be able to:

1. Gain insight into the background of Generative Adversarial Networks
2. Comprehend the GAN objective functions
3. Understand the process of controlled image-to-image conversion
4. Understand the process of unsupervised image-to-image translation

INTRODUCTORY EXAMPLE

"PixelWorks Solutions" is a prominent technology company that specializes in providing image editing and enhancement services. With the help of state-of-the-art Generative Adversarial Networks (GANs), PixelWorks has completely transformed the user experience when it comes to digital images. Imagine a situation where a user desires to effortlessly convert a black and white photograph into a vivid, visually striking work of art. Utilizing cutting-edge GAN technology, PixelWorks has developed a cutting-edge image editing software that effortlessly accomplishes this task. With the utilization of GAN-based image-to-image translation, PixelWorks empowers users to effortlessly manipulate and enhance their images with remarkable precision and lifelike quality, opening a world of limitless creative opportunities. This introductory example provides a glimpse of the incredible possibilities that GANs offer in the field of image editing and manipulation.

UNIT INTRODUCTION

The need to convert input images into corresponding output images arises from concerns regarding image handling, processor structure, and computer representation. Just like ideas can be conveyed through various languages, a presentation can be represented in different formats such as an RGB image, a slope field, a control map, or a semantic marker map, among other options. Automated language modification involves the transformation of one potential representation of an element into another, utilizing specific training data (Wang et al., 2018). This technique is commonly referred to as tailored image-to-image conversion. In the past, these jobs were carried out using different types of equipment, each designed for a specific purpose: predicting pixels by analyzing other pixels. This section seeks to offer a comprehensive and in-depth analysis of these matters. Significant progress has been made in this area, with convolutional neural networks (CNNs) becoming the favored method for addressing a range of image prediction tasks. CNNs strive to minimize the impact of a loss function, which measures the efficacy of results. Even though the learning process is automated, the development of impactful loss functions still demands significant human effort. Essentially, it is crucial to ensure that the desired information is consistently provided to CNN, with the aim of minimizing its impact (Esfahani & Latifi, 2019). Employing a primary approach and guiding CNN to minimize the Euclidean distance between projected and ground truth pixels might result in less precise outcomes. Various factors contribute to the reduction of Euclidean detachment, leading to distortion.

Mastering the art of crafting effective loss functions to steer the convolutional neural network (CNN) towards achieving specific objectives, like generating accurate and lifelike images, is a complex and demanding pursuit that requires expertise and finesse. It would be ideal to define a top-level objective, such as "attaining output that is virtually identical to reality," and subsequently train a suitable loss function automatically (Goodfellow et al., 2014). Generative adversarial networks (GANs) achieve this objective. GANs use a loss function to distinguish between real and fake images, while simultaneously training a generative model to minimize this loss. Images that are blurry or lack sharpness will not be approved as they create the perception of being computer-generated. Thanks to their ability to learn a flexible loss function from the data, GANs have proven to be highly versatile in tackling various tasks that previously required distinct loss functions (Kim et al., 2021).

6.1. GAN OBJECTIVE FUNCTIONS

Learning objectives

- Understand the loss challenges of GANs
- Comprehend the loss of discriminator in GANs
- Understand the concept of GAN loss minimax

GANs and their derivatives employ the objective function to quantify and decrease the disparity between the real and generated sample distributions. Although GANs have shown remarkable effectiveness in several tasks, the lack of dependable data has presented significant challenges such as gradient vanishing and model collapse. Simply modifying the existing technique will not adequately resolve these issues (Yuan et al., 2021). The architecture of GANs is truly one-of-a-kind. These problems can be addressed by reevaluating the objective function. Several goal functions have been proposed and categorized to enhance data quality and encourage sample diversity, while also addressing the limitations of the original GAN and its subsequent iterations. Understanding GAN loss functions can be challenging for beginners, despite the simplicity of GAN architecture (Komodakis & Tziritas, 2007).

6.1.1. GAN Loss Challenges

GAN engineering is normally defined by the minimax GAN loss; however the non-saturating loss function is often used. Contemporary GANs frequently utilize the least squares and Wasserstein loss functions as alternative loss functions.

Under the condition that all other elements, such as processing capacity and model hyperparameters, remain unchanged, the thorough assessment of GAN loss functions demonstrates negligible variance (Pan et al., 2020).

6.1.2. The Problem of GAN Loss

GAN has demonstrated remarkable efficacy in generating lifelike images of faces, environments, and several other objects. Although the GAN architecture is rather uncomplicated, understanding the notion of GAN loss functions may be somewhat intimidating for beginners (Zhu et al., 2020).

6.1.3. Loss of Discriminator

The goal of the discriminator is to increase the likelihood of accurately classifying both genuine and counterfeit photographs. The objective is to educate D so that it can accurately assign labels to both training examples and G samples, thereby increasing the likelihood of achieving success. The formal objective of the discriminator is to maximize the average logarithmic probability of authentic photographs while minimizing the probability of fake photos (Albuquerque et al., 2019).

$$\log(1 - D(G(z)) + \log(1 - D(G(z))$$

If this were to be directly implemented, modifications would be required to utilize stochastic ascent instead of stochastic descent. Usually, this is addressed as a standard binary classification issue, where the labels 0 and 1 represent synthetic and natural pictures, respectively. The approach aims to minimize the standard paired cross-entropy, often known as log loss (Choi & Han, 2022).

6.1.4. GAN Loss Minimax

The "min" and "max" terms are utilized to optimize the losses of the generator and discriminator, respectively, within the framework of minimizing and maximizing (D, G). The discriminator strives to maximize the mean logarithmic probability of genuine photos while minimizing the probability of counterfeit images, as previously elucidated. Practically, the loss function may not provide sufficient gradient for G to effectively gain learning. In the early stages of learning, when the ability to generalize is not yet strong, the discriminator can confidently identify and reject samples that deviate significantly from the training data (Gazzan & Sheldon, 2023). The discriminator is trained on a combination of genuine and synthetic images to accurately classify them as real or fake. Instead of training on the generator, the discriminator model is used. The discriminator has been meticulously crafted to compute the loss function of the generator. During a two-player game, the generator and discriminator models engage in a competition to enhance their performance. Evaluating the convergence of a model on a training dataset often involves maximizing the selected loss function. The outcome of a two-player game in a GAN is determined by a conjunction. Instead, the goal is to achieve a balanced harmony between the generator's loss and the discriminator's loss (Lee et al., 2021).

6.2. IMAGE-TO-IMAGE TRANSLATION

Learning objectives

- Understand the controlled image-to-image translation
- Comprehend the unsupervised image-to-image conversion

The CycleGAN algorithm was utilized for image-to-image translation tasks in the absence of pre-existing integrated models. When considering the path from source area A to objective space B, it is crucial to consider the potential losses in two-cycle consistency. DualGAN and DiscoGAN employ a self-guided learning method for image-to-image translation, leveraging unsupervised data and distinctive loss functions. HarmonicGAN is a method employed in unsupervised image-to-image interpretation. It incorporates spatial smoothing to maintain consistent mappings throughout its execution (Yi et al., 2017). Picture-to-picture interpretation is the procedure of arranging photographs from a source region together with images from a destination location. The uses of this technology encompass picture colorization, semantic labeling derived from photos, enhancing image resolution, and analyzing spatial variance. Typically, a picture-to-picture interpretation technique entails the identification of appropriate regions within the input pictures and devising a means to convert such regions into the desired target area. When operating in a context devoid of visual assistance, it is crucial to concentrate on the conceptual aspects that demand attention. Identifying regions of interest in the interpretation of one picture to another is a substantial task. The translation should prioritize a particular article rather than the entirety of the picture (Liu et al., 2017). Using CycleGANs, it is possible to smoothly go from one domain A to another domain B without requiring training sets that completely match each other. Assuming a vast range of photographs from area A and an unconnected arrangement of pictures from space B, it becomes necessary to include the capability to translate ideas across different groups. To do this, a planning function G(G: A→B) is established. It aims to efficiently plan the transformation of A to B. Currently, the comparison between actual and fake datasets is unfeasible due to the absence of matching data. By configuring a generator, domain B can be supplied with captivating photos when they are uploaded to domain A. Nevertheless, a possible obstacle occurs due to the inability to confine the generator's output to a straight connection with its input. This raises a concern known as mode breakdown, where a model might allocate different inputs from region A to produce a similar outcome from region B. Based on the given information, it is evident that the outcome should align with domain B and consider the provided data for that domain. For a more valuable contribution to the specific goal, it is recommended to incorporate an additional planning method known as reverse planning G'(G': →A) (Li et al., 2019). This method emphasizes planning from B to A. This requirement is known as the cycle-consistency imperative. After successfully translating from domain B back to A, one can expect to see a similar representation that was initially used. Through a thorough process of interpretation, one should ultimately arrive at a similar image to the one they started with. If the necessary conditions are fulfilled for the translation of images from space A to space B, it can be deduced that the image conversion from A to B is accurate

$$G_{\mathrm{AtoB}}(G_{\mathrm{AtoB}}(x))\approx x$$

CycleGAN indicates the accurate mapping of the model from one domain to another (Lin et al., 2018). To perform image-to-image translation, one must follow a specific sequence of steps:

a) Exploring the visualization of datasets
b) Establishing a suitable framework
c) Utilize a discriminator.
d) Utilization of residual blocks/functions
e) Utilize a generator.
f) The process of training
i. Calculating the discriminator and generator functions
ii. Utilize an optimizer to achieve optimal results (Xiong et al., 2019).

Recently, there has been a significant increase in the application of GAN-based methods for image-to-image translation, resulting in impressive results. The pix2pix framework employed the Conditional Generative Adversarial Network (cGAN) to train a model capable of converting a drawing into a lifelike image. The conditional generative adversarial network (cGAN) can generate a model that considers both the source and target domains by utilizing paired pictures throughout the training process. Zhu et al. developed a unique technique called CycleGAN to tackle the issues of non-paired image-to-image conversion (Alotaibi, 2020). To examine the mapping between foundation domain X and aim domain Y (and vice versa), they include two-cycle consistency losses. DiscoGAN and DualGAN apply unique loss functions for image-to-image translation, however, their learning technique lacks adequate proof. HarmonicGAN, designed for non-uniform image-to-image transformation, employs spatial regularization to guarantee seamless and uninterrupted mappings during the transformation procedure. The recently created UNIT (image-to-image conversion network) is constructed using coupled GANs and the shared-latent planetary assumption. This assumption implies that two related pictures from different domains may be transformed into the same underlying representation (Cherian & Sullivan, 2019).

Moreover, image-to-image conversion techniques operate under the assumption that the fundamental composition of pictures may be dissected into a significant and intricate domain, facilitating the generation of outputs with several modes. This study introduces a framework called MUNIT for converting images from one modality to another without the need for supervision. MUNIT leverages two latent vectors, one for style and one for content, to achieve this conversion (Lata et al., 2019). The image's content code is merged with diverse style drawings from the desired domain to convert one image into another. Lee et al. recently presented a new method for converting images called DRIT in research.

This approach employs extracted characteristics from unstructured data to divide the underlying elements into two components. The initial element is a domain-invariant space that captures common information, whereas the subsequent element is a domain-specific space that produces varied outputs with comparable content. The author proposed BranchGAN as a technique to transport pictures between various domains while ensuring that the distribution and encoder remain consistent for both domains (Dosovitskiy & Brox, 2016). Instagram uses object segmentation masks to carry out domain-to-domain image translation in many scenarios.

The incorporation of the context-preserving loss ensures that the backdrop is successfully preserved. However, Instagram's training process is limited when it does not have access to semantic separation labels, which offer detailed explanations at the pixel level. Supervised learning involves training a model to learn the relationship between an input picture and an output image by using a set of related pairs. The researchers employed Conditional Generative Adversarial Networks (cGAN) in the pix2pix framework to examine the correlation between picture pairings originating from distinct domains. BicycleGAN is a model configuration for cGANs that investigates the process of learning a distribution of possible outputs (Cao et al., 2018).

6.2.1. Controlled Image-to-Image Conversion

6.2.1.1. cGAN

Isola et al. explore the application of conditional argumentative networks (cGANs) as a flexible solution for tackling difficulties in image-to-image translation. Their approach showcases its efficacy in a range of tasks, including generating photos from label maps, reconstructing objects from edge maps, and enhancing images with color. This chapter explores the correlation between a perceptual image x and a random noise vector z and y. This is achieved by utilizing Conditional GANs. The generator G is trained to create outputs that closely resemble "authentic" pictures, due to an adversarially capable discriminator, D, which is trained to accurately identify the generator's "counterfeits." Presented in Figure 6.1 is a visual representation of the operational methodology (Kang et al., 2021).

6.2.1.2. BicycleGAN

This section aims to discuss the implementation of potential outputs in a scenario involving a convolutional neural network.

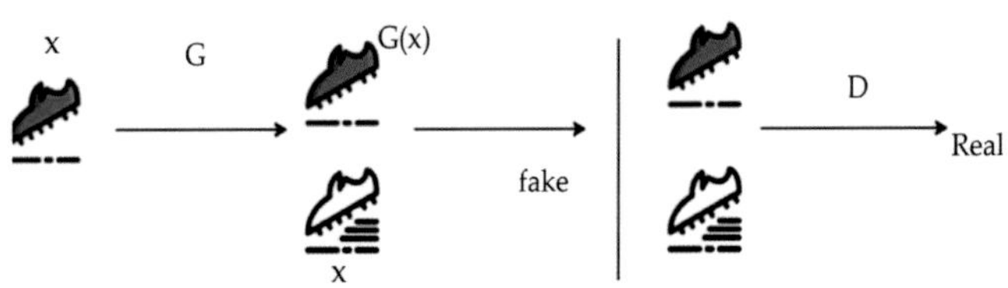

Figure 6.1. *Illustration of training a conditional GAN to map edges to photo.*

Source: Anuja Jadhav, Creative Commons License.

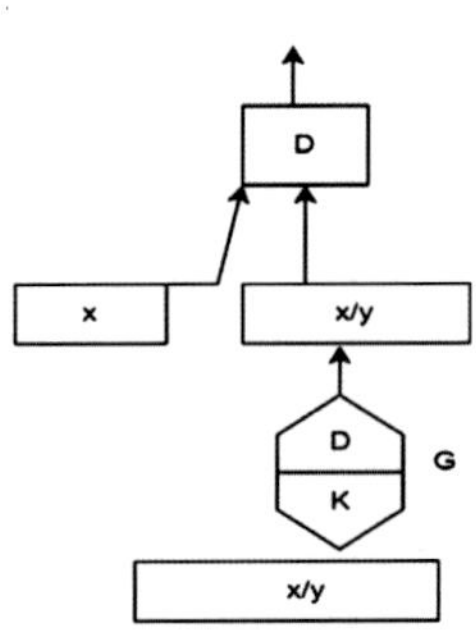

Figure 6.2. *Representation of SPA-GAN architecture.*

Source: Roshani Raut, Creative Commons License.

Combining BicycleGAN, cVAE-GAN, and aLR-GAN enhances the connection between latent encoding and output, resulting in improved representation. By avoiding a one-to-many plotting between the stationary coding and the product during training, it can effectively address the method collapse issue and achieve more diverse outcomes (Alharbi et al., 2019).

6.2.1.3. SPA-GAN

Emami et al. devised a pioneering technique known as SPA-GAN for converting images to images. They accomplished this by including the attention mechanism directly into the GAN architecture. SPA-GAN computes the discriminator's assessment and employs it to direct the generator's attention toward the most distinctive regions between the source and target domains. As shown in Figure 6.2, the discriminator produces spatial attention maps and categorizes the input pictures. The generator uses these maps to focus on the most salient features of the item. Furthermore, the blocks (b-1) and (b-2) exhibit the distinct phenomenon of map deterioration. The loss is determined by comparing the characteristic maps of the actual and produced pictures, namely in the first layer of the decoder. Image translation commonly uses the conventional map loss to maintain domain-specific attributes (Ding et al., 2022).

6.2.1.4. CE-GAN

Consistent entrenched generative accusatorial networks (CEGAN) aim to develop conditional cohort models that may produce visually accurate results and restrict the range of possible outcomes by employing complex networks within the picture and the hidden space. This approach efficiently tackles the issue of mode failure and yields a broader spectrum of accurate outcomes. As shown in Figure 6.3, the generator uses the participation picture X1 and the secret code z to recreate the original X2. To mitigate the problem of noise and redundancy, encryption is implied to convert the obtained sample yield X2 into a concealed code z utilizing method E. The goal is to accurately recreate both the hidden representation and visual output of the true data, to provide authentic and varied images within the specified category (Sampath et al., 2021).

Practice Problem

Examine the utilization of Generative Adversarial Networks (GANs) in the enhancement of picture resolution through the development of a framework that is based on GANs. The objective is to increase the quality of low-resolution photographs. Utilize a dataset comprising of paired low-resolution and high-resolution pictures to train the model and assess the efficacy of the super-resolution model.

Solution to Practice Problem

To develop a GAN-based model for enhancing picture resolution, one can employ a GAN architecture consisting of a generator and discriminator network. It is advisable to train the model by utilizing a dataset that contains both low-resolution and high-resolution pictures that are paired together, such as the DIV2K dataset. The generator is taught to comprehend the correlation between low-resolution images and their high-resolution counterparts, while the discriminator's function is to distinguish between authentic high-resolution images and artificially created ones. After the completion of training, the generator may be utilized to enhance the resolution of newly captured low-quality photos.

6.2.2. Unsupervised Image-to-Image Conversion

6.2.2.1. cycleGAN

Researchers have utilized cycleGAN to address the challenges of image-to-image translation in situations where paired samples are unavailable. There is a clear connection between the domains, allowing for the seamless incorporation of "cycle consistent" loss and argumentation losses on fields X and Y. By incorporating two-cycle consistency losses, a mapping was established between the foundation domain X and the aim domain Y (and vice versa) (Dwarkani et al., 2020).

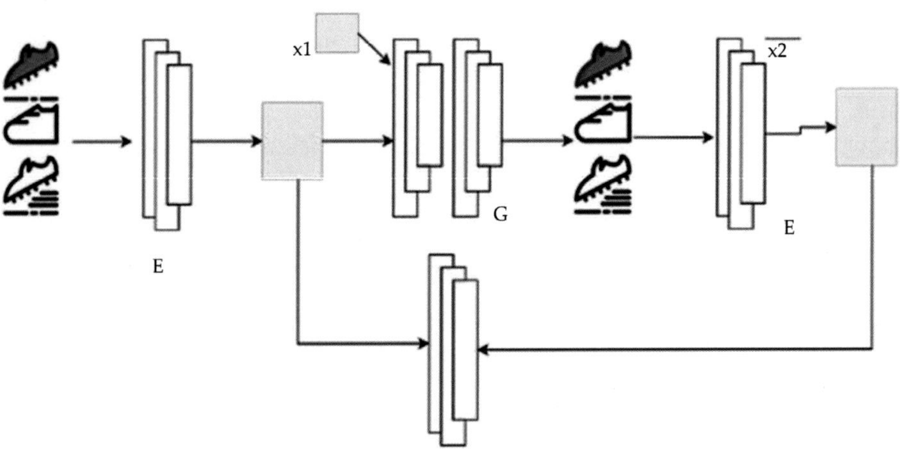

Figure 6.3. *Illustration of the model for image-to-image translation.*

Source: Swati Jasiwal, Creative Commons License.

6.2.2.2. DuGAN

Yi et al. (2017) provide a new dual-GAN method for training image classifiers by utilizing two separate sets of unlabeled photos from various domains. The early GAN is particularly adept at interpreting photos from domain U and mapping them to field V, given its distinctive design. In contrast, the dual GAN adopts a distinct strategy by emphasizing the inverse procedure through its unique and inventive architecture. The closed loop formed by primal and dual tasks enables the conversion and reconstruction of pictures from both domains. As a result, the translators might receive training by utilizing a loss function that takes into consideration any mistakes in picture reconstruction (Rossi & Cerveri, 2021).

6.2.2.3. UNIT

To address the problem, they introduced an unverified picture into an image transformation system known as UNIT. This system integrates GANs with the notion of latent planetary hypothesis. The latent planetary hypothesis proposes that two comparable pictures from distinct domains can be linked to a common latent space (Alami Mejjati et al., 2018).

6.2.2.4. MUNIT

The code used to process the image is combined with various style illustrations from the chosen domain to transform the picture into a different domain. Every hidden encoder consists of a code c and a code s that are carefully selected. The model is evaluated using argumentation goals that define the need for the generated images to have a fuzzy quality, relying on accurate descriptions in the target domain. Furthermore, the model's capacity to reconstruct both images and latent codes is assessed using bidirectional renovation objectives, which are depicted by dashed lines (Shen et al., 2019).

6.3. APPLICATIONS

The main applications are classified using the I2I taxonomy. I2I approaches are frequently employed to create realistic photos that closely match real-world environments by merging several forms of input data. A frequent job includes the procedure of semantic synthesis, in which a semantic segmentation mask is converted into real-world pictures. Person duplication synthesis is a technique that involves modifying the clothing and poses of the subject to turn one image into another. This technique depicts the same human in different outfits and settings (Alqahtani et al., 2021). This encompasses the utilization of virtual try-on technology and the transformation of skeletal structure and key elements to accurately correspond to the individual. Furthermore, there exist several methodologies that strive to depict the physical environment by transforming manually created drawings, written material, audio recordings, and paintings into visual representations. Before the development of I2I, several techniques depended on a laborious and time-intensive process of accessing pre-existing pictures and moving sections of those images to the corresponding region. The core focus of I2I image handling revolves around the manipulation of pictures, particularly in terms of modifying or adjusting a picture while preserving other features in their original state (Collins et al., 2020).

Semantic manipulation entails modifying the underlying significance of a picture, which includes the inclusion or exclusion of certain components (such as cosmetics). Attribute management includes the manipulation of binary representations or the utilization of landmarks to adjust different visual characteristics of an image, such as the subject's gender, hair color, presence of spectacles, and facial expression. Furthermore, it carries out other tasks such as reclassifying images, altering gaze, and simulating real-world situations. Moreover, image/video retargeting facilitates the smooth movement of information across several domains while maintaining the intended visual style of the target site (Sidorov, 2019). The I2I study places particular emphasis on the restoration of pixels that are absent from pictures. This encompasses methodologies for image inpainting and outpainting, which tackle distinct categories of obstructed images. The painting process employs the concept of human emotion as a visual depiction, yielding accurate and significant outcomes based on the provided input. This input involves covering the nose, mouth, and eyes, resulting in visually appealing and contextually correct outputs. Conversely, the process of creating a picture from a face that is highly veiled just requires the identification of the nose, mouth, and eyes. I2I significantly contributed to the creative output. Previously, reproducing an image in a specific artistic style required the skill of a proficient artist and a significant amount of labor. However, several experiments in the field of artificial intelligence have shown that automated methods can turn realistic photos into synthetic ones, hence reducing the requirement for human participation. The implementation of the I2I approach results in a successful transfer of elegance in this scenario (Isola et al., 2017). The primary goals of this technology are to convert a standard image into a specific artistic style, such as that of Monet or van Gogh, and to apply that style while maintaining the original content. Furthermore, image restoration may be accomplished using I2I. Image restoration aims to recover a degraded image to its initial form by employing a deprivation model.

To enhance the resolution of a picture, one can improve its clarity by using reduced versions of the original image as references. The process of removing noise from photographs involves the eradication of intentionally introduced aberrations. The goal of de-hazing and de-blurring procedures is to remove optical flaws from pictures shot in unfavorable settings or while the camera was moving, as well as from images of distant topographical or astronomical occurrences. Picture creation employs heuristic methods to generate visually captivating images that are esthetically attractive to the human eye. I2I demonstrates its efficacy in this field by highlighting its abilities in picture colorization and enhancing duplication quality. When applying color to a duplicate, it is necessary to envision the hue of each pixel purely based on its brightness. The objective of enhancing picture quality is to decrease the presence of colorful objects near edges, improve color precision, and limit noise in even shadows. Furthermore, this lesson offers guidance on combining multi-focus photos through the utilization of I2I approaches. It is important to note that I2I algorithms depend on two distinct forms of data for their respective responsibilities. Isolated sensing imaging is used to investigate animal habitats, whereas constructing abstract medical imaging is used for diagnosing illnesses, calculating dosages, and improving surgical training (Ling et al., 2021).

SUMMARY

- Recent advancements in cross-domain image-to-image translation have been remarkable, with unsupervised learning techniques now rivaling the performance of supervised approaches.
- In the future, there will be a greater push toward using unsupervised approaches in many applications due to the expensive or unfeasible nature of collecting paired training data.
- Furthermore, the aforementioned models can be classified as either unimodal or multimodal. UNIT, CycleGAN, and cGAN are all unimodal algorithms.
- Utilizing multimodal approaches can effectively mitigate the problem of model collapse and offer a wider range of diverse and lifelike images. In the future, multimodal and unsupervised approaches will likely become the standard for translating pictures into images.

MULTIPLE CHOICE QUESTIONS

1. Which neural networks are typically involved in a Generative Adversarial Network (GAN)?

a) Convolutional Neural Networks (CNNs) and Recurrent Neural Networks (RNNs)

b) Generator Networks and Discriminator Networks

c) Deep Neural Networks (DNNs) and Shallow Neural Networks (SNNs)

d) Autoencoders and Variational Autoencoders (VAEs)

2. What is the primary objective of the generator in a GAN?

a) To classify input images

b) To minimize the classification error of the discriminator

c) To generate realistic images that fool the discriminator

d) To maximize the classification accuracy of the discriminator

3. Which loss function is commonly used to train the discriminator in a GAN?

a) Mean Squared Error (MSE)

b) Binary Cross-Entropy Loss

c) Categorical Cross-Entropy Loss

d) Huber Loss

4. What is the objective of image-to-image translation using GANs?

a) To classify images into different categories

b) To generate new images from random noise

c) To convert images from one domain to another while preserving semantic content

d) To enhance the resolution of low-quality images

5. Controlled image-to-image translation involves:

a) Generating images without any constraints

b) Conditioning the generator on additional information to control the output images

c) Altering the loss function to improve image quality

d) Increasing the learning rate during training

REVIEW QUESTIONS

1. What are the two primary neural networks involved in a Generative Adversarial Network (GAN), and what are their roles in the image editing process?
2. Explain the objective functions used in GANs for training the generator and discriminator. How do these objective functions drive the training process?
3. Describe the concept of image-to-image translation using GANs. What are the key differences between controlled and unsupervised approaches to image translation?
4. How does controlled image-to-image translation work, and what additional information is typically used to condition the generator?
5. What are some common applications of controlled image-to-image translation using GANs? Provide examples of how this approach can be used for targeted image editing tasks.

Answers to Multiple Questions

1. (b) 2. (c) 3. (b) 4. (c) 5. (b)

REFERENCES

1. Alami Mejjati, Y., Richardt, C., Tompkin, J., Cosker, D., & Kim, K. I. (2018). Unsupervised attention-guided image-to-image translation. *Advances in Neural Information Processing Systems, 31*, 87–90.

2. Albuquerque, I., Monteiro, J., Doan, T., Considine, B., Falk, T., & Mitliagkas, I. (2019). Multi-objective training of generative adversarial networks with multiple discriminators. In *International Conference on Machine Learning*. PMLR. (Vol. 3, pp. 202–211).
3. Alharbi, Y., Smith, N., & Wonka, P. (2019). Latent filter scaling for multimodal unsupervised image-to-image translation. In *Proceedings of the IEEE/CVF Conference on Computer Vision and Pattern Recognition* (Vol. 3, pp. 1458–1466).
4. Alotaibi, A. (2020). Deep generative adversarial networks for image-to-image translation: A review. *Symmetry, 12*(10), 1705.
5. Alqahtani, H., Kavakli-Thorne, M., & Kumar, G. (2021). Applications of generative adversarial networks (GANs): An updated review. *Archives of Computational Methods in Engineering, 28*, 525–552.
6. Cao, Y. J., Jia, L. L., Chen, Y. X., Lin, N., Yang, C., Zhang, B., & Dai, H. H. (2018). Recent advances of generative adversarial networks in computer vision. *IEEE Access, 7*, 14985–15006.
7. Cherian, A., & Sullivan, A. (2019). Sem-GAN: Semantically-consistent image-to-image translation. In *2019 IEEE Winter Conference on Applications of Computer Vision (WACV)*. IEEE. (Vol. 2, pp. 1797–1806).
8. Choi, J., & Han, B. (2022). MCL-GAN: Generative adversarial networks with multiple specialized discriminators. *Advances in Neural Information Processing Systems, 35*, 29597–29609.
9. Collins, E., Bala, R., Price, B., & Susstrunk, S. (2020). Editing in style: Uncovering the local semantics of GANs. In *Proceedings of the IEEE/CVF Conference on Computer Vision and Pattern Recognition* (Vol. 2, pp. 5771–5780).
10. Ding, Z., Wang, Z., Wei, Y., Li, L., Ma, X., Zhang, T., & Zeng, T. (2022). SPA-GAN: SAR Parametric Autofocusing Method with Generative Adversarial Network. *Remote Sensing, 14*(20), 5159.
11. Dosovitskiy, A., & Brox, T. (2016). Generating images with perceptual similarity metrics based on deep networks. *Advances in Neural Information Processing Systems, 29*, 8971.
12. Dwarkani, A., Jain, M., Thakkar, J., & Kottursamy, K. (2020). Unpaired image-to-image translation using Cycle Generative Adversarial Networks. *International Journal of Engineering and Advanced Technology (IJEAT), 9*(6), 879–885.
13. Emami, H., Aliabadi, M. M., Dong, M., & Chinnam, R. B. (2020). SPA-GAN: Spatial attention GAN for image-to-image translation. *IEEE Transactions on Multimedia, 23*, 391–401.

14. Esfahani, S. N., & Latifi, S. (2019). Image generation with GANs-based techniques: A survey. *AIRCC's International Journal of Computer Science and Information Technology, 10*(3), 33–50.

15. Gazzan, M., & Sheldon, F. T. (2023). An enhanced minimax loss function technique in generative adversarial network for ransomware behavior prediction. *Future Internet, 15*(10), 318.

16. Goodfellow, I., Pouget-Abadie, J., Mirza, M., Xu, B., Warde-Farley, D., Ozair, S., & Bengio, Y. (2014). Generative adversarial nets. *Advances in Neural Information Processing Systems, 27*, 321–325.

17. Isola, P., Zhu, J. Y., Zhou, T., & Efros, A. A. (2017). Image-to-image translation with conditional adversarial networks. In *Proceedings of the IEEE Conference on Computer Vision and Pattern Recognition* (Vol. 3, pp. 1125–1134).

18. Jones, E. A., Wang, F. F., & Costinett, D. (2016). Review of commercial GaN power devices and GaN-based converter design challenges. *IEEE Journal of Emerging and Selected Topics in Power Electronics, 4*(3), 707–719.

19. Kang, S., Uchida, S., & Iwana, B. K. (2021). Tunable U-Net: Controlling image-to-image outputs using a tunable scalar value. *IEEE Access, 9*, 103279–103290.

20. Kim, H., Choi, Y., Kim, J., Yoo, S., & Uh, Y. (2021). Exploiting spatial dimensions of latent in GAN for real-time image editing. In *Proceedings of the IEEE/CVF Conference on Computer Vision and Pattern Recognition* (Vol. 3, pp. 852–861).

21. Komodakis, N., & Tziritas, G. (2007). Image completion using efficient belief propagation via priority scheduling and dynamic pruning. *IEEE Transactions on Image Processing, 16*(11), 2649–2661.

22. Lata, K., Dave, M., & Nishanth, K. N. (2019). Image-to-image translation using generative adversarial network. In *2019 3rd International Conference on Electronics, Communication and Aerospace Technology (ICECA)*. IEEE. (Vol. 2, pp. 186–189).

23. Lee, K. S., Tran, N. T., & Cheung, N. M. (2021). Infomax-GAN: Improved adversarial image generation via information maximization and contrastive learning. In *Proceedings of the IEEE/CVF Winter Conference on Applications of Computer Vision* (Vol. 3, pp. 3942–3952).

24. Li, Y., Tang, S., Zhang, R., Zhang, Y., Li, J., & Yan, S. (2019). Asymmetric GAN for unpaired image-to-image translation. *IEEE Transactions on Image Processing, 28*(12), 5881–5896.

25. Lin, J., Xia, Y., Qin, T., Chen, Z., & Liu, T. Y. (2018). Conditional image-to-image translation. In *Proceedings of the IEEE Conference on Computer Vision and Pattern Recognition* (Vol. 3, pp. 5524–5532).

26. Ling, H., Kreis, K., Li, D., Kim, S. W., Torralba, A., & Fidler, S. (2021). EditGAN: High-precision semantic image editing. *Advances in Neural Information Processing Systems, 34*, 16331–16345.

27. Liu, M. Y., Breuel, T., & Kautz, J. (2017). Unsupervised image-to-image translation networks. *Advances in Neural Information Processing Systems, 30*, 852–855.

28. Ma, Y., Liu, K., Guan, Z., Xu, X., Qian, X., & Bao, H. (2018). Background augmentation generative adversarial networks (BAGANs): Effective data generation based on GAN-augmented 3D synthesizing. *Symmetry, 10*(12), 734.

29. Pan, Z., Yu, W., Wang, B., Xie, H., Sheng, V. S., Lei, J., & Kwong, S. (2020). Loss functions of generative adversarial networks (GANs): Opportunities and challenges. *IEEE Transactions on Emerging Topics in Computational Intelligence, 4*(4), 500–522.

30. Rossi, M., & Cerveri, P. (2021). Comparison of supervised and unsupervised approaches for the generation of synthetic CT from cone-beam CT. *Diagnostics, 11*(8), 1435.

31. Sampath, V., Maurtua, I., Aguilar Martin, J. J., & Gutierrez, A. (2021). A survey on generative adversarial networks for imbalance problems in computer vision tasks. *Journal of Big Data, 8*, 1–59.

32. Shen, Z., Huang, M., Shi, J., Xue, X., & Huang, T. S. (2019). Towards instance-level image-to-image translation. In *Proceedings of the IEEE/CVF Conference on Computer Vision and Pattern Recognition* (Vol. 3, pp. 3683–3692).

33. Sidorov, O. (2019). Changing the image memorability: From basic photo editing to GANs. In *Proceedings of the IEEE/CVF Conference on Computer Vision and Pattern Recognition Workshops* (Vol. 1, pp. 890–895).

34. Wang, T. C., Liu, M. Y., Zhu, J. Y., Tao, A., Kautz, J., & Catanzaro, B. (2018). High-resolution image synthesis and semantic manipulation with conditional GANs. In *Proceedings of the IEEE Conference on Computer Vision and Pattern Recognition* (Vol. 2, pp. 8798–8807).

35. Xiong, F., Wang, Q., & Gao, Q. (2019). Consistent embedded GAN for image-to-image translation. *IEEE Access, 7*, 126651–126661.

36. Yi, Z., Zhang, H., Tan, P., & Gong, M. (2017). DualGAN: Unsupervised

dual learning for image-to-image translation. In *Proceedings of the IEEE International Conference on Computer Vision* (Vol. 3, pp. 2849–2857).

37. Yuan, R., Wang, B., Mao, Z., & Watada, J. (2021). Multi-objective wind power scenario forecasting based on PG-GAN. *Energy, 226*, 120379.
38. Zhang, G. Y., Tong, Y. Z., Yang, Z. J., Jin, S. X., Li, J., & Gan, Z. Z. (1997). Relationship of background carrier concentration and defects in GaN grown by metalorganic vapor phase epitaxy. *Applied Physics Letters, 71*(23), 3376–3378.
39. Zhu, X., Zhang, L., Zhang, L., Liu, X., Shen, Y., & Zhao, S. (2020). GAN-based image super-resolution with a novel quality loss. *Mathematical Problems in Engineering, 2020*, 1–12.

CHAPTER 7

PRACTICAL APPLICATIONS OF GANS

LEARNING OBJECTIVES

At the end of this chapter, readers will be able to:

1. Understand the versatility of GANs in different fields.
2. Comprehend the utilization of GANs in medicine.
3. Understand the benefits of utilizing GANs in the fashion industry.

INTRODUCTORY EXAMPLE

A pharmaceutical company named "MedTech Solutions" specializes in developing diagnostic tools for medical imaging. By leveraging Generative Adversarial Networks (GANs), MedTech Solutions aims to enhance the accuracy of its diagnostic algorithms by generating synthetic medical images for training. This enables the company to overcome limitations associated with small or imbalanced datasets and improve the performance of its diagnostic tools, ultimately leading to more precise and reliable medical diagnoses.

UNIT INTRODUCTION

While the applications of GANs extend beyond the realm of creating realistic handwritten digits and transforming objects, their potential in various fields is truly remarkable. This chapter explores the practical uses of GANs, showcasing their real-world usefulness. It appropriately highlights the areas in which GANs have been utilized for practical purposes. This exploration will encompass the driving forces behind these applications, their compatibility with advancements facilitated by GANs, and the strategies employed by creators for implementation (Alqahtani et al., 2021). The analysis will cover various applications of GANs in the fields of medicine and fashion, selected based on specific criteria:

a) They demonstrate the significant value of GANs, focusing on both academic and business perspectives. They demonstrate the practical applications of the cutting-edge research conducted by GAN scholars.

b) The chapter covers tools and techniques that make GAN models more accessible and comprehensible. Instead of exploring novel ideas, the potential applications of the models implemented beyond the MNIST dataset will be examined (Porkodi et al., 2023).

c) They can be easily comprehended without requiring specialized domain knowledge. For instance, the utilization of GANs in the fields of chemistry and physics can be quite challenging to grasp for individuals who do not possess a solid foundation in these areas (Saxena & Cao, 2021).

In addition, the selected fields and examples demonstrate the wide range of applications for GANs. In the field of medicine, the application of GANs becomes evident when dealing with scenarios where data is scarce. In the realm of fashion, the applications of GANs in situations where there is an abundance of extensive datasets are discussed. Regardless of the reader's field of study or personal interests, the knowledge and techniques discussed in this chapter have wide-ranging applications (Sorin et al., 2020).

7.1. GANS IN MEDICINE

Learning objectives

- Understand the usage of GANs to enhance diagnostic accuracy
- Comprehend the methodoly to enhance diagnostic accuracy

This section will explore various applications of GANs in the field of medicine (Gupta et al., 2020). Specifically, the utilization of synthetic data generated by GANs to augment a training dataset, thereby enhancing the accuracy of diagnostic procedures, is discussed (Jeong et al., 2022).

7.1.1. Using GANs to Improve Diagnostic Accuracy

The implementation of machine learning (ML) in medicine encounters various challenges that make it well-suited to benefit from GANs. One of the key challenges in obtaining training datasets for supervised ML algorithms is the difficulty in collecting sufficient medical data. Acquiring samples of health conditions can be quite costly and impractical. Acquiring datasets for optical character recognition (OCR) or self-driving cars is relatively straightforward, as they are readily available. However, obtaining examples of medical conditions is more challenging, as they necessitate specialized collection equipment (Maweu et al., 2021). Furthermore, it is crucial to imposessider the significant concerns surrounding patient privacy, which impose restrictions on the collection and utilization of medical data. Obtaining medical datasets can be quite challenging, especially when it comes to accurately labeling the data. This task often requires the expertise of individuals who are well-versed in a specific medical condition. Consequently, numerous medical applications have been unfit to take advantage of the progress made in deep learning and AI. Several methods have been devised to tackle the issue of limited labeled datasets (Segal et al., 2021).

In certain scenarios, when dealing with a substantial dataset, it can be advantageous to employ semi-supervised learning. This approach proves particularly useful when only a fraction of the dataset is labeled. In numerous medical applications, the presence of labels for a small fraction of the dataset poses a significant challenge. This limited portion of data often represents the entirety of available information. Put simply, numerous extra samples from the identical field that are ready to be labeled or utilized in a semi-supervised manner do not exist. Medical researchers are dedicated to addressing the issue of limited datasets through the utilization of data-augmentation techniques. When it comes to images, various adjustments and modifications can be made, such as scaling, translations, and rotations (Shah et al., 2022). These techniques enable the generation of multiple additional examples from a single one, effectively increasing the size of the dataset.

Figure 7.1 displays various data augmentations frequently employed in computer vision. Traditional data augmentation methods have several limitations. Additionally, slight adjustments result in examples that stay closely aligned with the original image. Consequently, the supplementary examples fail to contribute significant diversity in aiding the algorithm's ability to generalize. When it comes to handwritten digits, it's fascinating to explore the various writing styles that can be used to depict the number 6, rather than just seeing different versions of the same image (Marcadent et al., 2020). When it comes to medical diagnostics, it is crucial to have a variety of examples showcasing the identical underlying pathology. Expanding the dataset with artificial examples, like those generated by GANs, can enhance the existing data beyond conventional augmentation methods. That is precisely what the Israeli scientists Maayan Frid-Adar, Michal Amitai, Eyal Klang, Hayit Greenspan, and Jacob Goldberger aimed to explore (Tekchandani et al., 2020).

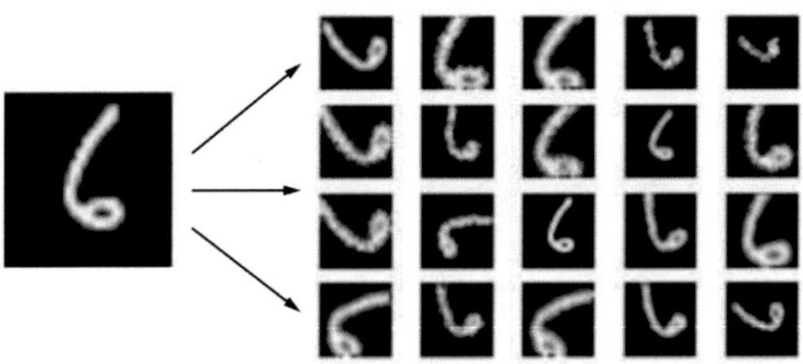

Figure 7.1. *Examples of data augmentations used in computer vision.*

Source: Bharath Raj, Creative Commons License.

Intrigued by the potential of GANs to generate realistic images across various fields, Frid-Adar and her fellow researchers embarked on a research journey to investigate the application of GANs in augmenting medical data. The researchers decided to concentrate their efforts on enhancing the categorization of liver lesions (Wali et al., 2023). One of the main reasons for their interest in the liver is its high prevalence as a site for metastatic cancer. In 2012, liver cancer alone accounted for over 745,000 deaths, making it one of the top three primary sites for this type of cancer. Accordingly, the development of methods and ML models that can assist doctors in diagnosing at-risk patients holds immense potential to save lives and enhance outcomes for numerous patients (Xiao et al., 2021).

Did You Know?

GANs have been used to generate synthetic medical images for various applications, including detecting tumors in MRI scans, identifying abnormalities in X-rays, and segmenting organs in CT scans.

7.1.2. Methodology

Frid-Adar and her colleagues faced a challenging predicament: they aimed to train a GAN to enhance a limited dataset, yet GANs inherently require a substantial amount of data for training purposes. Put simply, they aimed to utilize GANs to generate a substantial dataset. However, they faced the challenge of requiring a sizable dataset to initially train the GAN. Their solution was incredibly clever. Initially, conventional data-augmentation techniques were employed to expand the dataset. Furthermore, the dataset was utilized to train an academic model that generates synthetic examples (Vaccari et al., 2021). The researchers utilized the expanded dataset from the initial step in conjunction with the synthetic examples generated by the GAN in the subsequent step to train a classifier for liver lesions. Highlighting the versatility of GANs in various datasets and situations, Frid-Adar et al. found that they only needed to make minor adjustments and customizations to adapt the DCGAN to their specific requirements. As shown in Figure 7.2, certain adjustments were required for the model, specifically the dimensions of the layers that are hidden and the dimensions of the output of the Generator and input to the Discriminator network (Armanious et al., 2020).

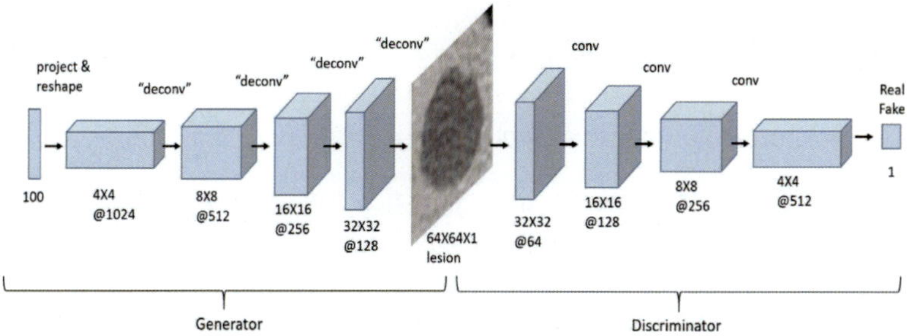

__Figure 7.2.__ Diagram of the DCGAN model architecture to generate synthetic images of liver lesions (Source: Maayan Frid-Adar, Creative Commons License).

This GAN focuses on images that have dimensions of 64 × 64 × 1, rather than the 28 × 28 × 1 sized image found in the MNIST dataset. As mentioned in their paper, Frid-Adar et al. also utilized 5 × 5 convolutional kernels. However, this adjustment to the network hyperparameters is relatively minor. Aside from the image size, which is determined by the training data, it is highly likely that all of these adjustments were made through a process of trial and error. The researchers continued to fine-tune the parameters till the model generated images that met their expectations (Uzunova et al., 2019).

7.1.3. Results

By employing DCGAN for data augmenting, Frid-Adar and her team were able to achieve a notable enhancement in classification accuracy when compared to the baseline approach of standard data augmentation alone (Lee et al., 2020). The findings are presented in Figure 7.3, illustrating the relationship between the total number of training instances (x-axis) and the classification accuracy (y-axis).

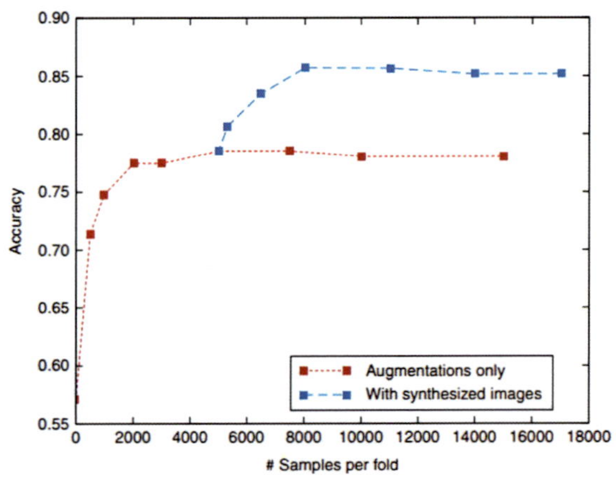

Figure 7.3. *Representation of the classification accuracy as new examples are added using two dataset augmentation strategies.*

Source: David Salomon, Creative Commons License.

The dashed line represents the classification performance when using traditional data augmentation techniques. As more training examples are added, the performance gets better. However, there comes a point where the improvement levels off at around 80% accuracy. Adding more examples beyond this point does not lead to any further improvement (Middel et al., 2019). The dotted line illustrates the further improvement in accuracy obtained by enhancing the dataset with synthetic examples generated by GANs. After reaching the limit where traditional augmented examples no longer improved accuracy, Frid-Adar et al. introduced synthetic data generated by their DCGAN model. The classification's performance saw a significant improvement, going from approximately 80% to over 85%. This showcases the practicality and effectiveness of GANs in this context. Data augmentation through synthetic examples produced by GANs can be highly beneficial for various data-constrained use cases in the field of medicine, including the improved categorization of liver lesions. As an illustration, a group of researchers at Imperial College London, led by Christopher Bowles, utilized advanced techniques in the field of ML to enhance brain segmentation tasks. Their work involved the application of cutting-edge methods such as Progressive GANs. Significantly, enhancing performance can greatly improve the practical applicability of a model, particularly in critical domains such as medicine, where precision can have life-saving implications (Kazeminia et al., 2020).

7.2. GANS IN FASHION

Learning objectives

- Comprehend the usage of GANs in fashion industry and understand the methodology.

In contrast to the challenges faced in medicine, fashion researchers have the advantage of having access to vast datasets. Popular social media platforms such as Instagram and Pinterest are filled with a vast array of images showcasing various outfits and clothing pieces. In addition, major online retailers like Amazon and eBay possess extensive data on several million purchases, ranging from garments to dresses. Aside from the abundance of data, numerous other factors make fashion a perfect fit for AI applications. Customer preferences in fashion can vary widely, and the potential for personalizing content offers valuable business advantages. Furthermore, the ever-changing nature of fashion trends necessitates swift reactions and adaptability from retailers and brands to cater to evolving customer preferences. This section discusses the creative applications of GANs in the realm of fashion (Sohn et al., 2020).

7.2.1. Using GANs to Design Fashion

Amazon has been making waves in the news with its futuristic ventures, ranging from drone shipping to cashier-less grocery stores. In 2017, Amazon achieved another milestone, this time focusing on the company's aspiration to create an AI fashion artist solely through advanced techniques. The article, featured in

MIT Technology Review, lacks specific information apart from the reference to utilizing GANs for creating products that align with a specific esthetic (Kato et al., 2019). Fortunately, a group of academics from Adobe and the University of California recently published a paper with a shared objective. Their approach provides insight into the inner workings of Amazon's AI research labs, which are dedicated to revolutionizing the fashion industry. With a vast dataset of numerous users, products, and reviews obtained from Amazon, Wang-Cheng Kang, the lead author, and his collaborators successfully developed two distinct models. One model focuses on providing fashion recommendations, while the other model specializes in generating fashion designs. Understanding the model's functionality is crucial: it provides a preference score for any person-item pair, indicating the suitability of the item based on the person's tastes (Cui et al., 2018). This model is a lot more innovative and captivating—not only due to its utilization of cutting-edge techniques but also because of the two imaginative applications Kang and his colleagues developed:

a) Designing fresh fashion pieces that perfectly align with an individual's unique fashion sense.
b) Recommending customized modifications to current items, tailored to an individual's specific fashion preferences.

This section delves into the methods employed by Kang and his team to accomplish these objectives (Singh et al., 2020).

7.2.2. Methodology

Kang and his colleagues utilize a Conditional GAN (CGAN), incorporating a product's group as the conditioning label. The dataset includes six categories, namely tops for both men and women, bottoms for both men and women and shoes for both men and women. As mentioned in Chapter 8, MNIST labels were used to instruct a CGAN in generating various handwritten digits according to varying preferences. Following a similar approach, Kang et al. utilize labeled categories to train their CGAN to generate fashion items that fall within a specific category (Ak et al., 2019). In a GAN, the Generator utilizes random noise and conditioning information to create synthetic images, while the Discriminator evaluates the authenticity of a given image-category pair. Through this adversarial process, GANs can generate remarkably realistic outputs. Figure 7.4 provides a comprehensive overview of the network architecture utilized by Kang et al. The diagram illustrates the different layers in the model. Each box represents a layer, with "fc" indicating a fully connected layer. The "st" notation represents the strides for the convolutional kernel, with the dimensions specified as the first two values in the conv/deconv layers (Mishra et al., 2024). The terms "deconv" and "conv" indicate the type of layer used, either a regular or a transposed convolution. The depth of the layer, or the total number of convolutional filters used, is determined by the number immediately following the conv or deconv. The use of batch normalization on the output of the ascribed layer is indicated. Additionally, it is worth mentioning that Kang et al. opted for the utilization of least squares loss as opposed to cross-entropy loss. With a CGAN at their disposal, capable of generating lifelike clothing items for various upper-level categories in their data set, Kang and his fellow researchers conducted experiments on two promising applications: designing unique personalized items and customizing existing items to suit individual preferences (Jetchev & Bergmann, 2017).

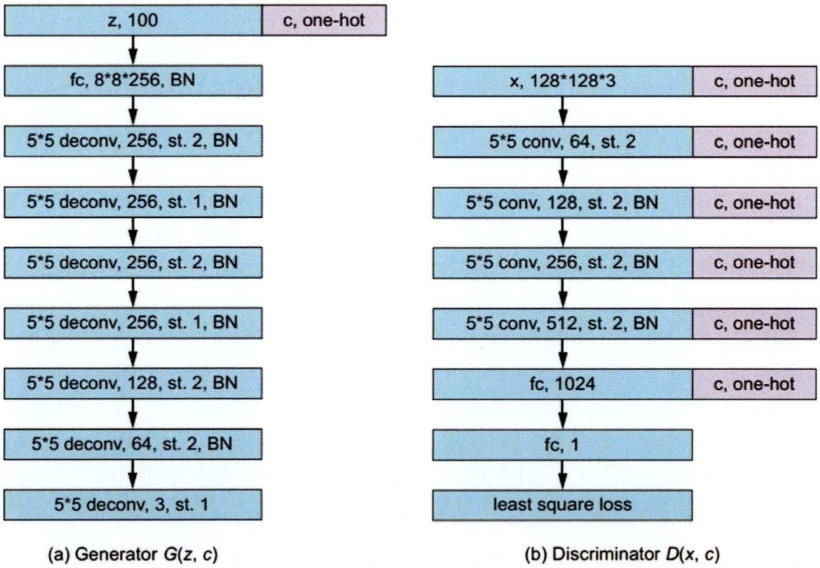

Figure 7.4. *Illustration of the architecture of CGAN Generator and Discriminator network used by Kang et al in their study.*

Source: Weng-Chang Kang, Creative Commons License.

Practice Problem

Evaluate the impact of GANs on enhancing the online shopping experience in the fashion industry. Compare and contrast the advantages and disadvantages of virtual try-on experiences enabled by GANs.

Solution to Practice Problem

GANs enhance the online shopping experience by providing virtual try-on experiences, allowing customers to visualize how clothing items would look on them without physically trying them on. This reduces the need for returns and increases customer satisfaction. However, challenges include accurately representing different body shapes and sizes and ensuring the realism of generated images.

7.2.3. Creating New Items Matching Individual Preferences

To ensure that the generated images cater to an individual's unique fashion preferences, Kang and his colleagues devised a clever methodology. They began with a fascinating observation: by generating new items that maximize the preference score assigned by their recommendation model, they could create items that perfectly match a person's style and taste (Liu et al., 2019). According to Kang et al., this process is referred to as preference maximization, drawing inspiration from economics and choice theory. What sets Kang et al.'s approach apart is that they go beyond the limitations of the training data or the entire Amazon catalog when considering the number of possible items. With the help of their CGAN, they can finely adjust the creation of novel items to an almost limitless level of detail. The next challenge that Kang and his coworkers faced was to ensure that the CGAN Generator could create a fashion item that would perfectly cater to individual preferences. Ultimately, their Conditional Generative Adversarial Network (CGAN) was specifically trained to generate visually convincing images within a specific category, rather than focusing on generating images of specific individuals (Kang et al., 2017).

One potential approach could involve continuously generating images and evaluating their preference scores until a satisfactory level of quality is reached. Nevertheless, considering the vast array of image possibilities that can be produced, this method would prove to be highly inefficient and time-consuming. Rather, Kang and his team approached the problem by reframing it as an optimization challenge: specifically, constraint maximization. The limitation of their algorithm is determined by the capacity of the latent space, which is defined by the vector z. Kang et al. utilized a conventional size of 100-dimensional vector, with each number falling within the range of -1 to 1. To ensure that the values can be utilized in an optimization algorithm, the authors of the study decided to apply the tanh function to each element in vector z. These elements were initially assigned random values. The researchers then utilized gradient ascent in their study. Gradient ascent is like gradient descent but with a different objective. Instead of minimizing a cost function by moving toward the steepest decrease, it aims to maximize a reward function by moving toward the steepest increase (Deldjoo et al., 2023).

The results by Kang et al. can be observed in Figure 7.5, where the three best images from the dataset are compared with the top three images generated for six distinct people. Kang et al.'s solution demonstrates remarkable ingenuity, as evidenced by the examples they generated. These examples received higher preference scores, indicating that they align more closely with the customer styles and preferences. The leftmost columns display the dataset items that have achieved the highest scores, while the rightmost columns showcase the generated items that have obtained the highest scores. According to the preference rating, the generated images align more closely with the shoppers' preferences. Kang and his team didn't stop there. They delved into the possibility of utilizing their developed model to customize existing items according to an individual's unique style, in addition to generating new ones. Considering the subjective aspect of fashion shopping, the ability to modify a garment until it meets the desired standards can bring substantial advantages to businesses (Yu et al., 2019).

***Figure** 7.5. Representation of top three results from datasets and GANs.*

Source: Julian McAuley, Creative Commons License.

Remember

GANs enable fashion designers to experiment with new designs and textile patterns by generating realistic images, accelerating the design process and fostering creativity and innovation.

7.2.4. Adjusting Existing Items to Match Individual Preferences

The values in the latent space, symbolized by the input vector z, hold significance in the real world. Additionally, vectors that are close to each other mathematically, measured by their separation in the high-dimensional space that they occupy, tend to generate similar images in terms of both content and style. As highlighted by Kang et al., a method to generate different versions of image A is to identify the latent vector zA, which the Generator utilizes to produce the image. Then, images can be generated by using vectors that are close to each other, resulting in similar images. Moreover, an input vector z' which, when passed through the Generator, generates an image depicting the number 9. If a vector z" that is very similar to z' in the 100-dimensional latent space is used as input, it will generate a slightly altered image of the number 8. This is depicted in Figure 7.6. In the realm of variational automatic encoders, the intermediate/compressed illustration functions identically to z in the realm of GANs (Men et al., 2020).

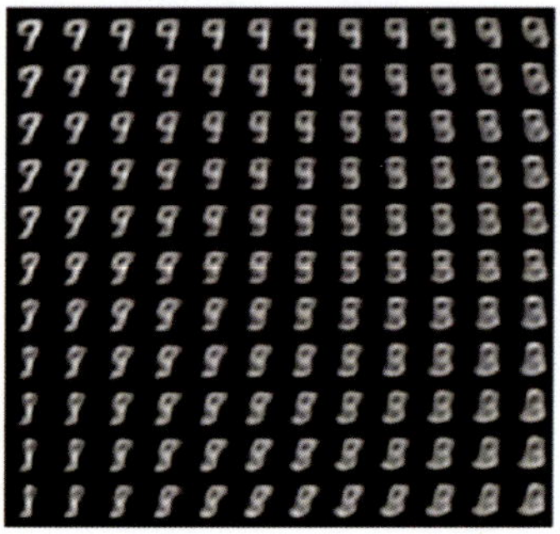

Figure 7.6. *Illustration of variations on digit 9 obtained by moving around in the latent space.*

Source: Jakub Langr, Creative Commons License.

Undoubtedly, in the realm of fashion, there exists a multitude of intricacies. Indeed, the complexity of a photograph of a dress far surpasses that of a grayscale picture of a numeral. Exploring the latent space using a vector can result in the creation of various T-shirt variations, including different colors, patterns, and styles such as V-neck or crewneck. It all comes down to the types of encoders and meanings that the Generator has internalized through training. Experimentation is key to gaining knowledge (Hsiao et al., 2019).

The next obstacle that Kang and his team had to tackle is discussed further. To successfully implement the method, it is essential to have the vector z corresponding to the image that requires modification. It would be quite simple if the intention was to alter a fabricated image. The track of the vector z could easily be kept every time an image was created, allowing it to be referenced at a later time (Cheng et al., 2021). The context becomes more complex when alterations to an actual image are required.

According to the definition, a genuine image cannot be created by the Generator, therefore the vector z does not exist. The goal is to identify a latent space illustration of a generated image that closely matches the one intended to be modified. In other words, it is necessary to locate a vector z that the Generator can utilize to create a synthetic image resembling the real image. This synthesized image can then serve as a substitute for the hypothetical z that could have generated the real image. That is exactly what Kang et al. accomplished in their research. As in previous instances, the scenario is initially framed as an optimization problem. A loss function is defined based on the reconstruction loss, which measures the distinction between two images. The magnitude of the loss indicates the level of dissimilarity between the images. After formulating the problem, Kang et al. proceeded to iteratively search for the most accurately generated image for any given real image using gradient descent, to minimize the reconstruction loss. After obtaining a fabricated image that closely resembles the authentic image, alterations can be made to it by manipulating the latent space. This is where the strategy devised by Kang and his fellow researchers demonstrates its full potential. By exploring the latent space, the ability to manipulate images to match the desired modifications is reached, all while considering the user's preferences (Wang et al., 2018).

Figure 7.7 illustrates the process at hand: From the left to the right in each row, shirts, as well as trousers, become increasingly customized. For example, the individual in the first row was seeking a more vibrant choice, while Kang et al. noted that the person in the fifth row appeared to prefer brighter colors and a more worn-out appearance. Additionally, it seems that the last person prefers skirts rather than jeans. This represents the pinnacle of hyper personalization. The first image on the left displays an authentic product taken from the training dataset, while the second image from the left showcases a generated image that closely resembles the real photo. This generated image served as the initial point for the personalization process. Every image is labeled with its preference rating. From left to right, the item is gradually optimized for the specific individual. The personalization process has shown significant improvement in matching items to the shopper's unique style and taste, as indicated by the rising scores (Jing et al., 2019).

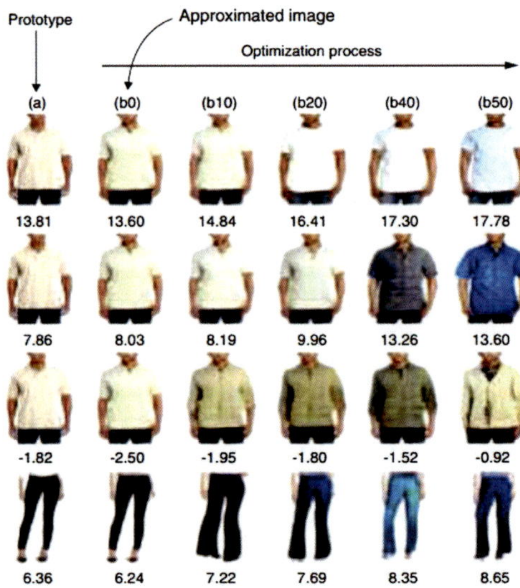

Figure 7.7. *Representation of the personalization process for six shoppers.*

Source: Chen Fang, Creative Commons License.

SUMMARY

- Due to the flexibility of GANs, they can be utilized for a diverse range of non-academic purposes and effortlessly adapted for applications beyond the MNIST dataset.
- In the field of medicine, GANs can generate artificial examples that can significantly enhance classification accuracy, surpassing the limitations of traditional dataset augmentation techniques.
- In the field of fashion, GANs have the potential to generate fresh designs and modify existing ones to align with individual preferences and personal styles. This is achieved by creating images that maximize the preference score given by a recommendation algorithm.
- The possibilities with GANs are far-reaching and extend beyond the applications discussed in this chapter. There are numerous applications in the fields of medicine and fashion, as well as in various other domains. It is undeniable that GANs have gone beyond the realm of academia and are now widely used in various applications that take advantage of their capability to generate lifelike data.

MULTIPLE CHOICE QUESTIONS

1. How are Generative Adversarial Networks (GANs) utilized in medicine?

a) Generating synthetic data for gaming applications

b) Creating virtual environments for therapy sessions

c) Generating synthetic medical images for training diagnostic models

d) Designing personalized treatment plans for patients

2. What role do GANs play in disease diagnosis?

a) Directly treating patients with medications

b) Generating realistic images of organs and tissues

c) Assisting in the development and evaluation of diagnostic algorithms

d) Conducting clinical trials for new drugs

3. How do GANs contribute to fashion design?

a) Generating synthetic music tracks for fashion shows

b) Designing virtual reality headsets for fashion events

c) Generating realistic images of clothing items and textile patterns

d) Producing 3D-printed accessories for fashion collections

4. What is one application of GANs in the fashion industry?

a) Designing virtual fitting rooms for online retailers

b) Manufacturing sustainable fabrics from recycled materials

c) Generating synthetic data for trend analysis

d) Developing biodegradable footwear for eco-friendly consumers

5. In which domain do GANs contribute to improving diagnostic accuracy and patient outcomes?

a) Agriculture

b) Finance

c) Healthcare

d) Transportation

REVIEW QUESTIONS

1. How are Generative Adversarial Networks (GANs) applied in the field of medicine? Provide examples of how GANs contribute to medical imaging and diagnosis.
2. Discuss the role of GANs in generating synthetic medical images for training diagnostic models. What are the potential benefits and challenges of using GANs in this context?
3. Explain how GANs are utilized in fashion design and retail. Describe specific applications of GANs in fashion, such as virtual try-on experiences and pattern generation.
4. What are some practical benefits of using GANs in the fashion industry? How do GANs enhance the online shopping experience for customers?
5. Compare and contrast the applications of GANs in medicine and fashion. What are the similarities and differences in how GANs are used in these two domains?

Answers to Multiple Questions

1. (c) 2. (c) 3. (c) 4. (a) 5. (c)

REFERENCES

1. Ak, K. E., Lim, J. H., Tham, J. Y., & Kassim, A. A. (2019). Attribute manipulation generative adversarial networks for fashion images. In *Proceedings of the IEEE/CVF International Conference on Computer Vision* (Vol. 2, pp. 10541–10550).
2. Alqahtani, H., Kavakli-Thorne, M., & Kumar, G. (2021). Applications of generative adversarial networks (GANs): An updated review. *Archives of Computational Methods in Engineering, 28*, 525–552.
3. Armanious, K., Jiang, C., Fischer, M., Küstner, T., Hepp, T., Nikolaou, K., & Yang, B. (2020). MedGAN: Medical image translation using GANs. *Computerized Medical Imaging and Graphics, 79*, 101684.
4. Cheng, W. H., Song, S., Chen, C. Y., Hidayati, S. C., & Liu, J. (2021). Fashion meets computer vision: A survey. *ACM Computing Surveys (CSUR), 54*(4), 1–41.
5. Cui, Y. R., Liu, Q., Gao, C. Y., & Su, Z. (2018). Fashion GAN: Display your fashion design using conditional generative adversarial nets. *Computer Graphics Forum, 37*, 109–119.
6. Deldjoo, Y., Nazary, F., Ramisa, A., Mcauley, J., Pellegrini, G., Bellogin, A., & Noia, T. D. (2023). A review of modern fashion recommender systems. *ACM Computing Surveys, 56*(4), 1–37.
7. Gupta, R., Sharma, A., & Kumar, A. (2020). Super-resolution using GANs for medical imaging. *Procedia Computer Science, 173*, 28–35.
8. Hsiao, W. L., Katsman, I., Wu, C. Y., Parikh, D., & Grauman, K. (2019). Fashion++: Minimal edits for outfit improvement. In *Proceedings of the IEEE/CVF International Conference on Computer Vision* (Vol. 2, pp. 5047–5056).
9. Jeong, J. J., Tariq, A., Adejumo, T., Trivedi, H., Gichoya, J. W., & Banerjee, I. (2022). Systematic review of generative adversarial networks (GANs) for medical image classification and segmentation. *Journal of Digital Imaging, 35*(2), 137–152.
10. Jetchev, N., & Bergmann, U. (2017). The conditional analogy GAN: Swapping fashion articles on people images. In *Proceedings of the IEEE International Conference on Computer Vision Workshops* (Vol. 1, pp. 2287–2292).
11. Jing, Y., Yang, Y., Feng, Z., Ye, J., Yu, Y., & Song, M. (2019). Neural style transfer: A review. *IEEE Transactions on Visualization and Computer Graphics, 26*(11), 3365–3385.
12. Kang, W. C., Fang, C., Wang, Z., & McAuley, J. (2017). Visually-aware

fashion recommendation and design with generative image models. In *2017 IEEE International Conference on Data Mining (ICDM)* (Vol. 2, pp. 207–216). IEEE.

13. Kato, N., Osone, H., Oomori, K., Ooi, C. W., & Ochiai, Y. (2019). GANs-based clothes design: Pattern maker is all you need to design clothing. In *Proceedings of the 10th Augmented Human International Conference 2019* (Vol. 1, pp. 1–7).
14. Kazeminia, S., Baur, C., Kuijper, A., van Ginneken, B., Navab, N., Albarqouni, S., & Mukhopadhyay, A. (2020). GANs for medical image analysis. *Artificial Intelligence in Medicine, 109*, 101938.
15. Lee, D. H., Li, Y., & Shin, B. S. (2020). Generalization of intensity distribution of medical images using GANs. *Human-Centric Computing and Information Sciences, 10*, 1–15.
16. Liu, L., Zhang, H., Ji, Y., & Wu, Q. J. (2019). Toward AI fashion design: An Attribute-GAN model for clothing match. *Neurocomputing, 341*, 156–167.
17. Marcadent, S., Hofmeister, J., Preti, M. G., Martin, S. P., Van De Ville, D., & Montet, X. (2020). Generative adversarial networks improve the reproducibility and discriminative power of radiomic features. *Radiology: Artificial Intelligence, 2*(3), 190035.
18. Maweu, B. M., Shamsuddin, R., Dakshit, S., & Prabhakaran, B. (2021). Generating healthcare time series data for improving diagnostic accuracy of deep neural networks. *IEEE Transactions on Instrumentation and Measurement, 70*, 1–15.
19. Men, Y., Mao, Y., Jiang, Y., Ma, W. Y., & Lian, Z. (2020). Controllable person image synthesis with attribute-decomposed GAN. In *Proceedings of the IEEE/CVF Conference on Computer Vision and Pattern Recognition* (Vol. 2, pp. 5084–5093).
20. Middel, L., Palm, C., & Erdt, M. (2019). Synthesis of medical images using GANs. In L. S. Jiao, F. R. Wong, J. Luo, Q. Zhang, & S. Chang (Eds.), *Uncertainty for Safe Utilization of Machine Learning in Medical Imaging and Clinical Image-Based Procedures: First International Workshop, UNSURE 2019, and 8th International Workshop, CLIP 2019, Held in Conjunction with MICCAI 2019, Shenzhen, China, October 17, 2019, Proceedings* (Vol. 2, pp. 125–134). Springer International Publishing.
21. Mishra, A., Kaintura, S., Yadav, Y. S., Joshi, V., Vaidya, H., & Kapruwan, A. (2024). GANs and augmented reality in virtual clothing try-on. In *2024 International Conference on Intelligent and Innovative Technologies in Computing, Electrical and Electronics (IITCEE)* (Vol. 2, pp. 1–6). IEEE.

22. Porkodi, S. P., Sarada, V., Maik, V., & Gurushankar, K. (2023). Generic image application using GANs (generative adversarial networks): A review. *Evolving Systems, 14*(5), 903–917.

23. Saxena, D., & Cao, J. (2021). Generative adversarial networks (GANs) challenges, solutions, and future directions. *ACM Computing Surveys (CSUR), 54*(3), 1–42.

24. Segal, B., Rubin, D. M., Rubin, G., & Pantanowitz, A. (2021). Evaluating the clinical realism of synthetic chest x-rays generated using progressively growing GANs. *SN Computer Science, 2*(4), 321.

25. Shah, P. M., Ullah, H., Ullah, R., Shah, D., Wang, Y., Islam, S. U., & Rodrigues, J. J. (2022). DC-GAN-based synthetic X-ray images augmentation for increasing the performance of Efficient Net for COVID-19 detection. *Expert Systems, 39*(3), 12823.

26. Singh, M., Bajpai, U., V, V., & Prasath, S. (2020). Generation of fashionable clothes using generative adversarial networks: A preliminary feasibility study. *International Journal of Clothing Science and Technology, 32*(2), 177–187.

27. Sohn, K., Sung, C. E., Koo, G., & Kwon, O. (2020). Artificial intelligence in the fashion industry: Consumer responses to generative adversarial network (GAN) technology. *International Journal of Retail & Distribution Management, 49*(1), 61–80.

28. Sorin, V., Barash, Y., Konen, E., & Klang, E. (2020). Creating artificial images for radiology applications using generative adversarial networks (GANs)–A systematic review. *Academic Radiology, 27*(8), 1175–1185.

29. Tekchandani, H., Verma, S., & Londhe, N. (2020). Performance improvement of mediastinal lymph node severity detection using GAN and Inception network. *Computer Methods and Programs in Biomedicine, 194*, 105478.

30. Uzunova, H., Ehrhardt, J., Jacob, F., Frydrychowicz, A., & Handels, H. (2019). Multi-scale GANs for memory-efficient generation of high-resolution medical images. In *Medical Image Computing and Computer Assisted Intervention–MICCAI 2019: 22nd International Conference, Shenzhen, China, October 13–17, 2019, Proceedings, Part VI* (Vol. 2, pp. 112–120). Springer International Publishing.

31. Vaccari, I., Orani, V., Paglialonga, A., Cambiaso, E., & Mongelli, M. (2021). A generative adversarial network (GAN) technique for internet of medical things data. *Sensors, 21*(11), 3726.

32. Wali, A., Ahmad, M., Naseer, A., Tamoor, M., & Gilani, S. A. M. (2023). StynMedGAN: Medical images augmentation using a new GAN model for

improved diagnosis of diseases. *Journal of Intelligent & Fuzzy Systems*, (Preprint), 7(2), 1–18.

33. Wang, T. C., Liu, M. Y., Zhu, J. Y., Tao, A., Kautz, J., & Catanzaro, B. (2018). High-resolution image synthesis and semantic manipulation with conditional GANs. In *Proceedings of the IEEE Conference on Computer Vision and Pattern Recognition* (Vol. 2, pp. 8798–8807).
34. Xiao, Y., Wu, J., & Lin, Z. (2021). Cancer diagnosis using generative adversarial networks based on deep learning from imbalanced data. *Computers in Biology and Medicine, 135*, 104540.
35. Yu, C., Hu, Y., Chen, Y., & Zeng, B. (2019). Personalized fashion design. In *Proceedings of the IEEE/CVF International Conference on Computer Vision* (Vol. 2, pp. 9046–9055).

CHAPTER 8

ADVANCED CONCEPTS IN GANS

LEARNING OBJECTIVES

At the end of this chapter, readers will be able to:

1. Understand the role of GANs in semi-supervised learning
2. Comprehend the responsibility of GANs for domain adaption
3. Comprehend integration of GANs with reinforcement learning
4. Gain knowledge about attention mechanisms in GANs
5. Understand the intersection of GANs and quantum computing
6. Recognize GANs in edge computing and IoT
7. Comprehend the theoretical limits of GANs

INTRODUCTORY EXAMPLE

In the realm of advanced technology solutions, "TechAdvance Innovations" stands as a pioneering company at the forefront of cutting-edge research and development. Leveraging its expertise in machine learning and artificial intelligence, TechAdvance Innovations has been exploring the frontier of Generative Adversarial Networks (GANs) to address complex challenges and unlock new opportunities in various domains.

Recently, TechAdvance Innovations embarked on a project to deploy GAN-based solutions in semi-supervised learning scenarios. Recognizing the potential of GANs to leverage unlabeled data for improved learning, the company aims to revolutionize the way machine learning models are trained and deployed across diverse industries.

As part of their initiative, TechAdvance Innovations is exploring novel applications of GANs in domains such as healthcare, finance, and autonomous systems. By harnessing the power of GANs for semi-supervised learning, the company seeks to enhance the performance and efficiency of machine learning algorithms, ultimately driving innovation and delivering value to their clients and partners.

UNIT INTRODUCTION

Generative Adversarial Networks (GANs) have quickly become a fundamental tool in the field of artificial intelligence (AI) and machine learning (ML) due to its unmatched capability to produce extremely lifelike data samples. GANs consist of two neural networks, namely a generator and a discriminator, that are trained concurrently in a competitive manner. The generator's objective is to generate data that is indistinguishable from real data, while the discriminator's goal is to accurately differentiate between real data and the data produced by the generator. The adversarial training enhances the ability of GANs to learn complicated and complex data distributions, allowing them to generate realistic images, text, audio, and other forms of data.

As the technology behind GANs becomes more developed, researchers are focusing more on investigating sophisticated themes that expand the potential of GANs beyond basic data creation jobs. The advanced topics covered in this context include a wide range of areas such as semi-supervised learning domain adaptation, integration with reinforcement learning, attention mechanisms, few-shot learning, data generation for graphs, quantum computing, adversarial attacks and robustness, applications in edge computing and IoT, transfer learning, and the generation of multimodal data. The purpose of this section is to establish a fundamental comprehension of these complex subjects, preparing the way for a thorough exploration of each area in the next sections (Saxena & Cao, 2021).

a) **Semi-Supervised Learning:** GANs have been successfully incorporated into semi-supervised learning frameworks, which represents a notable progress in their application. GANs utilize both labeled and unlabeled data in these configurations to enhance model performance, particularly in scenarios when acquiring labeled data is limited or costly (Sajun & Zualkernan, 2022).

b) **Domain Adaptation:** GANs play a crucial role in domain adaptation, which involves adapting models trained in one domain (source) to perform effectively in another domain (target), even when there is no labeled data available in the target domain. GANs enable this process by acquiring the ability to transform data from the original domain to the desired domain. This allows for the training of models using a diverse set of labeled data and subsequently applying them to distinct yet interconnected domains (Gu et al., 2019).

c) **Reinforcement Learning:** GANs have also been applied in reinforcement learning, specifically in contexts where conventional approaches face difficulties due to scant or misleading outputs. Here, GANs can produce artificial experiences that influence the learning process, effectively molding the reward environment to support the acquisition of intricate strategies (Willard et al., 2022).

d) **Attention Mechanisms:** Integrating attention mechanisms into GAN structures is a new area of advancement in GAN innovation. Attention methods enhance the quality of generated data and increase the stability and efficiency of GAN training by allowing models to concentrate on the key aspects of the data (Cui et al., 2024).

e) **Few-Shot Learning:** Few-shot learning with GANs is a study field focused on producing authentic data samples using a limited number of examples. This skill has substantial ramifications for situations in which data is scarce or costly to gather (Xi et al., 2020).

f) **Graph Data Generation:** With the growing prevalence of graph-based data in domains including social networks, biological networks, and communication networks, GANs have been modified to produce graph-structured data. This advancement creates new opportunities for enhancing, creating, and examining data in applications that utilize graphs (Blanchard et al., 2021).

g) **Quantum Computing:** The convergence of GANs and quantum computing is an emerging and auspicious field of study that investigates how quantum algorithms can augment the efficiency and capacities of GANs, potentially resulting in significant advancements in both domains (Hoo Teo et al., 2021).

h) **Malicious Attacks:** Comprehending and enhancing the resilience of GANs against malicious attacks is crucial for their secure implementation in practical scenarios. This entails the creation of techniques to identify and counteract attacks that are intended to deceive the models (Hashemi & Mozaffari, 2019).

i) **Edge Computing and IoT:** Utilizing GANs in edge computing and IoT devices allows for the generation and processing of data locally, which lessens the reliance on cloud-based services and tackles issues surrounding bandwidth, latency, and privacy (Hashemi & Mozaffari, 2019).

j) **Transfer Learning:** GANs are being utilized to enable transfer learning, where a model trained on one task is adjusted to perform a different but related task. This is especially valuable in situations where there is a scarcity of data available for the target task (Elaraby et al., 2022).

k) **Multimodal Data Generation:** GANs are currently being investigated for their ability to generate multimodal data by combining information from various data types. This results in the creation of diverse and intricate data samples that have a wide range of applications (Yuan et al., 2023).

Exploring these advanced topics expands the scope and applicability of GANs while also tackling the fundamental challenges of training and deploying them. The following sections will explore each of these topics extensively, providing insights into the most recent research discoveries, practical applications, and the potential influence of these advancements on the field of AI (Kadurin et al., 2017).

8.1. ROLE OF GANS IN SEMI-SUPERVISED LEARNING

Learning objectives

- Understand the integration of GANs in semi-supervised learning
- Comprehend the challenges of GANs in semi-supervised learning

GANs have demonstrated impressive capabilities in producing lifelike data from latent dimensions. Their distinctive architecture, which involves a generative network (G) pitted against a discriminative network (D), enables them to acquire knowledge of intricate data distributions. GANs have proven to be valuable in semi-supervised learning paradigms, showcasing their versatility beyond generative tasks. This section explores the incorporation of GANs into semi-supervised learning, providing a comprehensive analysis of the methodologies, advantages, and obstacles associated with this approach (Kumar et al., 2017).

Semi-supervised learning is a technique that falls between supervised and unsupervised learning methods. It makes use of both labeled and unlabeled data to train models. This learning methodology is especially beneficial in situations where obtaining labeled data is costly or impractical, but there is an abundance of unlabeled data. Through the integration of GANs into semi-supervised frameworks, model performance can be improved, even when there is a scarcity of labeled data (Dai et al., 2017).

Incorporating GANs into semi-supervised learning often requires making adjustments to the discriminator D so that it can handle more than just differentiating between "real" and "fake" samples. In this context, the discriminator D functions as a multi-task classifier. It not only determines the authenticity of inputs but also categorizes the samples into their respective classes, which includes an additional class for the generated samples (Chen & Chang, 2020).

Imagine a scenario with a semi-supervised setting where there are K real classes. Next, the discriminator D is expanded to produce K + 1 scores, representing the K classes and an extra class for the generated (or fake) samples. The result of D is a softmax function applied to K + 1 classes. This approach enables the discriminator to effectively learn from both labeled and unlabeled data. When working with labeled data, the cross-entropy loss is computed for the correct class, which makes D to enhance its classification accuracy. When working with unlabeled data, the discriminator is trained to differentiate between real and generated samples, helping to understand the underlying data distribution (Ding et al., 2018).

Training a GAN for semi-supervised learning requires a careful equilibrium between the generator and discriminator functions. One of the main difficulties in using GANs for semi-supervised learning is ensuring that the generator and discriminator perform at a similar level. An excessively strong generator has the ability to create fake samples that are so similar to the real ones that the discriminator is unable to effectively learn meaningful patterns from the data. On the other hand, an overly strong discriminator can effortlessly distinguish between genuine and generated samples, which can impede the generator's progress (Njima et al., 2022).

Another challenge in semi-supervised learning with GANs is the potential for model collapse, where the generator produces a limited variety of samples. This can be quite problematic, especially when trying to achieve balance in the generated data. To tackle these challenges, one must meticulously fine-tune model architectures, training procedures, and hyperparameters. Despite the difficulties, the application of GANs in semi-supervised learning has shown great promise in a wide range of fields, such as image classification, speech recognition, and natural language processing. Through the strategic utilization of unlabeled data, GANs within semi-supervised learning frameworks have the potential to achieve significant enhancements in performance, even when faced with limited amounts of labeled data (Chang et al., 2018).

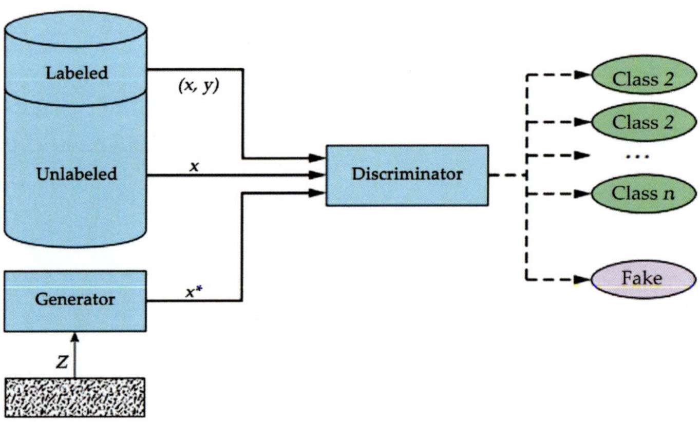

Figure 8.1. *Schematic of SGAN architecture.*

Source: Jakub Langr, Creative Commons License.

8.2. THE ROLE OF GANS IN DOMAIN ADAPTATION

Learning objectives

- Identify and understand the domain adaptation techniques
- Comprehend the challenges and potential applications of GANs in domain adaption

Domain adaptation is a significant hurdle in the realm of machine learning. The objective is to adjust a model that was trained on one domain so that it can effectively perform on a different, yet similar, domain. This becomes especially important when there is a lack of labeled data in the target domain or when such data is completely unavailable. GANs are a powerful tool for tackling this challenge. They can learn to transform instances from the source domain to match the appearance of the target domain, all while maintaining the underlying structure (Nidadavolu et al., 2019).

a) **Adversarial Domain Adaptation with GANs:** The fundamental concept consists of two primary steps. First, a GAN is trained on the data from the target domain, effectively learning the distribution of that particular domain. Afterwards, the generator that has been trained is utilized to convert the data from the source domain into a format that closely resembles the target domain. This process can be seen as a form of domain translation.

b) **Approach:** The process of GAN-based domain adaptation can be broken down into the following essential components:
   - The generator is responsible for transforming the data from the source domain to closely resemble the data in the target domain.
   - The discriminator is responsible for classifying data as either part of the target domain or generated by G.

c) **Objective Function:** The training objective can be represented as a min-max game between G and D, formally expressed by the equation(Balaji et al., 2020):

$$\min_G \max_D V(D,G) = \mathbb{E}_{x\sim p_{data}(x)}[\log D(x)] + \mathbb{E}_{z\sim p_z(z)}[\log(1-D(G(z)))]$$

where x is data from the target domain, and z is data from the source domain that has been mapped into the target domain by G.

8.2.1. Domain Adaptation Techniques

Several approaches enhance the basic domain adaptation capability of GANs:

a) **Feature-level Domain Adaptation:** It involves aligning the features of source and target domains in a shared feature space. GANs can be employed to learn a mapping that minimizes the distributional discrepancy between the domains at the feature level.

b) **Instance-level Domain Adaptation:** This technique focuses on transforming individual instances from the source domain to have the appearance of target domain instances, thus performing instance-wise adaptation (Song et al., 2020).

8.2.2. Cycle-Consistency

In order to maintain the important characteristics of the original instances, it is possible to introduce a cycle-consistency loss to ensure that the learned transformation is effective. This process follows a loop where an instance from the source domain is translated to the target domain and then back to the source domain. The goal is to minimize the disparity between the original source instance and the cycled source instance (Zhang et al., 2022).

8.2.3. Case Studies and Applications

Domain adaptation using GANs has proven to be effective in a wide range of domains. It has been applied successfully in computer vision to translate images, in natural language processing for style transfer, and in robotics to transfer simulations to real-world scenarios. These applications demonstrate the versatility and power of GANs in connecting various domains (Singhal et al., 2023).

GAN-based domain adaptation is a remarkable breakthrough in the realm of transfer learning and presents exciting opportunities for further investigation. Through ongoing improvements to the adversarial training methods and the integration of additional losses and constraints, it becomes feasible to attain greater accuracy in domain adaptation tasks.

This content provides a thorough exploration of domain adaptation using GANs, encompassing fundamental concepts, methodologies, objective functions, techniques, and potential applications (Choi et al., 2019).

8.3. INTEGRATION OF GANS WITH REINFORCEMENT LEARNING

Learning objectives

- Comprehend the approaches of integrating GANs with reinforcement learning.

Generative Adversarial Networks (GANs) and Reinforcement Learning (RL) are two highly influential paradigms in the field of machine learning, each possessing unique mechanisms and a wide range of applications. The combination of GANs and RL aims to harness the creative abilities of GANs and the problem-solving skills of RL to tackle intricate problems that are too challenging for either model on its own. This section delves into the integration of GANs with RL, discussing the advantages, difficulties, and practical uses of this combination (Kasgari et al., 2020).

An effective method for combining GANs with RL involves shaping the reward signal. Traditional RL algorithms typically focus on learning policies that aim to maximize the expected cumulative reward. Nevertheless, creating a suitable reward function can be quite difficult. Using GANs, it is possible to generate a curriculum of training scenarios that have varying levels of difficulty. This can greatly improve the training process for reinforcement learning.

This approach not only helps in tackling situations with limited and misleading rewards, but also fosters the exploration of novel strategies by the RL agent through ongoing adjustments to the environment's complexity. One approach to integrating the GAN's generator and the RL agent is through direct interaction. In this scenario, the actions of the RL agent have the ability to impact the training of the GAN's generator. As a result, the quality of the generated samples is affected, creating a feedback loop that benefits both models (Paul et al., 2022).

For example, picture an RL agent that is learning how to navigate through a virtual environment. An agent's current mastery level could be used to task a GAN with generating new and believable environments. As the agent continues to advance, the GAN adjusts the complexity of the generated environments, ensuring that the agent is always learning at the forefront of its capabilities.

Integrating GANs with RL has proven to be successful in domain adaptation. In this scenario, an RL agent trained in a source environment, which is generated by a GAN, can be adapted to perform effectively in a slightly different target environment. This is especially beneficial in situations where gathering extensive real-world data is not feasible.

Nevertheless, this integration presents certain difficulties. Ensuring the progression of GAN-generated environments aligns with the learning pace of the RL agent, maintaining the diversity and quality of generated samples, and optimizing computational efficiency are all crucial considerations that demand meticulous attention (Tian et al., 2020).

Applications of GANs integrated with RL are found in various fields. For example, in autonomous driving simulators, cars are able to learn how to navigate through environments that constantly change. Similarly, in game AI, agents are able to learn intricate strategies in environments that adapt to the agent's abilities.

In conclusion, the combination of GANs and RL presents exciting opportunities for further exploration and practical use. Through the integration of GANs' generative power and RL's decision-making abilities, the realm of AI can be expanded, resulting in Al systems that are more adaptable, efficient, and capable.

This section aims to give readers a comprehensive understanding of how GANs can be successfully combined with reinforcement learning. It will demonstrate the methodologies and potential implications of this integration through theoretical explanations and practical examples (Wang et al., 2017).

8.4. ATTENTION MECHANISMS IN GANS

Learning objectives

- Understand the rationale behind attention in GANs
- Comprehend the approach of implementing attention in GAN architectures
- Identify the impacts of attention mechanisms on GAN performance

GANs have made significant strides in a wide range of applications, mastering the art of generating data that closely resembles real data. Integrating attention mechanisms has been a crucial advancement in improving GAN performance. Attention mechanisms enable the model to direct its focus towards specific sections of the input data, resulting in enhanced quality and precision of the generated outputs (Daras et al., 2020).

8.4.1. Rationale behind Attention in GANs

Traditional GAN architectures may face difficulties in capturing long-range dependencies within the data or distributing computation resources evenly across different parts of an image. Attention mechanisms solve these problems by allowing the model to adaptively concentrate on important aspects of the input data while it is being trained.

When it comes to GANs, attention mechanisms can be incredibly useful for tasks like image generation. These mechanisms allow the model to focus on specific details, resulting in high-quality outputs. When generating faces, focusing on important features like the eyes or mouth can greatly improve the realism of the resulting images (Rice et al., 2023).

8.4.2. Implementing Attention in GAN Architectures

Attention mechanisms in GANs can be implemented in various ways. One common approach is to incorporate an attention layer into the generator and/or discriminator models. This layer is designed to learn how to prioritize different parts of the input data, enabling the model to concentrate on the most relevant areas for the given task.

This self-attention mechanism involves processing the input feature map to generate query, key, and value representations. The attention map is calculated by applying the softmax function to the dot product of the query and key. This map is then utilized to determine the weight of the value representation. The output feature map is generated by computing a weighted sum of the value representations, which enables the model to selectively focus on particular sections of the input (Ma et al., 2018).

8.4.3. Impacts of Attention Mechanisms on GAN Performance

Incorporating attention mechanisms into GAN architectures has been shown to result in several benefits:

a) **Improved Image Quality:** By focusing on salient parts of the image, GANs can generate more detailed and realistic images. This is especially noticeable in tasks requiring high reliability or fine-grained details.

b) **Enhanced Model Capabilities:** Attention allows GANs to handle more complex dependencies and patterns in the data, expanding their applicability to a wider range of tasks and datasets.

c) **Increased Efficiency:** By prioritizing certain parts of the input data, attention mechanisms can reduce the computational burden on the model, leading to faster training times and lower resource consumption.

However, the integration of attention mechanisms also presents challenges, such as increased model complexity and the need for careful tuning to avoid overfitting. Nevertheless, the benefits often outweigh these challenges, making attention a valuable component in the development of advanced GAN architectures (Ghaffarian et al., 2021).

8.5. GANS FOR GRAPHICAL DATA GENERATION

Learning objectives

- Understand the concept of graphical GANs
- Comprehend the training challenges and solution of graphical GANs

GANs have demonstrated impressive achievements in producing lifelike and top-notch images, texts, and audio. However, their application goes beyond these data modalities and includes more structured data types, like graphs. Graphs are found everywhere, depicting intricate connections in different fields such as social networks, biological networks, and communication networks.

Generating graph data presents distinct challenges due to the discrete nature of graph structures and the requirement to preserve valid connectivity patterns. This section will delve into the customization of GANs for generating graph data. The unique challenges, methodologies, and potential applications associated with this process will also be discussed (Figueira & Vaz, 2022).

In order to fully comprehend the utilization of GANs in graph data, it is crucial to have a solid understanding of the fundamental principles of graph theory. A graph G = (V,E) is made up of a collection of vertices V and a collection of edges E. Each edge e € E represents a connection between two vertices, indicating a relationship between them. Graphs have different types such as directed or undirected, weighted or unweighted. They can also have intricate patterns of connectivity that are significant in various applications. The main objective in graph generation is to create a graph G' that closely resembles a real graph G in terms of its structure, vertex properties, and edge distribution (Dinh et al., 2020).

Generating graphs using conventional GAN frameworks poses significant challenges. First of all, graphs have a discrete nature, while GANs generally function in a continuous space. Additionally, graphs can come in various sizes and topologies, posing a challenge when trying to utilize fixed-length vectors that are typically employed in GANs. In order to tackle these challenges, experts in the field have put forward GAN models that are specifically tailored for graph data (Tang et al., 2023).

8.5.1. Graphical Generative Adversarial Networks (GraphGANs)

GraphGAN is a novel approach that merges the traditional GAN architecture with graph representation learning, as introduced by Wang et al. The generator in GraphGAN is designed to generate adjacency matrices that represent graphs, while the discriminator's role is to differentiate between real and generated adjacency matrices. GraphGAN utilizes a Graph Convolutional Network (GCN) as a component of the generator to effectively handle the discrete nature of graphs. This allows the model to learn how to map noise to graph structures.

Creating adjacency matrices in GraphGAN poses a significant challenge of generating valid and realistic graphs. This is accomplished by utilizing a discriminator that assesses the authenticity of graphs by analyzing their structural characteristics and leveraging properties from graph theory (Kossaifi et al., 2018).

8.5.2. Challenges and Solutions

Training GANs for graph data generation presents extra difficulties. One of the main concerns revolves around mode collapse, where the generator tends to generate a limited range of graphs. To address this, one can apply techniques like feature matching and minibatch discrimination. In addition, it is important to consider the diversity of generated graphs, which can be achieved by using custom loss functions that discourage similarity and promote structural diversity (Zhu et al., 2022).

The application of GANs to graph data generation has far-reaching implications across a wide range of fields. GAN-generated graphs are commonly used in bioinformatics to model protein-protein interaction networks, which are crucial for drug discovery. Similarly, through social network analysis, researchers have the ability to simulate social structures in order to study the spread of information or diseases. In the field of telecommunications, GANs can be utilized to generate network topologies for the purpose of testing and optimization.

With the continuous evolution of GANs, their integration with graph theory and network science opens up exciting possibilities for cutting-edge research and practical applications. Further advancements in model development are expected to tackle current limitations, including the ability to generate large-scale graphs and enhance the accuracy and variety of the generated structures. With these advancements, GANs for graph data generation have the potential to completely transform the way to model, analyze, and comprehend intricate systems in various scientific and engineering fields (Pan et al., 2019).

Practice Problem

Discuss the challenges and opportunities in generating graph-structured data using GANs. Explore the applications of GANs in generating graphs with diverse topologies and attributes. Analyze the key considerations in training GANs for graph data generation tasks.

Solution to Practice Problem

Generating graph-structured data using GANs presents unique challenges due to the non-Euclidean nature of graphs and the complex relationships between nodes and edges. GAN-based approaches for graph generation typically involve learning a latent representation of the graph structure and generating new graphs from the learned representation. Challenges include ensuring graph consistency, preserving structural properties, and handling diverse graph topologies and attributes.

8.6. THE INTERSECTION OF GANS AND QUANTUM COMPUTING

Learning objectives

- Understand the development of quantum GANs
- Gain insight into potential applications of quantum GANs

The convergence of GANs and quantum computing is an exciting frontier in the realm of advanced ML and quantum information science. This section delves into the ways in which quantum computing principles can elevate GANs, the creation of quantum GANs (QGANs), and the possible applications of these cutting-edge computational models.

Quantum computing is based on the principles of quantum mechanics, where quantum bits or qubits are utilized instead of classical bits. Quantum computers have the remarkable ability to handle enormous amounts of data at incredible speeds, surpassing the capabilities of classical computers when it comes to solving specific problems. The combination of quantum computing and GANs presents exciting possibilities for enhancing the efficiency and capabilities of GAN algorithms. This integration has the potential to greatly improve the handling of complex datasets and speed up the training process (Pise et al., 2023).

8.6.1. Development of Quantum GANs (QGANs)

QGANSs utilize the unique properties of qubits to generate and differentiate data, harnessing superposition and entanglement. The structure of a QGAN closely resembles that of a classical GAN, comprising a generator and a discriminator. However, in a QGAN, these components consist of quantum circuits that manipulate quantum data. The quantum generator generates quantum states that represent data samples, while the quantum discriminator assesses and evaluates these states. During the training process, the quantum circuits of the generator and discriminator are fine-tuned to minimize the disparity between the generated quantum data and real quantum data (Kao et al., 2023).

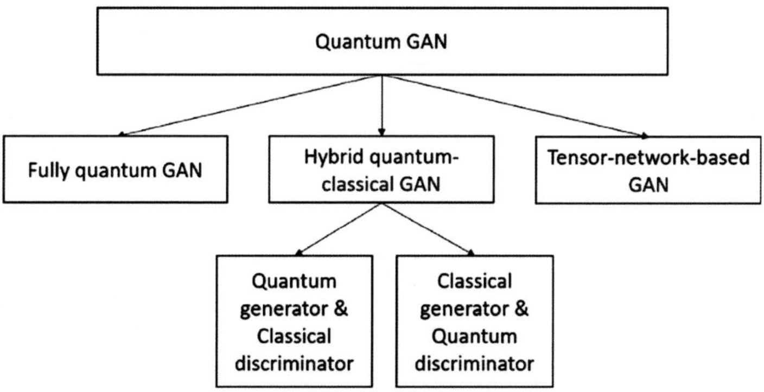

Figure 8.2. *Representation of QGAN structures.*

Source: Yahya Ibrahim, Creative Commons License.

The development of QGANs involves several key components:

a) **Quantum Circuits:** The design of quantum circuits for the generator and discriminator is crucial. These circuits must be capable of capturing the complexities of the data while being efficient enough to run on current quantum hardware.

b) **Hybrid Quantum-Classical Training:** Given the current stage of quantum technology, QGANs often employ a hybrid approach, where quantum circuits are optimized using classical computers. This involves the calculation of gradients through quantum circuit simulations or parameter shift rules.

c) **Quantum Data Encoding:** Encoding classical data into a quantum form is a significant challenge. Various encoding schemes, such as amplitude encoding and qubit encoding, are investigated to efficiently represent classical data in the quantum domain (Niu et al., 2022).

8.6.2. Potential Applications of QGANs

QGANs hold promise for a broad range of applications, including but not limited to:

a) **Drug Discovery:** By generating molecular structures as quantum states, QGANs can expedite the discovery of new drugs.

b) **Financial Modeling:** QGANs can simulate financial markets and instruments with complex quantum models, providing new insights into market dynamics.

c) **Quantum Data Compression:** QGANs can be used to compress quantum information, enabling more efficient use of quantum memory and transmission channels (Agliardi & Prati, 2022).

8.6.3. Challenges and Future Directions

Despite their potential, QGANs face several challenges:

a) **Hardware Limitations:** Current quantum computers have limited qubits and suffer from high error rates, constraining the size and complexity of QGANs that can be practically implemented.

b) **Scalability:** Scaling QGANs to handle larger datasets and models requires advancements in quantum hardware and algorithmic efficiency.

c) **Theoretical Understanding:** The theoretical framework for QGANs is still developing. A deeper understanding of their convergence properties, capacity, and limitation is needed.

Advancements in quantum technologies and algorithmic design are poised to tackle these challenges, opening up possibilities for widespread use of QGANs. The synergy between quantum computing and GANs promises to revolutionize machine learning, providing an exciting glimpse into a future where quantum-powered models can solve intricate problems that traditional computational methods cannot handle.

This section offers a comprehensive analysis of the emerging field that combines GANs and quantum computing. It delves into the development and potential of QGANs, while also discussing the challenges and future prospects in this exciting domain (Javeed et al., 2023).

8.7. ADVERSARIAL ATTACKS AND GANS' ROBUSTNESS

Learning objectives

- Comprehend the concept of GANs' robustness against adversarial attacks

GANs have shown impressive achievements in a wide range of domains, including image generation and natural language processing. However, similar to other ML models, GANs are susceptible to adversarial attacks. These attacks involve incorporating carefully designed alterations into the input data, which are typically undetectable by humans, yet have the potential to lead the model to produce incorrect results. Adversarial attacks carry significant consequences, especially in critical areas such as security and autonomous driving (Stutz et al., 2019).

There are two main types of adversarial attacks against GANs:

i. Training-Time Attacks

   These attacks are designed to disrupt the training process of a GAN. Injecting malicious data into the training dataset can lead to the generator producing undesirable outputs. When working with a conditional GAN, the generator's role is to generate output based on specific input conditions. However, it's important to be aware of potential attacks that can occur. These attacks involve manipulating the conditioning information, which can result in biased or incorrect model outputs (Pope et al., 2020),

ii. Test-Time Attacks

   On the other hand, test-time attacks center around manipulating the inputs to a trained GAN's generator or discriminator in order to produce inaccurate outputs. For instance, small adjustments to the input image may cause the discriminator to mistakenly classify a generated image as authentic (or the other way around).

Researching ways to enhance the robustness of GANs is crucial in addressing these vulnerabilities. There have been different strategies that have been suggested, including:

a) **Adversarial Training:** Incorporating adversarial examples into the training set can help improve the resilience of GANs. This method involves generating adversarial inputs and teaching the network to correctly handle them during training.

b) **Feature Squeezing:** This technique reduces the degrees of freedom available to an attacker by compressing the input data, thereby making it harder to craft effective adversarial examples.

c) **Detector Models:** Another approach involves training a separate model to detect adversarial inputs. This detector model works alongside the GAN, screening inputs and preventing adversarial examples from affecting the GAN's outputs.

d) **Defensive Distillation:** Defensive distillation involves training the GAN using outputs from a previously trained version of the model, which has been processed to make it harder for attackers to extract actionable information. This process can help in obscuring the gradients that attackers use to craft adversarial examples.

Despite ongoing efforts, the competition between those who create and those who protect against GANs remains relentless. Continual research aims to develop more robust defenses and gain deeper insights into the underlying vulnerabilities of GANs. Exploring the intrinsic vulnerabilities in the GAN architecture and developing new architectures that are naturally more resilient to adversarial manipulations is an exciting area of research.

When applying adversarial training, it is crucial to carefully design the perturbation function (δ). It is important for δ to generate adversarial examples that pose a challenge for the model while still staying close to the original data distribution. This ensures a balance between robustness and model fidelity.

In short, GANs provide impressive capabilities for generative modeling, but their vulnerability to adversarial attacks is a significant concern that needs to be addressed. Through the implementation of various defensive techniques like adversarial training, feature squeezing, detector models, and defensive distillation, one can significantly improve the resilience of GANs. With the continuous improvement in understanding vulnerabilities and defenses, the research on developing inherently robust GAN architectures holds great promise for the future (Chaudhury et al., 2021).

8.8. GANS IN EDGE COMPUTING AND IOT

Learning objectives

- Understand the process of optimizing GANs for edge deployment
- Comprehend GANs for data augmentation in IoT

GANs have revolutionized the field of AI, opening up exciting possibilities for a wide range of applications in various domains. When delving into the incorporation and application of GANs in Edge Computing and the Internet of Things (IoT), it becomes crucial to grasp the distinct possibilities and obstacles that arise in these settings. This segment explores the application of GANs in edge computing scenarios, with a focus on minimizing power consumption, decreasing latency, and safeguarding the privacy and security of data in IoT systems.

Edge Computing signifies a significant shift in data processing, moving away from centralized systems and towards the network's edge, where data is actually produced. This method optimizes speed, cuts down on expenses for transmitting data, and improves the overall performance of applications by handling data on a local level. When combined with IoT, which involves a vast network of interconnected devices generating large amounts of data, Edge Computing becomes crucial for time-sensitive applications by enabling real-time data processing (Pandey et al., 2023).

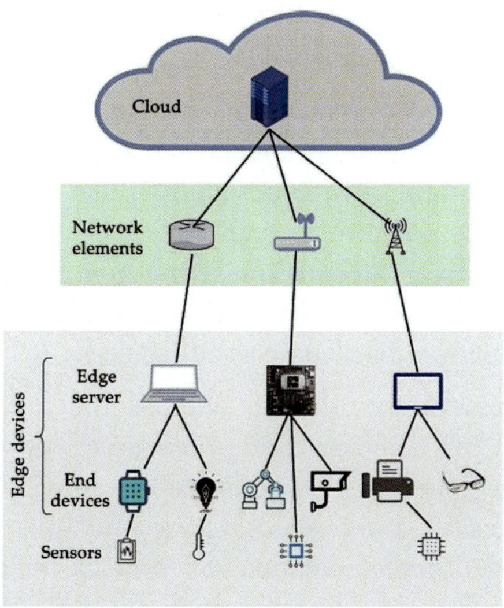

Figure 8.3. *Architecture of edge computing.*

Source: Visio Suite, Creative Commons License.

8.8.1. Optimizing GANs for Edge Deployment

Deploying GANs in resource-constrained environments, like edge devices in IoT systems, is a significant challenge due to the computational complexity arising from their dual-network architecture. Researchers have been working on creating GAN models that are both lightweight and computationally efficient, without compromising on their generative performance (Naeem et al., 2022).

8.8.2. GANs for Data Augmentation in IoT

Data augmentation is a key application of GANs in the realm of Edge Computing and IoT. For numerous IoT applications, the availability of labeled data is often restricted due to factors such as cost, privacy concerns, or the challenges involved in acquiring labels. GANs have the ability to create synthetic data, which can be incredibly useful for enhancing real datasets. This can greatly enhance the performance of ML models, all without the hassle of requiring large amounts of labeled data. The synthetic data generated is valuable for tackling the limited availability of training samples, especially in situations where gathering real-world data is difficult or impossible due to privacy issues or logistical limitations (Nie et al., 2021).

8.8.3. Privacy-Preserving Data Generation

Another important application of GANs in the realm of IoT involves creating synthetic datasets that protect privacy. IoT devices frequently gather sensitive data, which can lead to substantial concerns regarding privacy and security. GANs are useful for creating synthetic datasets that accurately replicate the statistical characteristics of the original data, all while guaranteeing the exclusion of any sensitive information. This approach enables the use of synthetic datasets for research and development purposes while safeguarding the privacy of individuals whose data was collected by IoT devices.

GANs offer a hopeful solution to address the inherent difficulties in Edge Computing and IoT, such as limited resources, privacy issues, and the lack of labeled data. Through the optimization of GAN architectures for edge deployment, the utilization of GANs for synthetic data generation and augmentation, and the implementation of privacy measures through the generation of synthetic datasets, the integration of GANs into Edge Computing and IoT has the potential to greatly improve the performance, efficiency, and security of these systems (Tabassum et al., 2022).

8.9. THE ROLE OF GANS IN GENERATING MULTIMODAL DATA

Learning objectives

- Understand the concept of conditioned GANs
- Comprehend cross-modal data generation

GANs are a powerful class of neural networks that have the ability to generate complex and high-dimensional data distributions. Generating multimodal data is an advanced application of GANs. The goal is to create outputs that encompass various modes or types of data, like texts, images, and sounds, using just one model. This potential has great potential to enhance the versatility of GANs in various fields such as multimedia content generation, data augmentation for machine learning, and improving human-computer interaction systems.

GANs are particularly useful for generating multimodal data because they can effectively grasp and reproduce the underlying distribution of input datasets that contain various data modalities. To accomplish this, specialized architectures and training techniques are utilized, designed to effectively handle the complexity and diversity of multimodal data (Kanezaki et al., 2019).

8.9.1. Conditioned Generative Adversarial Networks

Conditioning the generative model on additional information is a common approach in multimodal data generation with GANs. This additional information helps guide the generation process. As an example, a Conditional GAN (cGAN) has the ability to be trained in order to generate images based on textual descriptions. This allows for a translation from text to image, opening up new possibilities. By providing conditioning information, the GAN is able to understand the desired output mode and generate corresponding multimodal outputs (Duarte et al., 2019).

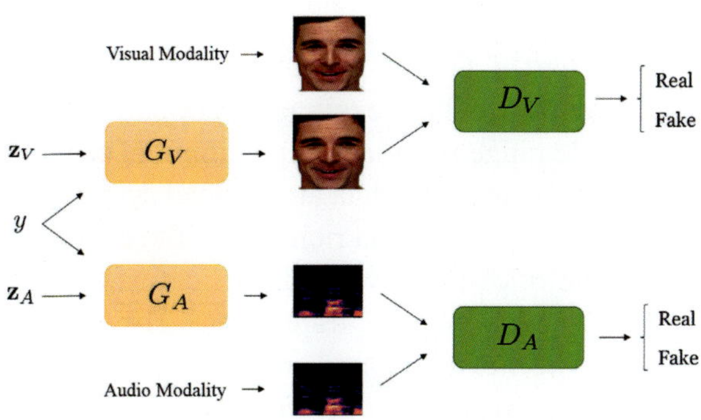

Figure 8.4. *Structure of multimodal conditional GAN.*

Source: Yang Li, Creative Commons License.

8.9.2. Multimodal Unsupervised Image-to-Image Translation (MUNIT)

The MUNIT framework is a significant advancement in generating multimodal data using GANs. It utilizes unsupervised learning to effectively convert images from one domain to another, while also preserving multiple potential outcomes for a single input image, resulting in a multimodal approach. MUNIT breaks down images into a content space that is shared by both domains, and a style space that captures the unique characteristics of each domain. By breaking down the input, MUNIT has the ability to manipulate style representations and generate a wide range of outputs in the desired domain. This showcases its capability to produce diverse multimodal data from a single input (Huang et al., 2018).

8.9.3. Cross-Modal Data Generation

GANs excel not only in translating data between different modalities, but also in creating brand new data examples that align across modalities. For instance, they can generate a textual description for an image or vice versa. Through the use of models that can learn joint distributions over different types of data, it becomes possible to synthesize related content across these modalities.

When it comes to modeling joint distributions, it is crucial to adapt GANs to effectively handle the unique characteristics and structures that are inherent in various data types. One way to achieve this is by integrating specialized network layers and architectures into the GAN framework. This helps to ensure that the generated content remains faithful and meaningful across different types of data.

With the combination of GANs and techniques designed for handling multimodal data, researchers now have exciting new opportunities for exploration and application in a wide range of fields. Expanding the capabilities of GANs to go beyond generating single-mode data and instead synthesizing multimodal data can greatly enhance the variety and richness of the content produced. This opens up exciting possibilities for advanced applications in content creation, data augmentation, and cross-domain translation. The continuous progress in this field highlights the flexibility and immense capabilities of GANs in modeling and generating intricate data distributions across various modalities (Hao et al., 2018).

8.10. THEORETICAL LIMITS OF GANS

Learning objectives

- Gain insight into the theoretical limits of GANs

GANs have made remarkable strides in the field of generative models in machine learning, paving the way for exciting applications in image synthesis and natural language processing. Nevertheless, ML models, including GANs, have certain theoretical and practical limitations that restrict their capabilities. Recognizing these limitations is essential for researchers and practitioners who want to enhance the effectiveness and efficiency of GANs.

GANs operate on the principle of an adversarial game, where a generator and a discriminator learn simultaneously through a minimax optimization framework. The generator's goal is to create data that is virtually identical to real data, while the discriminator's objective is to distinguish between real and generated data.

In this competitive setup, the goal is for the generator to replicate the data distribution so accurately that the discriminator cannot differentiate between real and generated samples. Nevertheless, attaining this balance in reality is filled with obstacles (Foschini & Gans, 1998).

One of the primary challenges with GANs is the issue of achieving convergence during the training process. Training GANs can be quite challenging due to their inherent instability and sensitivity to various factors such as hyperparameters, network architecture, and initial starting points of the generator and discriminator. GAN optimization is filled with challenges such as local minima, saddle points, and divergent behaviors, which can make it quite tricky to reach a stable Nash equilibrium.

The training dynamics are further complicated by the non-convex nature of the optimization problem. Efforts have been made to tackle these problems through theoretical advancements. As an illustration, the implementation of the Wasserstein loss function has demonstrated its ability to enhance the robustness of GAN training by offering a more significant evaluation of the disparity between the actual and generated data distributions. Despite the advancements made, establishing a training process that is globally stable continues to be a significant challenge.

One important limitation to consider is mode collapse, which occurs when the generator only produces a small range of samples and ignores other important parts of the data distribution. This phenomenon happens because the generator discovers ways to deceive the discriminator without fully understanding the entire data distribution. Various strategies have been suggested to address mode collapse, such as minibatch discrimination and unrolled GANs. However, it is important to note that no single solution has proven to be universally effective (Agrawal et al., 2019).

Expanding on the problem of mode collapse is the issue of sample diversity, which is closely related to the ability of GANs to create unique data points. In theory, a flawless GAN would accurately model the target data distribution.

However, in reality, finding the right balance between diversity (covering the entire range of the data distribution) and fidelity (accuracy of individual samples) is a challenging task.

In addition, the theoretical foundations of GANs indicate that although they are powerful generative models, their practical usefulness is greatly hindered by the complex and vast spaces in which they function. The issue of dimensionality has a significant impact on both the training process and the evaluation of GANs. Traditional metrics such as the Inception Score or Frechet Inception Distance may not provide a complete understanding of model performance and can be misleading or inadequate.

Although GANs are a remarkable type of generative models, their theoretical boundaries emphasize the challenges of learning data distributions in high-dimensional spaces. To overcome these limitations, it is crucial to constantly innovate in areas such as model architecture, loss functions, training algorithms, and more. As the field continues to develop, it is essential to grasp and explore the theoretical limits in order to fully unleash the potential of GANs across various applications (Farias et al., 1996).

SUMMARY

- This chapter explores how GANs can be leveraged in semi-supervised learning settings, where labeled data is scarce but unlabeled data is abundant.
- The chapter discusses the use of GANs for domain adaptation, where the goal is to learn a mapping between different domains with varying distributions.
- It examines the integration of GANs with reinforcement learning techniques to enable agents to generate realistic and diverse outcomes in interactive environments. GANs enhance the exploration-exploitation trade-off in reinforcement learning by providing a structured approach to sample generation.
- This chapter also explores the incorporation of attention mechanisms into GAN architectures to improve the generation of high-resolution and coherent images. The application of GANs for generating graph-structured data, such as molecular structures or social networks are also discussed. GAN-based models learn to generate realistic graphs by capturing the underlying graph topology and node attributes.
- The intersection of GANs and quantum computing, where quantum-inspired approaches are applied to enhance the efficiency and scalability of GAN training are part of this chapter. Quantum-inspired GANs leverage quantum computing principles to accelerate optimization and sampling processes.
- Finally, the chapter explores the use of GANs for generating multimodal data, including images, text, and audio, with diverse characteristics. GAN-based multimodal models enable the synthesis of data across different modalities, facilitating tasks such as image captioning and speech synthesis.

MULTIPLE CHOICE QUESTIONS

1. What is the primary objective of using GANs in semi-supervised learning?

a) Maximizing discriminative loss

b) Enhancing feature extraction

c) Leveraging unlabeled data for improved learning

d) Minimizing generative loss

2. How do GANs facilitate domain adaptation?
   a) By learning domain-specific features
   b) By minimizing the domain discrepancy
   c) By maximizing adversarial loss
   d) By increasing model complexity

3. What is the key advantage of integrating GANs with reinforcement learning?
   a) Improved convergence speed
   b) Enhanced exploration-exploitation trade-off
   c) Reduced computational complexity
   d) Increased model interpretability

4. What role do attention mechanisms play in GAN architectures?
   a) Enhancing discriminative loss
   b) Improving model regularization
   c) Focusing on relevant input regions
   d) Increasing model diversity

5. In which domain are GANs commonly used for generating graph-structured data?
   a) Computer vision
   b) Natural language processing
   c) Molecular design
   d) Speech synthesis

REVIEW QUESTIONS

1. How can GANs be utilized in semi-supervised learning?
2. Explain the concept of domain adaptation in the context of GANs. Discuss the challenges associated with domain adaptation.
3. What are some potential applications of integrating GANs with reinforcement learning?
4. How do attention mechanisms improve the performance of GAN architectures?
5. Describe the process of generating graph-structured data using GANs. What are the key challenges in generating realistic graph data, and how do GAN-based approaches address these challenges?

Answers to Multiple Questions

1. (c) 2. (b) 3. (b) 4. (c) 5. (c)

REFERENCES

1. Agliardi, G., & Prati, E. (2022). Optimal tuning of quantum generative adversarial networks for multivariate distribution loading. *Quantum Reports, 4*(1), 75–105.
2. Agrawal, A., Gans, J. S., & Goldfarb, A. (2019). Exploring the impact of artificial intelligence: Prediction versus judgment. *Information Economics and Policy, 47*, 1–6.
3. Balaji, Y., Chellappa, R., & Feizi, S. (2020). Robust optimal transport with applications in generative modeling and domain adaptation. *Advances in Neural Information Processing Systems, 33*, 12934–12944.
4. Blanchard, A. E., Stanley, C., & Bhowmik, D. (2021). Using GANs with adaptive training data to search for new molecules. *Journal of Cheminformatics, 13*, 1–8.
5. Chang, C. Y., Chen, T. Y., & Chung, P. C. (2018). Semi-supervised learning using generative adversarial networks. In *2018 IEEE Symposium Series on Computational Intelligence (SSCI)* (Vol. 3, pp. 892–896). IEEE.
6. Chaudhury, S., Roy, H., Mishra, S., & Yamasaki, T. (2021). Adversarial training time attack against discriminative and generative convolutional models. *IEEE Access, 9*, 109241–109259.
7. Chen, K. M., & Chang, R. Y. (2020). Semi-supervised learning with GANs for device-free fingerprinting indoor localization. In *GLOBECOM 2020-2020 IEEE Global Communications Conference* (Vol. 3, pp. 1–6). IEEE.
8. Choi, J., Kim, T., & Kim, C. (2019). Self-ensembling with GAN-based data augmentation for domain adaptation in semantic segmentation. In *Proceedings of the IEEE/CVF International Conference on Computer Vision* (Vol. 2, pp. 6830–6840).
9. Cui, Z., Chen, Q., Liu, G., & Xun, L. (2024). SA RelayGANs: A Novel Framework for the Characterization of Complex Hydrological Structures Based on GANs and Self Attention Mechanism. *Water Resources Research, 60*(1), 6546–6548.
10. Dai, Z., Yang, Z., Yang, F., Cohen, W. W., & Salakhutdinov, R. R. (2017). Good semi-supervised learning that requires a bad GAN. In *Advances in Neural Information Processing Systems, 30*, 324–330.
11. Daras, G., Odena, A., Zhang, H., & Dimakis, A. G. (2020). Your local GAN: Designing two-dimensional local attention mechanisms for generative

models. In *Proceedings of the IEEE/CVF Conference on Computer Vision and Pattern Recognition* (Vol. 1, pp. 14531–14539).

12. Ding, M., Tang, J., & Zhang, J. (2018). Semi-supervised learning on graphs with generative adversarial nets. In *Proceedings of the 27th ACM International Conference on Information and Knowledge Management* (Vol. 3, pp. 913–922).
13. Dinh, T. Q., Xiong, Y., Huang, Z., Vo, T., Mishra, A., Kim, W. H., & Singh, V. (2020). Performing group difference testing on graph structured data from GANs: Analysis and applications in neuroimaging. *IEEE Transactions on Pattern Analysis and Machine Intelligence, 44*(2), 877–889.
14. Duarte, A. C., Roldan, F., Tubau, M., Escur, J., Pascual, S., Salvador, A., & Giro-i-Nieto, X. (2019). WAV2PIX: Speech-conditioned Face Generation using Generative Adversarial Networks. In *ICASSP 2019* (Vol. 2019, pp. 8633–8637).
15. Elaraby, N., Barakat, S., & Rezk, A. (2022). A conditional GAN-based approach for enhancing transfer learning performance in few-shot HCR tasks. *Scientific Reports, 12*(1), 16271.
16. Farias, T. L., Köylü, Ü. Ö., & Carvalho, M. D. G. (1996). Range of validity of the Rayleigh–Debye–Gans theory for optics of fractal aggregates. *Applied Optics, 35*(33), 6560–6567.
17. Figueira, A., & Vaz, B. (2022). Survey on synthetic data generation, evaluation methods and GANs. *Mathematics, 10*(15), 2733.
18. Foschini, G. J., & Gans, M. J. (1998). On limits of wireless communications in a fading environment when using multiple antennas. *Wireless Personal Communications, 6*, 311–335.
19. Ghaffarian, S., Valente, J., Van Der Voort, M., & Tekinerdogan, B. (2021). Effect of attention mechanism in deep learning-based remote sensing image processing: A systematic literature review. *Remote Sensing, 13*(15), 2965.
20. Gu, Y., Ge, Z., Bonnington, C. P., & Zhou, J. (2019). Progressive transfer learning and adversarial domain adaptation for cross-domain skin disease classification. *IEEE Journal of Biomedical and Health Informatics, 24*(5), 1379–1393.
21. Hao, W., Zhang, Z., & Guan, H. (2018). Cmcgan: A uniform framework for cross-modal visual-audio mutual generation. In *Proceedings of the AAAI Conference on Artificial Intelligence* (Vol. 32, pp. 78–80).
22. Hashemi, A. S., & Mozaffari, S. (2019). Secure deep neural networks using

adversarial image generation and training with Noise-GAN. *Computers & Security, 86*, 372–387.

23. Hoo Teo, K., Zhang, Y., Chowdhury, N., Rakheja, S., Ma, R., Xie, Q., & Palacios, T. (2021). Emerging GaN technologies for power, RF, digital, and quantum computing applications: Recent advances and prospects. *Journal of Applied Physics, 130*(16), 9872–9875.
24. Huang, X., Liu, M. Y., Belongie, S., & Kautz, J. (2018). Multimodal unsupervised image-to-image translation. In *Proceedings of the European Conference on Computer Vision (ECCV)* (Vol. 2, pp. 172–189).
25. Javeed, D., Saeed, M. S., Ahmad, I., Adil, M., Kumar, P., & Islam, A. N. (2023). Quantum-Empowered Federated Learning and 6G Wireless Networks for IoT Security: Concept, Challenges and Future Directions. *Quantum, 96*, 1–8.
26. Kadurin, A., Nikolenko, S., Khrabrov, K., Aliper, A., & Zhavoronkov, A. (2017). druGAN: An advanced generative adversarial autoencoder model for de novo generation of new molecules with desired molecular properties in silico. *Molecular Pharmaceutics, 14*(9), 3098–3104.
27. Kanezaki, A., Kuga, R., Sugano, Y., & Matsushita, Y. (2019). Deep learning for multimodal data fusion. In A. K. Roy-Chowdhury & S. Sariyanidi (Eds.), *Multimodal Scene Understanding* (pp. 9–39). Academic Press.
28. Kao, P. Y., Yang, Y. C., Chiang, W. Y., Hsiao, J. Y., Cao, Y., Aliper, A., & Lin, Y. C. (2023). Exploring the advantages of quantum generative adversarial networks in generative chemistry. *Journal of Chemical Information and Modeling, 63*(11), 3307–3318.
29. Kasgari, A. T. Z., Saad, W., Mozaffari, M., & Poor, H. V. (2020). Experienced deep reinforcement learning with generative adversarial networks (GANs) for model-free ultra reliable low latency communication. *IEEE Transactions on Communications, 69*(2), 884–899.
30. Kaur, I., Lydia, E. L., Nassa, V. K., Shrestha, B., Nebhen, J., Malebary, S., & Joshi, G. P. (2022). Generative adversarial networks with quantum optimization model for mobile edge computing in IoT big data. *Wireless Personal Communications, 8*(4), 1–21.
31. Kossaifi, J., Tran, L., Panagakis, Y., & Pantic, M. (2018). Gagan: Geometry-aware generative adversarial networks. In *Proceedings of the IEEE Conference on Computer Vision and Pattern Recognition* (Vol. 2, pp. 878–887).
32. Kumar, A., Sattigeri, P., & Fletcher, T. (2017). Semi-supervised learning with GANs: Manifold invariance with improved inference. In *Advances in Neural Information Processing Systems, 30*, 987–992.

33. Ma, S., Fu, J., Chen, C. W., & Mei, T. (2018). Da-GAN: Instance-level image translation by deep attention generative adversarial networks. In *Proceedings of the IEEE Conference on Computer Vision and Pattern Recognition* (Vol. 1, pp. 5657–5666).
34. Naeem, F., Kaddoum, G., Khan, S., Khan, K. S., & Adam, N. (2022). IRS-empowered 6G networks: Deployment strategies, performance optimization, and future research directions. *IEEE Access, 10*, 118676–118696.
35. Nidadavolu, P. S., Kataria, S., Villalba, J., & Dehak, N. (2019). Low-resource domain adaptation for speaker recognition using cycle-GANs. In *2019 IEEE Automatic Speech Recognition and Understanding Workshop (ASRU)* (Vol. 2, pp. 710–717). IEEE.
36. Nie, L., Wu, Y., Wang, X., Guo, L., Wang, G., Gao, X., & Li, S. (2021). Intrusion detection for secure social internet of things based on collaborative edge computing: A generative adversarial network-based approach. *IEEE Transactions on Computational Social Systems, 9*(1), 134–145.
37. Niu, M. Y., Zlokapa, A., Broughton, M., Boixo, S., Mohseni, M., Smelyanskyi, V., & Neven, H. (2022). Entangling quantum generative adversarial networks. *Physical Review Letters, 128*(22), 220505.
38. Njima, W., Bazzi, A., & Chafii, M. (2022). DNN-based indoor localization under limited dataset using GANs and semi-supervised learning. *IEEE Access, 10*, 69896–69909.
39. Pan, S., Hu, R., Fung, S. F., Long, G., Jiang, J., & Zhang, C. (2019). Learning graph embedding with adversarial training methods. *IEEE Transactions on Cybernetics, 50*(6), 2475–2487.
40. Pandey, C., Tiwari, V., Imoize, A. L., Li, C. T., Lee, C. C., & Roy, D. S. (2023). 5GT-GAN: Enhancing data augmentation for 5g-enabled mobile edge computing in smart cities. *IEEE Access, 11*, 120983–120996.
41. Paul, N., Tasgaonkar, V., Walambe, R., & Kotecha, K. (2022). Integrating the generative adversarial network for decision making in reinforcement learning for industrial robot agents. *Robotics, 11*(6), 150.
42. Pise, S., Agarkar, A. A., & Jain, S. (2023). Unleashing the Power of Generative AI and Quantum Computing for Mutual Advancements. In *2023 3rd Asian Conference on Innovation in Technology (ASIANCON)* (Vol. 2, pp. 1–7). IEEE.
43. Pope, P., Balaji, Y., & Feizi, S. (2020). Adversarial robustness of flow-based generative models. In *International Conference on Artificial Intelligence and Statistics*. PMLR. (Vol. 2, pp. 3795–3805).

44. Rice, W. L., Shellhorn, J., Bloomgren, V., Booth, L., Duncan, S., Elias, J., & Winckler, C. (2023). The impact of graphic design on attention capture and behavior among outdoor recreationists: Results from an exploratory persuasive signage experiment. *Journal of Outdoor Recreation and Tourism, 42*, 100606.

45. Sajun, A. R., & Zualkernan, I. (2022). Survey on implementations of generative adversarial networks for semi-supervised learning. *Applied Sciences, 12*(3), 1718.

46. Saxena, D., & Cao, J. (2021). Generative adversarial networks (GANs) challenges, solutions, and future directions. *ACM Computing Surveys (CSUR), 54*(3), 1–42.

47. Singhal, P., Walambe, R., Ramanna, S., & Kotecha, K. (2023). Domain adaptation: Challenges, methods, datasets, and applications. *IEEE Access, 11*, 6973–7020.

48. Song, R., Cao, P., Yang, J., Zhao, D., & Zaiane, O. R. (2020). A domain adaptation multi-instance learning for diabetic retinopathy grading on retinal images. In *2020 IEEE International Conference on Bioinformatics and Biomedicine (BIBM)*. IEEE. (Vol. 2, pp. 743–750).

49. Stutz, D., Hein, M., & Schiele, B. (2019). Disentangling adversarial robustness and generalization. In *Proceedings of the IEEE/CVF Conference on Computer Vision and Pattern Recognition* (Vol. 1, pp. 6976–6987).

50. Tabassum, A., Erbad, A., Lebda, W., Mohamed, A., & Guizani, M. (2022). FedGAN-IDS: Privacy-preserving IDS using GAN and federated learning. *Computer Communications, 192*, 299–310.

51. Tang, H., Zhang, Z., Shi, H., Li, B., Shao, L., Sebe, N., & Van Gool, L. (2023). Graph transformer GANs for graph-constrained house generation. In *Proceedings of the IEEE/CVF Conference on Computer Vision and Pattern Recognition* (Vol. 2, pp. 2173–2182).

52. Tian, Y., Wang, Q., Huang, Z., Li, W., Dai, D., Yang, M., & Fink, O. (2020). Off-policy reinforcement learning for efficient and effective GAN architecture search. In *Computer Vision–ECCV 2020: 16th European Conference, Glasgow, UK, August 23–28, 2020, Proceedings, Part VII*. Springer International Publishing. (Vol. 2, pp. 175–192).

53. Wang, K., Gou, C., Duan, Y., Lin, Y., Zheng, X., & Wang, F. Y. (2017). Generative adversarial networks: Introduction and outlook. *IEEE/CAA Journal of Automatica Sinica, 4*(4), 588–598.

54. Willard, J., Jia, X., Xu, S., Steinbach, M., & Kumar, V. (2022). Integrating scientific knowledge with machine learning for engineering and environmental systems. *ACM Computing Surveys, 55*(4), 1–37.

55. Xi, Y., Yan, G., Hua, J., & Zhong, Z. (2020). JointFontGAN: Joint Geometry-Content GAN for Font Generation via Few-Shot Learning. In *Proceedings of the 28th ACM International Conference on Multimedia* (Vol. 3, pp. 4309–4317).
56. Yuan, C., Marion, T., & Moghaddam, M. (2023). DDE-GAN: Integrating a data-driven design evaluator into generative adversarial networks for desirable and diverse concept generation. *Journal of Mechanical Design, 145*(4), 041407.
57. Zhang, Z., Li, Y., & Shin, B. S. (2022). C2 GAN: Content consistent generative adversarial networks for unsupervised domain adaptation in medical image segmentation. *Medical Physics, 49*(10), 6491–6504.
58. Zhu, Y., Du, Y., Wang, Y., Xu, Y., Zhang, J., Liu, Q., & Wu, S. (2022). A survey on deep graph generation: Methods and applications. In *Learning on Graphs Conference*. PMLR. (Vol. 2, pp. 47–51).

INDEX

M

N

O

P

Q

R

S

FSC
www.fsc.org
MIX
Papier | Fördert gute Waldnutzung
FSC® C083411

Kolibri 360 GmbH
Ferdinand-Jühlke-Straße 7
99095 Erfurt, Deutschland
produktsicherheit@kolibri360.de